'In this powerful book, Natasha Saunders challenges us to think about refugees in terms of their struggles for rights, sanctuary, and international mobility. Gone is the figure of the refugees as an abject humanitarian victim. Instead, Saunders provides the conceptual tools to perceive refugees as people enacting themselves as political beings. This is a bold and highly recommended intervention into the growing field of critical refugee studies.'

— *Peter Nyers, Associate Professor of Political Science, McMaster University*

'Saunders' brilliantly interrogates and in true Foucauldian fashion uniquely cuts the hard-shelled "refugee problem" in two to reveal the problem refugees face and the problem they are deemed to pose. Confronting the former, Saunders compellingly explores Arendt's thought and decidedly pragmatic efforts like sanctuary provisions to bring us ever closer to understanding how displaced persons might again find their place in the world.'

— *Randy K. Lippert, Professor of Criminology, University of Windsor*

International Political Theory and the Refugee Problem

'The refugee problem' is a term that has become almost impossible to escape. Although the term is used by a wide range of actors involved in work related to forced migration, these actors do not often explain what exactly 'the problem' is that they are working to solve, leading to an unfortunate conflation of two quite different 'problems': the problems that refugees face and the problems that refugees pose.

Beginning from the simple, yet too often overlooked, observation that how one conceives of solving a problem is inseparable from what one understands that problem to be, Saunders' study explores the questions raised about how to address 'the refugee problem' if we recognise that there may not be just one 'problem', and that not all actors involved with the refugee regime conceive of their work as addressing the same 'problem'. Utilising the work of Michel Foucault, the book first charts how different 'problems' lend themselves to particular kinds of solutions, arguing that the international refugee regime is best understood as developed to 'solve' the refugee (as) problem, rather than refugees' problems. Turning to the work of Hannah Arendt, the book then reframes 'the refugee problem' from the perspective of the refugee, rather than the state, and investigates the extent to which doing so can open up creative space for rethinking the more traditional solutions to the refugee (as) problem. Cases of refugee protest in Europe, and the burgeoning Sanctuary Movement in the UK, are examined as two sub-state and popular movements which could constitute such creative solutions to a reframed problem.

The consequences of the 'refugee' label, and of the discourses of humanitarianism and emergency, are topics of critical concern, and as such, the book will form important reading for scholars and students of (international) political theory and forced migration studies.

Natasha Saunders is a lecturer at the University of St Andrews. Her research interests fall within the field of international political theory, with a focus on issues of human rights, migration, statelessness, inclusion/exclusion, and identity.

Routledge Research on the Global Politics of Migration

International Political Theory and the Refugee Problem

Natasha Saunders

Routledge
Taylor & Francis Group

LONDON AND NEW YORK

First published 2018 by Routledge

2 Park Square, Milton Park, Abingdon, Oxfordshire OX14 4RN

52 Vanderbilt Avenue, New York, NY 10017

Routledge is an imprint of the Taylor & Francis Group, an informa business

First issued in paperback 2019

Library of Congress Cataloging in Publication Data
A catalog record for this book has been requested

ISBN: 978-1-138-23566-3 (hbk)
ISBN: 978-0-367-37269-9 (pbk)

Typeset in Times New Roman
by Wearset Ltd, Boldon, Tyne and Wear

To my family and friends: my home in the world

Contents

Acknowledgements

The initial research for this book was made possible by the generous support of the UK Economic and Social Research Council, and could not have been completed without the counsel, advice, and camaraderie of my colleagues and friends in the School of International Relations at the University of St Andrews. I wish particularly to thank Patrick for the integral role he has played in the development of this book. Patrick, for your patience, your friendship, and for the invaluable guidance that you have given me over the years I will be forever grateful. Truly.

This book began its life as a PhD research project, and over the years I have presented ideas and papers that became its chapters at a range of conferences, workshops, and seminars. At each of these gatherings I received invaluable questions, comments, and suggestions. But while I remember many of those questions, I remember only a few of the people asking them. And so, I would like to send my thanks here to all of you, in the hope that this book, and my gratitude, do indeed find their way to you.

This book would be no more than an idea without the hard work of my editorial team at Routledge. I owe many thanks to Natalja, Lillian and Maria. From my first tentative email to the delivery of the manuscript you have made this process immeasurably less stressful and more enjoyable than I feared it would be. I hope that the final product will repay the faith that you have placed in me and my ideas.

I count myself lucky to have had the companionship of so many people – more than I can name – with whom I have laughed, cried, and debated over the years, and whose own passions, pursuits, and ideas have contributed in no small way to my own development as a scholar and as a person. To Antonio, Filippo, Kieran, Helga, Faye, Jenna, Selbi, Chris, Andreas (A and P), Hannah, and to Sarah and Josh: I thank, and love, you all.

And finally, I wish to thank my family: my father, Geoff; my brother, Nick; my sister, Francesca; and my beloved late mother, Jacqueline. I dedicate this book to you.

NB: A revised version of Chapter 1 appears as "Paradigm Shift or Business as Usual? An historical reappraisal of the 'shift' to securitisation of refugee protection" in *Refugee Survey Quarterly* 33(3) (September 2014) © 2014 Oxford University Press. I thank OUP for their permission to reproduce this work.

Abbreviations of books by Michel Foucault and Hannah Arendt

Michel Foucault

AK	*The Archaeology of Knowledge*
BB	*The Birth of Biopolitics*
DP	*Discipline and Punish*
EWE	*Essential Works 1954–1985, Volume 1: Ethics*
EWP	*Essential Works 1954–1985, Volume 3: Power*
HS	*The History of Sexuality, Volume 1: The Will to Knowledge*
SMD	*Society Must Be Defended*
STP	*Security, Territory, Population*

Hannah Arendt

BPF	*Between Past and Future*
CR	*Crises of the Republic*
EJ	*Eichmann in Jerusalem*
EU	*Essays in Understanding*
HC	*The Human Condition*
JW	*The Jewish Writings*
LK	*Lectures on Kant's Political Philosophy*
MDT	*Men in Dark Times*
OR	*On Revolution*
OT	*The Origins of Totalitarianism*
OV	*On Violence*
PP	*The Promise of Politics*
RJ	*Responsibility and Judgment*

Introduction

Out of Profound Concern – For Whom?

A critique does not consist in saying that things aren't good the way they are. It consists in seeing on what type of assumptions, of familiar notions, of established, unexamined ways of thinking the accepted practices are based.

(Foucault, EWP: 456)

In 2017, 66 years since the drafting of the United Nations *Convention relating to the Status of Refugees*, international refugee policy has stagnated. Since the outbreak of civil war in Syria in 2011, the global displaced population has skyrocketed to its highest rate since the Second World War: 65.3 million people, or roughly 1 in every 113 people globally is now 'displaced' (UNHCR, 2017). The three so-called 'durable solutions' to the refugee problem – repatriation, assimilation, and resettlement – each appear to be beyond the grasp of increasing numbers of displaced people, as conflicts in refugees' countries of origin drag on preventing return; countries of first asylum fight local assimilation amid a combination of security and economic concerns, which are exacerbated by being made to shoulder more and more responsibility for relief of the displaced; as developed countries close off access to asylum and resettlement.

Detention of refugees is becoming a more frequent occurrence, as those seeking protection of states other than their own are joined in the public imagination with criminals and terrorist threats, regardless of whether such linkages have any grounding in reality. In the global North this detention tends to take the form of 'temporary' incarceration in a range of different holding-, transit-, processing- and immigration detention centres and, in some cases, even in formal prisons. In the global South this detention tends to take the form of enforced encampment, placing refugees under the governance of humanitarian organisations and the United Nations High Commissioner for Refugees (UNHCR). While enforced encampment may be the preferred go-to 'solution' for states in the global South, many refugees seek to 'self-settle' in urban areas, refusing to be encamped and trying to 'go it alone'. The price paid for such agency is often an even more precarious existence than that awaiting refugees within the "humanitarian spaces without exit" (Dubernet, 2001) into which hundreds of millions of donor dollars are poured each year, but which seem to provide less and less protection and opportunity as time passes. Self-settled refugees live in constant risk of arrest, imprisonment, and deportation, since they often lack papers and prior authorisation from state authorities to seek a life outside of the camp archipelago.

Refugees from the Syrian civil war are the latest group to join this global population, and they have propelled the refugee problem to the forefront of global politics once more. Since 2015, often driven by a lack of security and opportunity in the countries bordering Syria to which they had initially fled, hundreds of thousands took their fate into their own hands once more and attempted the perilous journey across the Aegean or the Mediterranean to seek new lives in Europe. Suddenly, European press and politics were awash once again with talk about 'the refugee problem' or 'the refugee crisis', and our television screens and the front pages of our newspapers were plastered with pictures of anonymous masses crowded into rickety boats, or of the bloated bodies of small children washed up on the golden beaches of Europe's southern border.

Almost 70 years ago, in the same year as the Refugee Convention was opened for signature, Hannah Arendt, a political theorist and German-Jewish refugee, characterised international efforts addressing refugees as animated by a single overarching imperative: how to make the refugee deportable again (Arendt, OT: 284). This imperative seems an equally fitting characterisation of our situation today.

'The Refugee Problem'

This is not, however, a book about Syrian refugees, or about any specific group of refugees. This is a book about words, and about three words in particular: 'the refugee problem'. This might sound odd as surely all work on refugees is about 'the refugee problem'? But I mean something very specific when I say that my focus is 'the refugee problem': I mean that I am focused on it as a term, a turn of phrase, a place-holder or shorthand, so to speak. This is a term about which I have long had misgivings. It is a term that is used prolifically and by a wide range of different actors, and yet it has never been clear to me that these actors all mean the same thing when they use these words, or that those to whom these words are spoken recognise the same 'problem' to which they are being referred. When the High Commissioner for Refugees, Filippo Grandi, speaks of the "stories of loss" told by Sudanese refugees and appeals for "global solutions" and for states to "share responsibility" (UNHCR, 2016), does he have the same 'problem' in mind as the state representatives he is addressing? Or the Sudanese refugees of whom he speaks? Do Southern states within which the overwhelming majority of refugees and internally displaced persons reside, and Northern states which provide most of the financial support for UNHCR and its activities in these Southern states, understand themselves as addressing the same 'problem'? Do polling companies and the ordinary people they poll recognise the same referent object when they ask, or are asked, about the effectiveness of European responses to 'the refugee problem' (Pew Research Center, 2016: Q5)? Are

charitable organisations, refugee advocacy groups, and NGOs lobbying governments for more liberal approaches to 'the refugee problem' talking about the
same thing as the Ministers they seek to influence? And do refugees and refugee
regime actors seek solutions to a singular 'refugee problem'?

Why, one might ask, does this matter? Put simply: if the way in which we
approach or try to 'solve' a problem, and how we measure the 'success' of those
solutions, is dependent, at least in part, upon what we understand that problem to
be, then it matters a great deal. As has been made all too clear across the global
North since the start of the Syrian civil war (but in ways which will be eerily
familiar to scholars of forced migration), it does not appear to matter how vocal
organisations such as Amnesty International or Human Rights Watch, or refugees themselves, are in their criticism of policies which deny access to protection and result in human rights violations and, increasingly, in death (Amnesty
International, 2017), as states seem undeterred in their pursuit of these policies.
And yet, both 'sides' employ the same terminology: both assert that they are
seeking to address 'the refugee problem'. It is perhaps tempting to write off
states' professions to address 'the refugee problem' as disingenuous, but we can
only do so if we assume a priori that 'the problem' to which 'the refugee
problem' refers is necessarily the problem that refugees themselves face. If,
instead, we do not start from such an assumption, comforting as it may be, or
from the assumption that states are simply being disingenuous when they employ
the term, then an interesting and important series of questions are opened to
scrutiny. The international refugee regime, the key components of which are the
1951 Refugee Convention (as amended by its 1967 Protocol) and the UNHCR,
was established in order to solve 'the refugee problem', but if we recognise that
there may not be just one 'refugee problem' then we must ask which 'problem'
the refugee regime was established to solve. If it was established to solve more
than one problem, we have to ask to what extent it is able to address each
problem, and investigate the potential for, and consequences of, the possibility
that these problems may clash. The Refugee Convention itself seems to move
uneasily 'between problems', so to speak. If we look just to the Preamble we can
see that at first the Convention is portrayed as motivated by a "profound
concern" for the plight of the displaced, but not two short paragraphs later it
adopts a more adversarial mode towards refugees, highlighting how *they* are a
"problem" for the international system and how the Convention is, at least in
part, intended to prevent the problem of the refugee from becoming "a source of
tension between states" (United Nations, 1951: Preamble; Johns, 2004: 588). If
we recognise that there may not be just one 'refugee problem', then we must ask
who gets to have a say in how these different problems are solved. If we recognise that there may not be just one 'refugee problem' then we must ask what
assumptions and interests underpin each problem and the ways in which solutions to it are conceived. This book seeks to address these issues. But my goal in
doing so is a modest one. In drawing upon and bringing together somewhat dis-
parate (but in my view connected) critiques of various aspects of refugee policy
and discourse, in the attempt to 'unpack' 'the refugee problem', my goal is that

we – scholars, politicians, aid workers, decision-makers, advocates, ordinary citizens – are prompted to "think what we are [saying]" (Arendt, HC: 5) when we refer to 'the refugee problem'. My goal is that we become more attentive to how the ways in which we construct and speak about 'problems' will either open up or close off different kinds of 'solutions', and how different 'problems', and the different 'solutions' to which they lend themselves, have different consequences for those people supposedly at the heart of all of our concerns: refugees themselves.

In pursuit of this goal I turn to the work of two of the twentieth century's most influential political theorists: Michel Foucault and Hannah Arendt; two thinkers who sought explicitly to problematise unreflective ways of thinking and doing. Originally trained in philosophy and psychiatry, Foucault was a thinker whose work reverses the Enlightenment goal of critique by "revealing in what is given to us as universal, necessary, obligatory, what place is occupied by whatever is singular, contingent, and the product of arbitrary constraints" (Foucault, EWE: 315). As will be explained in more detail later in this chapter, Foucault is a theorist driven by the need to understand the emergence of 'problems' – why certain problems, or certain kinds of problems, emerge at certain points in time – and the consequences of certain modes of problematisation – how the ways in which certain phenomena or beings are problematised constrain or enable certain kinds of action. Hannah Arendt was originally trained in philosophy, but consciously turned away from philosophy (which she came to consider as a decidedly 'unworldly' enterprise) and towards political theory (an enterprise fundamentally grounded 'in the world') after being forced to flee Nazi Germany in 1933 (Arendt, EU: 2–4). Arendt's particular approach to 'doing' political theory was to shine a spotlight on the language we use to describe or explain phenomena, in recognition that "language is rarely neutral but often already steers discussion and debate into a certain direction, or, more importantly still, comes to function as a blanket, warming its users but obscuring relevant issues and opinions from view" (Klabbers, 2012: 230). It is my contention that the somewhat unreflective use of the terminology 'the refugee problem' acts as just such a blanket and, whether intended to or not on the part of those who use it, conflates two quite different, although related, problems: the problems that refugees *face* and the problems that refugees *pose*. While these two problems are undoubtedly connected, in that displacement poses a problem not only to the international community but also to the displaced themselves, it is far from clear, although it is often assumed, that solving the problem that refugees pose results automatically, or unproblematically, in solving the problems that refugees face. I contend that these two problems need to be understood separately, rather than being collapsed together, since they imply quite different approaches to addressing 'the refugee problem'. I contend that the problems that refugees *pose*, 'the refugee (as) problem', really lies at the root of the international refugee regime, and that shifting our focus to refugees' problems – the problems that refugees *face* – necessitates a quite different approach to the 'population management' orientation of 'the refugee (as) problem'. In exploring how certain ways of understanding, or framing, 'the refugee problem' influence the way this 'problem' is addressed, this book draws upon and seeks to bring together several important developments in scholarship on refugees and forced migration, by utilising the thought of Foucault and Arendt as an overarching framework.

Situating the Book

Contemporary developments in refugee policy, such as those highlighted above, are often framed as a violation of, or at the very least, a betrayal of the principles underpinning, the refugee regime and of the requirements of the Refugee Convention. It is often argued that there has been a "paradigm shift" away from humanitarianism and international law, towards politics, securitisation, and migration management since the end of the Cold War (Hyndman and Mountz, 2008; Haddad, 2008a). International refugee lawyers, in particular, tend to be vocal critics of the practices pursued by states such as Australia and the member states of the EU, particularly those which seek to prevent arrival, to detain – sometimes indefinitely – those seeking asylum, and the proliferation of 'lesser' forms of protective status which enable states not to fulfil the full range of their obligations towards the displaced (Goodwin-Gill, 2001 and 2011). UNHCR has also been criticised for providing support for, or enabling, many of these actions (Hathaway, 2007b). While these voices are certainly critical of state and UNHCR policies, and highlight the problems they pose to the ability of the displaced to access the protections to which they may be legally (and morally) entitled, the implicit assumption operative in much of this work is that the refugee regime exists, first and foremost, to protect the rights of refugees, even if its work may be vulnerable to the vagaries of high politics (Betts, 2004; Gibney, 1999; Goodwin-Gill, 2008; Hathaway, 2007a and 2007b).

The humanitarian credentials of the refugee regime have, however, come under scrutiny from a number of different angles, most notably in terms of humanitarianism's consequences and its claim to be 'above politics'. Humanitarian practices, as well intentioned as they may be, have both the ability and the propensity to 'silence' and marginalise recipients of humanitarian assistance. Humanitarian practices abstract refugees' predicaments from specific political, historical and cultural contexts, by rendering refugees an undifferentiated mass of victims in need of charity (Malkki, 1995 and 1996). While it would be difficult to deny the unfortunate need for humanitarian relief efforts – we can hardly address the problems that refugees face, the argument goes, if they have already died from starvation – these same practices have the effect of producing "anonymous corporeality and speechlessness" (Malkki, 1996: 389). The logistical challenges of delivering humanitarian assistance and running large-scale relief operations, such as in refugee camps, often entail an approach to the management of displaced populations that produces dehumanising effects (Agier, 2011; Hyndman, 2000). Seemingly mundane management needs and tasks, such as getting an accurate 'head count' of the number of refugees in a camp, can strip refugees of their humanity by practices such as herding them like cattle into pens to facilitate the counting exercise, and 'branding' each refugee with a tag to indicate that they have been 'recorded' (Hyndman, 2000: 127–131). The anonymity, corporeality, and silence produced by humanitarian practices 'on the ground' is reproduced in the process of raising the resources and 'awareness' that these organisations need in order to deliver often life-saving assistance. Barbara Harrell-Bond, founder of the Refugee Studies Centre, once stated that "to attract money, refugees must be visible" (Harrell-Bond, 1986: 8). In 'making refugees visible', often by means of photographs, it is rarely the individuality of refugees – it is rarely refugees them*selves* – that is put before potential donors, be they organisations or the general public. It is, rather, 'the refugee' as victim; the poverty-stricken, traumatised, helpless, and, increasingly, feminised and infantilised victim, incapable of speech and action and in need of a saviour (Johnson, 2011; Nyers, 2006a; Rajaram, 2002). Such practices are often justified by the 'emergency' nature of refugee flows, but this discourse of emergency serves a double function. While it may be a powerful fundraising tool, and while describing a mass exodus of people from, say, a warzone, as an emergency may be entirely justified on a human level, the logic of 'the emergency' also serves to insulate from critique and to shield from view the structural features of a system which seems to continually produce mass displacement (Nyers, 2006a). Not only, then, is there a politics of humanitarianism – in the sense that humanitarian management creates and entrenches hierarchies, and functions according to certain rules and practices – but there is a sense in which humanitarianism itself is fundamentally political. Humanitarianism, and the discourse or logic of emergency which underpins it, can be understood as "tools of statecraft" (Soguk, 1999), which serve the important function of keeping the international system of sovereign states intact by responding to the crises this same system produces in ways which not only fail to challenge, but themselves reproduce, the underlying principles and practices by which it functions. If refugee flows are 'emergencies' or 'crises' then they must be dealt with quickly with 'practical', 'technical' and 'operational' solutions (Nyers, 2006a: xvi), rather than by addressing the possibility that these flows may be such frequent occurrences because of the underlying structure of the sovereign state system itself (Haddad, 2008; Soguk, 1999). Rather than an 'external actor' created to ameliorate the effects of 'breakdowns' in the proper functioning of (international) political life, then, the refugee regime can be understood as part and parcel of the sovereign state system itself (Soguk, 1999). Organisations such as UNHCR, while popularly framed as working on behalf of the displaced, are, in fact, acting on behalf of states (Barutciski, 1996; Scheel and Ratfisch, 2014). This is perhaps nowhere more evident than in the ways in which securitised discourses of refugees and migrants have proliferated not only among states but also within supposedly 'humanitarian' organisations (Bigo 2002; Dauvergne, 2007; Hammerstad, 2010; Newman and Van Selm, 2003; Salter, 2006; Walters, 2002; Watson, 2009).

That humanitarian practices silence refugees, and render them non-political subjects, is becoming an accepted fact within studies of refugees and forced migration. But attention is now being turned to the reactions of these 'humanitarian' subjects to the practices that silence them, thereby challenging their status as voice-less victims who should simply receive aid with gratitude rather than speak up and seek to exert influence on the politics of their protection. Redclift (2013) and Rygiel (2012), for example, both examine how everyday life within camp spaces is infused with the agency of those caught within them. Moulin and Nyers' (2007) analysis of refugee protest in Cairo examines the challenge posed to UNHCR over defining populations of care, and who is empowered to speak on the subject of refugee status and protection. Johnson's (2014) study on rethinking politics from irregularity charts the everyday experiences of the politics of migration control on the part of irregular migrants in Tanzania, Australia, and Morocco, demonstrating that while the system seeks to render these migrants powerless and voiceless, they nevertheless exert agency and enact a series of challenges to the practices which seek to control them. Critical Citizenship Studies is an approach that has developed within the broader field of the study of citizenship, and seeks to problematise the status of the citizen as the political subject *par excellence*, and the casting into abjection of those whose legal status renders them 'outsiders'. Political movements of non-status migrants agitating for employment rights, protests by refugees and asylum seekers, and acts of resistance – such as hunger strikes and lip-sewing – by imprisoned migrants have all been examined from the perspective of the 'politics of citizenship'. In exercising agency, in a variety of verbal and non-verbal forms, actors traditionally conceived of as non-political subjects challenge the state's closely guarded prerogative to distinguish between insiders and outsiders, "chal-lenging the drawing of lines between citizens and non-citizens" (Johnson, 2014: 196) (Beltran, 2009; McNevin, 2006, 2011, and 2009; Monforte and Dufour, 2011; Nyers, 1999, 2003, 2006b). Isin and Nielsen (2008) argue that such acts on the part of non-citizen 'others' should be understood as "acts of citizenship", whereby cit-izenship ceases to be understood as a legal status but as a practice which *creates* citizens. On such an understanding, subjects enact themselves as citizens through creative and performative acts. This approach to citizenship enables a shift in the focus of political action to more diffuse, diverse, and unpredictable spaces, sub-jects, and issues, and the reconceptualisation of political subjectivity and practice from the territorially bound to the mobile (Nyers and Rygiel, 2012; Squire, 2010).

Work on refugees and forced migration has, thus, problematised the conven-tional wisdom of the humanitarian nature of the refugee regime, highlighted the consequences of humanitarian management of/on the displaced, and begun to examine the ways in which these subjects attempt to shake off this 'human-itarian' identity and insert themselves into the politics of their protection. In the pages that follow I seek to bring together under one roof, so to speak, and to build upon, such work originating from across a range of disciplines and utilis-ing a range of theoretical and methodological approaches. These critiques can be brought together through situating the roots of these various practices in par-ticular conceptualisations of 'the refugee problem': 'the refugee (as) problem', and refugees' own problems. I understand this enterprise as one of (international) political theory, first and foremost. Isaiah Berlin suggests that the project of political theory is

> an inquiry concerned ... with the critical examination of presuppositions and assumptions, and the question of the order of priorities and ultimate ends ... in a society in which there is not total acceptance of any single end.
>
> (Quoted in Zivi, 2012: 10)

On this account, political theory is

> part of an effort to make visible dominant ways of thinking so that we can recognise their value and their limits, so they can be modified or rejected if need be, always knowing full well that the modifications suggested are open to contestation.
>
> (Zivi, 2012: 10)

Political theory has traditionally been focused on 'the inside' of societies, usually of states. The 'international' (which can literally mean 'inter-national' (Lang, 2015), or can be used, as I do here, as a synonym for 'global' or the 'world') has tended to be left to the attention of International Relations theorists. That such a distinction between 'inside' and 'outside' has never been so clear-cut in practice (Walker, 1993: 7–8) has not prevented such disciplinary entrenchments. However, these disciplinary boundaries have become much more porous in recent decades, with growing and promising 'cross fertilisation'. 'International political theory' is the moniker given to this cross-fertilisation, or inter-disciplinarity, which seeks, on the one hand, to bring the tools, approaches and insights of political theory – the concepts and approaches developed by political theorists – to bear on questions of global concern, such as human rights, world order, climate change, peace and conflict, globalisation and, of course, migration; and which seeks, on the other hand, to analyse the connections between these 'global' practices and traditionally 'domestic' concerns such as social justice, representation, democracy, citizenship, political agency, legitimacy, authority and accountability.

Giorgio Agamben has been by far the most influential political theorist for scholars of refugees and forced migration, including for many of those already examined above and more (Darling, 2009; Diken, 2004; Edkins, 2000; Edkins and Pin-Fat, 2005; Jenkins, 2004; Rajaram and Grundy-Warr, 2009). Drawing on Hannah Arendt, Michel Foucault, Walter Benjamin and Carl Schmitt, Agamben (1998; 2000) presents a theory of sovereignty which he considers to be the 'hidden truth' of Western political life since Aristotle. Sovereignty – the supreme governing principle of international and domestic political life – constitutes the body politic by deciding on who is excluded from it. Agamben utilises Aristotle's distinction between 'forms of life', the differentiation between *zoe* – what Agamben calls "bare life" – and *bios* – which he refers to as "politically qualified life" – and argues that the state, or the sovereign, is the one who decides which individuals count as politically qualified life, and are thus subject to the law, and which individuals will be excluded from the protection of the law and be rendered bare life. All politics is, by necessity, therefore (bio)politics. To be declared bare life is to be declared *homo sacer*, a figure from Roman law who could be killed with impunity but not sacrificed. *Homo sacer* is thus included in the legal order precisely through his exclusion from it. The ability to declare someone *homo sacer* is fundamental to sovereignty and is thus an ever-present danger to all. Importantly, since this ability is the most fundamental and constitutive aspect of sovereignty, it is not the exclusive purview of authoritarian or totalitarian states. It is also, and, Agamben argues, increasingly, operative in liberal democratic societies. The allure of Agamben for those studying refugees and the refugee problem lies in the space of the 'state of exception'. To be *homo sacer* is to live within a state of exception – in which the law is completely suspended – and as states make increasing use of this most basic of sovereign powers, camps for the warehousing of bare life have become an ever-present and permanent feature of the political landscape, such that the camp actually forms the paradigmatic space under modernity, and the figure of the refugee kept within it, the hidden cipher of politics. The refugee camp, and the detention centre, should be understood as spaces of exception, within which people are reduced to bare life, and not as benign spaces for the distribution of aid or speedy determination of refugee status. Further, the existence and reproduction of spaces of exception and the reduction of increasing numbers of people to bare life should be understood not as an unfortunate exception to the normal functioning of a liberal democratic system, but as the most fundamental expression of the hidden logic of that system.

Agamben's work has not, however, gone without criticism. The *totality* of the life of abjection that those rendered bare life are cast into has been brought into doubt as it leaves little room for understanding how, in the face of such abjection, these individuals are in fact able to act and to act politically (Ellermann, 2010; Johnson, 2014; Walters, 2008). While the camp is in many ways a space of domination, exploitation, and inequality, it cannot be conceived solely as such, as the social and political relations that emerge within any given space, including a camp, are dependent upon the historical, spatial, and material specificities operative in that space (Redclift, 2013; Sigona, 2015). From a purely theoretical perspective, Fitzpatrick (2001) dissects Agamben's historical moves in his reconstruction of *homo sacer*, and puts his interpretation of Roman law in doubt. Kalyvas (in Ek, 2006) questions the utility of Agamben's insights for a politics that could resist the seemingly unstoppable march of sovereignty and the reduction of individuals to bare life. Blencowe (2010) seeks to recover the enterprises of Arendt (as does Owens, 2010) and Foucault from Agamben's self-proclaimed 'corrections' of them. She argues that whatever the merits of Agamben's work may be, the biopolitics that he describes is not the biopolitics of either Arendt or Foucault, and his work should not, therefore, be considered a substitute for, or cognate of, theirs. Finally, Colatrella claims that Agamben's trans-historical account of sovereignty and *homo sacer* leaves too many vital questions unanswered for anyone seeking to utilise his theory of (bio)politics:

An explanation of historical or political phenomena must address the question of why? Why now and not later, or before? Why in this place and not the other? Why the differences in degree between places or times? Why is this group under attack and not another one? … Why is a discourse of bio-politics, or of changing methods of social discipline and control emerging in a given century instead of another?

(Colatrella, 2011: 103)

In making sovereignty as the decision on the exception the hidden foundation of all politics since Aristotle, Agamben's theory is not able to answer questions such as these, which seek more historically grounded explanations and insights. I turn, therefore, not to Agamben, but to two of the thinkers that he drew inspiration from: Arendt and Foucault.

Foucault never took the refugee, or 'the refugee problem', as a subject of his historico-political investigations, notwithstanding his interest in the plight of the Vietnamese Boat People in the 1970s and 1980s (Foucault, EWP: 474–475). There is, however, a growing body of work on refugees that draws on Foucault's broader insights on politics, and on his conception of governmentality and of biopolitics (Lippert, 1998, 1999 and 2004; Lui, 2004; Muller, 2004; Soguk, 1999). A smaller group of scholars have also begun to utilise his reflections on the relationship between power, knowledge, and the subject (Doná, 2007), often focused on the practice of asylum seeking (Fassin and d'Halluin, 2005; Hardy, 2003; McGhee, 2000). These two 'strands' of Foucault's thought are not often brought together, however, and much of the work on governmentality or biopolitics tends to focus solely on contemporary practices in refugee protection, rather than on the historical development of 'the refugee problem' (Soguk's and Lippert's works being notable exceptions). In Chapter 2 I seek to utilise Foucault's reflections on governmentality within a much longer historical time-frame, to explore the development of 'the refugee problem'. Chapter 3 then seeks to bring Foucault's reflections on the relationship between power, knowledge and the subject to bear on how this 'problem' is then managed.

A focus on the utility of Foucault's reflections to contemporary practice is particularly evident in the field of migration studies, and the conceptualisation of 'migration management' as a 'new' approach being taken to address population movement (Andrijasevic and Walters, 2010). In a recently published edited volume, the first to explore a similarly popular 'catchphrase' to 'the refugee problem' – 'migration management' – Geiger and Pécoud argue that 'migration management' is a term, coined in 1993, that refers to at least three different trends. It is a "notion mobilised by actors to conceptualise and justify their increasing interventions in the migration field"; a range of *practices* that are now part of migration policies, including counter-trafficking efforts and 'capacity building' activities; and a set of discourses and new narratives "regarding what migration is and how it should be addressed" (Geiger and Pécoud, 2010: 1–2). In the post-Cold War era, migration has been recognised as possessing the potential to generate real crises, and "a global and holistic regime of rules and norms was needed to successfully address the phenomenon and turn it into a more orderly, predictable and manageable process" which both facilitated a "regulated openness" towards 'beneficial' migratory flows and the restriction of 'unwanted' migration (Geiger and Pécoud, 2010: 2). In analysing this 'new' trend of migration management, many of the contributors to Geiger and Pécoud's volume draw explicitly on Foucault's concept of 'governmentality' – the organised practices through which the government of subjects and phenomena is produced. As I will show in Chapter 2, however, Foucault's reflections on governmentality, when brought to bear upon the historical development of the state and 'the refugee problem', reveal that this 'new' migration management approach is actually much older than is assumed, and forms the very foundation upon which a 'refugee problem' is able to emerge at all. What arguably *is* 'new' about 'migration management' today is the availability of bio-political techniques to enable the state and other actors to achieve – or to believe that they can achieve – this 'management' (Muller, 2004).

Hannah Arendt is a much more familiar name to scholars of forced migration, and her reflections on refugees, the nation-state, and human rights have had a marked influence on the study of refugees. References to her analysis of the systemic origins of forced displacement outlined in *The Origins of Totalitarianism* can now be found in a great many works (e.g. Agier, 2008; Haddad, 2008b; Johnson, 2014; Malkki, 1995 and 1996; Marfleet, 2006; Nyers, 2006a and b; Owens, 2010). But while it is very common to refer to these reflections, it is much less common, in refugee studies, to engage her broader body of work in any substantial way (Gündoğdu (2015) and Hayden (2009) being the obvious exceptions here). Arendt's ability to contribute to the search for solutions to 'the refugee problem' is often considered to be limited, certainly for those scholars interested in the political action of refugees, due to what many commentators regard as the narrowness of her conception of politics and political agency and its inapplicability to questions of social and economic marginalisation – experiences particularly acute for many refugees. It is, thus, increasingly common to recognise the influence of Arendt's work, but then to turn away from her towards a more 'useful' theorist such as Rancière (Nyers, 2003), Warner (Beltran, 2009), or Lefèbvre (Squire and Darling, 2013), or to question the continued utility of her insights on refugees at all (Bradley, 2013). In Chapter 4, however, I contend that Arendt's work is indeed relevant to 'the refugee problem' today, and that the criticisms of her conception of politics and agency are mistaken and based on a highly selective reading of her vast body of work. Ayten Gündoğdu (2015) is the rare scholar of (forced) migration who has engaged with Arendt's entire oeuvre. Her focus is on Arendt's 'aporetic thinking' as the key to understanding the continued relevance of her reflections on human rights to the struggles of migrants today. For my purposes, however, it is Arendt's quite unique understanding of 'the world' and how people come to be 'at home' in it that holds the key to her continued relevance in understanding and addressing 'the refugee problem'. In unpacking 'the refugee problem', then, this book utilises Michel Foucault's concept of 'governmentality' and the intimate relationship he charts between power, knowledge, and the subject, and Hannah Arendt's concept of 'the world' as an overarching framework.

Why Foucault *and* Arendt?

Foucault and Arendt are not often utilised together. On the surface, they appear to be engaged in fundamentally different enterprises: Arendt is a thinker concerned with classical macro-political themes, such as the nature of political regimes, revolution, and the public sphere; whereas Foucault is fascinated by micro-political contexts such as prisons and asylums, suggesting that the obsession with the macro-political context of states and sovereignty is precisely what has led political theory astray (Foucault, EWP: 122). Arendt celebrates power and politics, whereas Foucault paints a darker and more suspicious picture (Allen, 2002: 131). However, this initial characterisation of their differences is premature. Both Foucault and Arendt are committed to historicising political and philosophical inquiry; they both reject the Hegelian/Marxist philosophy of history, and "traditional metaphysical accounts of truth and foundationalist epistemologies" (Allen, 2002: 131); both share a concern with race thinking in modern political thought and practice; and they have a similar approach to political enquiry and recognition of the importance of language to human understanding and action.

Genealogy and Storytelling

As a thinker, Foucault's main concern – the drive behind his diverse examinations of madness, medicine, punishment, sexuality, and the human and social sciences – is with understanding and revealing how different kinds of (problematic) subjects are created by different modes of thought and practice. His interest in psychiatry lay in charting how 'the insane person' is a subject created by the functions of modern psychiatry as a discipline and practice, and how the 'problem' of 'insanity' is constructed so as to control such subjects. His interest in punishment lay in the emergence of 'the delinquent' and the role that the 'problem' of 'recidivism' comes to play in the development of contemporary practices of criminal punishment. Foucault takes a historical approach to studying these 'problems' and problematic subjects, but it is history of a particular kind. Rather than examining continuity, or searching for 'origins', and thus approaching documents as ambassadors of historical continuity, Foucault is interested in ruptures, in breaks, and refuses to grant a privileged place to 'the subject' as the *creator* of history – which might see 'the delinquent' as the driving force behind the development of modern techniques of criminal punishment – positing instead that 'the subject' is *created* by (historically contingent) 'power-knowledge' complexes (Shiner, 1982: 387).

Foucault begins from the position that at any given period there are substantial constraints, beyond those of grammar and logic, on how people are able to think and speak, and that these 'discursive' practices can be recovered through the study of the material traces left behind by a particular historical period and culture – an 'archive' (Foucault, AK). However, this examination of the historical 'archive' is not a hermeneutical one in which the document, text, or statement is 'interpreted' or 'translated' to reveal a 'true' meaning lying behind that text. Rather than seeking to "render into discourse the unsaid", Foucault's approach is to concentrate his focus precisely on what *is* said (Dean, 2002: 16). Language, or discourse, is, on this account, not merely instrumental but is a source of thought in its own right. Foucault's earlier works, examining madness, medicine, and the emergence of the human and social sciences – dubbed 'archaeologies' – are not focused on the specific bodies of knowledge (*connaissance*) of disciplines such as psychology/psychiatry, medicine, or economics, but the deeper epistemic context and conditions (*savoir*) within which such bodies of knowledge became intelligible and authoritative (Rousse, 2005: 96). Foucault argued that particular investigations were structured by

> which concepts and statements were intelligible together, how those statements were organised thematically, which of those statements counted as 'serious', who was authorised to speak seriously, and what questions and procedures were relevant to assess the credibility of those statements.
>
> (Rousse, 2005: 96)

These 'rules' form a kind of "'general politics' of truth" (Foucault, EWP: 131), which govern what kinds of discourses are considered to 'be true'. These studies revealed, for Foucault, that there were important shifts over time in what counted as serious discussions of madness, disease, wealth, and so on, but he came to the realisation that the rules of discourse alone could not explain the occurrence of these shifts, or why they took the form that they did. Foucault's later 'genealogical' works – on punishment and sexuality – supplement this archaeological analysis of discourse with a complementary analysis of the relation of discursive knowledge to the power structures of society (Gutting, 1989: 260). There is nothing to be gained, Foucault states, from describing autonomous layers of discourses unless one can relate them to other layers, practices, institutions, social and political relations, and it is this relationship which "ha[d] always intrigued" him (Foucault: 1967: 284–285).

Every society, Foucault claims, has its 'regime of truth'. In societies like ours – contemporary Western society – our 'political economy of truth' is characterised by a number of important traits:

> 'Truth' is centred on the form of scientific discourse and the institutions which produce it; it is subject to constant economic and political incitement (the demand for truth, as much for economic production as for political power); it is the object, under diverse forms, of immense diffusion and consumption (circulating through apparatuses of education and information whose extent is relatively broad in the social body ...); [and] it is produced and transmitted under the control, dominant if not exclusive, of a few great political and economic apparatuses (university, army, writing, media) ...
>
> (Foucault, EWP: 131–132)

In this system of truth, Shiner explains, there are many forms of excluded and subjugated knowledge:

> Those who occupy the lowest status in various institutions and conditions of life all find their knowledge discounted. They are part of a system of power that invalidates their discourse ... continuously by a set of implicit rules concerning what sorts of concepts and vocabulary are acceptable and what credentials and status are essential for one's discourse to count as knowledge.
>
> (Shiner, 1982: 384)

It is the operation of these systems of power-knowledge, and the exclusions that they produce, which is the focus of Foucault's genealogical 'method'. While Foucault may be unconcerned with the scientific 'validity' of the disciplines of power-knowledge that he critiques, he is certainly not *politically* neutral about them, as he is concerned precisely with their *effects*. Revealing the effects of subjugation and normalisation behind these practices of power-knowledge is the moral/normative imperative behind genealogy as an approach to investigating social and political practices.

Hannah Arendt also takes a historical approach to political theory, turning to the past in order to 'illuminate' the present. But this illumination is not achieved through the recovery of causation or of the 'origins' of contemporary practices. Although Arendt almost never discussed 'methods' or 'methodology' (Vollrath, 1977: 161), in order to differentiate her approach both from traditional historiography, and from the positivist methods of the social sciences, she calls her 'method' – her way of 'doing political theory' – "my old-fashioned storytelling", precisely, Disch argues, to signal her resistance to the dictate that theory remove itself to an Archimedean point 'beyond' the social world in order to understand its happenings and adjudicate its conflicts of interest (Disch, 1993: 668). The very concepts of theory and method in the social and political sciences presuppose that a theory – and theorist – can remain detached from its object, but Arendt's political thinking regards political events not as objects to be explained but as *phenomena* to be understood which, by definition, include those to whom they appear – the theorist as well as others – along with the space in which they occur. Since phenomena always occur within a "web of human relationships from which the theorist cannot extricate herself", the 'objectivity' of method and theory can only be achieved at the expense of the understanding of the phenomenon itself (Vollrath, 1977: 163–164; Arendt, 1953). Understanding, and not explanation or prediction, is the goal of political theory for Arendt, and understanding is oriented, fundamentally, towards *meaning*; towards the production of meaning to enable action in the future. This is an enterprise which Arendt felt became particularly important in the wake of a catastrophe such as totalitarianism – the phenomenon that prompted her turn away from philosophy and towards the political realm. In seeking to understand totalitarianism – both its nature as a truly novel form of government and how it was possible for such a form of government to emerge at all – she felt compelled to analyse it 'historically' in a way that sought not to preserve it but destroy it; to write its 'history' in a decidedly un-deterministic way that would reveal how it was made possible but without the impression that its appearance was inevitable. For this reason, despite the unfortunate choice of title, *The Origins of Totalitarianism* is not really an analysis of its 'origins' at all, but of certain 'elements' that she identified as having 'crystallised' into totalitarianism. In a response to Eric Voegelin's review of *The Origins of Totalitarianism* she takes issue with his characterisation of her enterprise, stating that she did not describe

> a "gradual revelation of the essence of totalitarianism from its inchoate forms in the eighteenth century to the fully developed" because this essence, in my opinion, did not exist before it had not [*sic*] come into being. I therefore talk only of 'elements', which eventually crystallise into totalitarianism, some of which are traceable to the eighteenth century, some perhaps even farther back.
>
> (Arendt, 1953: 81)

Rather than a 'history' of totalitarianism, strictly speaking, *Origins* is Arendt's 'story' of the emergence and nature of totalitarianism. The chief task of storytelling is to recover the 'pearls' of past experience to frame a story which can orient the mind to the future (Benhabib, 1990: 171). Arendt's 'method' thus requires an "'attentiveness to reality' that is [perhaps] more the mark of a political actor than a scholar" (Luban, 1983: 248).

The notion of political theorist as storyteller is perhaps even clearer in Arendt's most 'theoretical' work, *The Human Condition*, which she frames as a "reconsideration of the human condition from the vantage point of our newest experiences and our most recent fears" – namely totalitarianism and the advent of the nuclear age. It is, she continues, an attempt "to think what we are doing" (Arendt, HC: 5). An examination of the three fundamental activities of man insofar as he is an active being – labour, work, and action – *The Human Condition* attempts to think through (in both senses) these concepts. In much the same way as what Foucault would later dub his 'genealogical' method, Arendt's story of the development of these concepts seeks to identify moments of rupture, displacement and dislocation, as it is in such moments, Benhabib explains, that "our language is witness to more profound transformations taking place in human life" (Benhabib, 1990: 190). Arendt's fascination with language and concepts lies not in their ability to help us build abstract theories with which to explain or give order to human life, but in the recognition that language and concepts really began as particular experiences:

> no matter how abstract our theories may sound or how consistent our arguments may appear, there are incidents and stories behind them which, at least for ourselves, contain as in a nutshell the full meaning of whatever we have to say.
>
> (Arendt quoted in Disch, 1993: 669)

Such a history of concepts is "an act of remembering, in the sense of a creative act of rethinking which sets free the lost potentials of the past" (Benhabib, 1990: 190).

Arendt and Foucault thus seem to be engaged in quite similar historico-political enterprises, despite their different choice of subject matter. Both seek to unpack the notion of history/historiography as a positivist/objectivist cataloguing of causal factors, and see political theory, instead, as a mode of storytelling – of reconstructing how we have arrived at a particular discourse of political events, of how particular events are made *possible*, and thus how it might be possible to change them moving forward.

This book does not search for the ultimate *cause* of population displacement, or for the *origin* of 'the refugee problem' as a term. Rather, it seeks to understand their development as political concerns, how it has become possible to 'know' anything about them, and what the consequences of particular conceptualisations of the 'problem' and our drive to know it are. It asks, ultimately, if understanding this process allows us to rethink the problem in need of a solution; if it presents us with the opportunity to tell a different story of 'the refugee problem' and, there-fore, to conceptualise different kinds of solutions. Genealogy and storytelling, as ways of 'doing political theory', are ideally suited to this enterprise because they are modes of investigation which seek to understand the conditions (social, eco-nomic, political, philosophical, epistemological and discursive) which *make pos-sible* the emergence and development of particular problems, and the discourses we produce about them, and reveal how these discourses already circumscribe par-ticular solutions, thereby rendering others irrational, impractical, unthinkable, or unworkable. As decidedly un-deterministic approaches to (historically informed) political investigation, genealogy/storytelling reveal the radically contingent nature of our socio-political and epistemic structures. Recognising this contingency opens up the possibility of conceiving of 'the refugee problem' in different, and poten-tially less constraining, ways.

These discussions might give the impression that Arendt and Foucault are so similar as to render the use of both theorists, rather than one or the other, a redundant enterprise. While the initial characterisation of the differences between the two thinkers mentioned above (the micro/macro difference in focus, and the pessimistic/optimistic approaches to the potentials of politics) might be premature, it is not entirely inaccurate, and it is these two initial dif-ferences which make both thinkers helpful for this project. In other words, their similarities make them compatible enough to be used together, while their differences make it *necessary* to do so. When engaging the work of multiple theorists there is a delicate balance to be struck between addressing each in sufficient depth to demonstrate their relevance and utility, while avoiding unnecessary or unhelpful repetition, and also avoiding a treatment of each the-orist in isolation. This book does not seek to bring Foucault and Arendt directly 'into conversation' with each other. They are, rather, two similar ana-lytical lenses through which 'the refugee problem' can be analysed, but with important and useful differences in focus.

Foucault and Arendt tell remarkably similar stories of the rise of the modern state and state system (addressed in Chapters 2 and 4 of this book), but where Foucault's examination illuminates the inner workings of the governmental *rationality* by which they function, which enables the emergence of a distinct 'refugee problem' – 'the refugee (as) problem' – and provides a framework within which to 'manage' it, Arendt's examination puts the consequences and *meaning* of this rationality for the refugee (and others) at the forefront. While Foucault's work thus forms the framework for understanding the emergence of 'the refugee (as) problem', and the ways in which such a problem is managed, Arendt's work can begin to shift our perspective from an understanding of the problem from the perspective of the state – the refugee (as) problem – to that of the refugee. Supplementing her story of the rise of the modern state (system) with the theoretical and philosophical reflections in her other works reveals first why being cut off from the system – being made superfluous and, thus, world-less – is so problematic for the refugee, and second why the three durable solutions of the refugee regime are not as equipped as we might think to solve 'the refugee problem' when understood in this way. In using her insights to reframe 'the problem' itself, we can also begin to reframe the search for solutions (undertaken in Chapter 5). Utilising Arendt's work can help us to recast the 'durability' of solutions we may seek in a way that more closely addresses problems for refugees rather than the problem of the refugee.

Outline of the Book

Chapter 1 examines the relationship between 'the refugee problem' and the refugee regime, exploring how a particular understanding of 'the refugee problem' provides the foundation of the international refugee regime that persists to this day: 'the refugee (as) problem'. Understanding how the dominance of the framework of 'the refugee (as) problem' has been present since the very earliest days of international concern with population displacement reveals that the rationale behind contemporary state practices such as those highlighted above are not novel developments which 'betray' an earlier, humanitarian, guiding conception of 'the refugee problem', but have been present since the very beginning. To do this, the chapter turns to the archives of the League of Nations and the United Nations between 1921 and 1951, to understand not simply how we have formally *defined* 'the refugee', 'refugee problem' and the solutions to it, but to examine the characterisations and assumptions upon which these definitions rest, and how, together, they form a distinct discourse which governs how the refugee and refugee problem are spoken about to this day. This discourse constructs 'the refugee problem' in need of a solution as the very existence of the refugee herself, and the economic and social burdens she places on the state and state system. In order to 'solve' this problem, states created an international regime of solutions governed by (economic) self-interest, a drive to limit the burden of the care of refugees on the states and shift it to charitable organisations, and to portray the problem to be solved as one of humanitarian concern and action rather than one of political organisation requiring political solutions.

Chapter 2 turns to Michel Foucault's lectures at the Collège de France to understand why the problem in need of a solution is conceptualised as 'the refugee (as) problem', and why it emerges when it does – in the late nineteenth and early twentieth century. I argue that while people have always moved between communities and attempted to escape from violence and persecution, it was only with the development of the *political rationality* underpinning the rise of the modern state and state system that the 'refugee' and 'refugee (as) problem' emerge as distinct subjects and problems in need of sustained attention. That refugees are an inevitable by-product of the state system is now accepted wisdom on the part of refugee studies scholars and political theorists interested in forced migration, but the focus of this line of argumentation has overwhelmingly been on the nationalisation of the state – i.e. the role that the development of the state as *nation*-state plays in the production of refugees – and with the emergence of refugees as subjects. This chapter seeks to move beyond this focus on the nationalisation of the state and pay due attention to the *state* side of the nation-state partnership. Further, it seeks to elucidate not the emergence of 'the refugee', per se, but the emergence of 'the refugee problem' – i.e. how it becomes possible for a distinct refugee problem to emerge at all. As such I argue that with the emergence of population as a distinct entity, the management of which becomes the responsibility of government, migration becomes a phenomenon in need of regulation, and migrants themselves become anomalies in need of management. This necessitates the development of a nascent migration management regime, which itself enables the birth of a distinct refugee problem, when groups of individuals emerge onto the international scene who cannot conform to the rules of the new regime.

Building upon the insight that a problem can only be managed by being known, and the more 'accurately' it can be known the more 'effectively' it can be managed, Chapter 3 examines the role that knowledge production plays in the effective management of 'the refugee (as) problem'. Turning to Foucault's work on the relationship between knowledge, truth, power, and the subject, I argue that in order for the international refugee regime to effectively manage 'the refugee (as) problem' in line with its principles of burden shifting/limiting and self-interest, both the individual 'on the move' and the phenomenon of forced migration must be 'known', and that the knowledge and management of one necessitates and facilitates knowledge and management of the other. Two practices, or processes, of knowledge production in relation to 'the refugee (as) problem' are examined: the refugee status determination process, and the development of Refugee Studies as a discipline. The chapter argues that these two practices of knowledge production serve as both the legitimation for, and a key component of, managing access to Refugee status as a way to manage 'the refugee (as) problem'. The production of academic knowledge provides a 'grid of specification' against which different categories of migrant – or different subjectivities – can be produced; and the status determination process then works to assign individuals to one of these subject positions. This joint operation enables states and UNHCR to more 'accurately' sift populations on the move so as to more 'effectively' manage them. This practice differentially restricts or enables the legitimate exercise of choice and agency on the part of such migrants in seeking solutions to their displacement, or to the problems for which displacement is itself a partial solution, and keeps them locked within the statist framing of the problem of migration management. Beyond exploring how knowledge production facilitates effective management of 'the problem', the chapter illuminates how the consequences, for the displaced, of the operation of this power-knowledge-subject nexus necessitates a rethinking of 'the problem' in need of a solution.

Chapter 4 shifts our understanding of 'the refugee problem' and the search for solutions from the problem that refugees pose to states, to the problems faced by refugees in becoming displaced. The chapter begins by revisiting Hannah Arendt's well-known analysis of the structural causes of displacement, and then situates these reflections within the context of her philosophical and political reflections on the 'world' and 'world alienation', in order to bring to light what makes this structural problem of displacement such a personal problem for those who are displaced. I posit that this is best understood, in Arendtian terms, as 'worldlessness' and 'superfluity'. These insights are then utilised to reveal why the three durable solutions to 'the refugee (as) problem', focused as they are on formal/legal remedies to structural problems, are not as well equipped as we might think to address the problems that *being* a refugee presents for those ejected from the state-citizen-territory trinity. It does so through resituating Arendt's now famous conception of the 'right to have rights' within her critique of the state and citizenship as modes of political belonging in modernity, and argues that, because of the profound problems that Arendt identifies with both of these institutions, the right to have rights needs to be understood as *more* than simply a right to nationality or a right to citizenship. The right to have rights, therefore, does not directly, or without significant problems, map on to the three durable solutions to 'the refugee (as) problem'.

Building on Arendt's insight that to become displaced is to lose one's place in the world, in the sense of our lived experience of belonging to particular communities, the final chapter investigates the potential of refugee protest, and the UK City of Sanctuary movement, as ways in which to address the problems of worldlessness and superfluity. It reflects upon refugee protest as instances of performative rights-claiming, a practice which not only reveals the refugee as a political actor but also begins the work of building new 'worlds' to which to belong with others, through the mutual recognition of rights between those engaged in the protests. However, due to the dynamic nature of power relations and efforts by the state to reclaim the political ground from the refugee evident in these protests, these actions stand in need of greater support if refugees are to mount an effective challenge to their exclusion. It is necessary, therefore, not only to focus on the political action of these 'non-political' subjects, but also on the role to be played by those already 'included' in the community in supporting such action. The UK City of Sanctuary movement is therefore presented as one such avenue of support. An examination of its activities, the role that refugees play within it, and its focus on refashioning the city as a place of belonging for all those resident within it, reveals the potential the movement possesses to enable, or perhaps prompt, citizens to act in solidarity with those claiming rights and inclusion. While growing attention is being paid to the political action of supposedly non-political subjects (such as refugees), much less attention has been paid by this same literature to the actions of those already 'on the inside'. Turning to Arendt's work on understanding, storytelling and judgement, and how these relate to (political) action, we can see how these two movements can be – but are not inevitably – mutually reinforcing.

To conclude I return to the primary insight of the introduction and starting point for the book: that how one conceives of solving a problem is inseparable from what one understands that problem to be. The solution to 'the refugee (as) problem' is to find places to put people who have been ejected from the state-citizen-territory trinity, until such time as their state of origin can be recognised by the international community as 'home' again. To understand home in this way is to reduce it to a function of legal status expressed as a physical point on a map. An Arendtian understanding of the refugee problem as the problems of worldlessness and superfluity *for* the refugee lends itself to an understanding of home as 'world', and requires an approach to addressing the problem from an understanding of the *character* of this thing called 'world', and how what we do, or fail to do, can undermine its existence and, thus, our human existence within it. In other words, it requires an approach oriented by the lived experience of being in the world and the different modes that such being takes, and is not reducible to legal status or simply having a physical space to which to 'belong'. The 'durability' or 'permanence' of refugee protest and the City of Sanctuary movement as 'solutions', and the challenges of spatiality, belonging, and responsibility that they raise are discussed, clarifying that the call made by this book to problematise our use of 'the refugee problem' and to challenge the dominant, statist framework of solutions, is not a call to dispose with the durable solutions of repatriation, resettlement and assimilation. It is, however, a call to *diversify* the kind of solutions that we seek, and to recognise that an awareness of the different nature of the problems in need of solutions can have an important role to play in the task of reconfiguring the games of truth and domination in which we all – citizens and refugees alike – find ourselves governed, and to *begin* to reconfigure the nature of the communities to which the right to have rights can correspond.

References

Agamben, G., *Homo Sacer* (Stanford, CA: Stanford University Press, 1998)

Agamben, G., *Means Without End: Notes on Politics* (Minneapolis: University of Minnesota Press, 2000)

Agier, M., *On the Margins of the World: The Refugee Experience Today* (Cambridge: Polity Press, 2008)

Agier, M., *Managing the Undesirables: Refugee Camps and Humanitarian Government* (Cambridge: Polity Press, 2011)

Allen, A., "Power, Subjectivity and Agency: Between Arendt and Foucault" in *International Journal of Philosophical Studies* 10(2) (2002): 131–149

Amnesty International, "EU–Turkey deal: a shameful stain on the collective conscience of Europe" (17 March 2017), available at: www.amnesty.org/en/latest/news/2017/03/eu-turkey-deal-a-shameful-stain-on-the-collective-conscience-of-europe/ (last accessed 5 June 2017)

Andrijasevic, R., and Walters, W., "The International Organization for Migration and the International Government of Borders" in *Environment and Planning D: Society and Space* 28 (2010): 977–999

Arendt, H., *The Origins of Totalitarianism* (New York: Harcourt, 1973) (originally published 1951)

Arendt, H., "[The Origins of Totalitarianism]: A Reply" in *The Review of Politics* 15(1) (1953): 76–84

Arendt, H., "'What Remains? Language Remains': A Conversation with Gunter Gaus" [1964] in *Essays in Understanding 1930–1954: Formation, Exile, and Totalitarianism* (New York: Schocken Books, 1994): 1–23

Barutciski, M., "The Reinforcement of Non-Admission Policies and the Subversion of UNHCR: Displacement and Internal Assistance in Bosnia-Herzegovina (1992–94)" in *International Journal of Refugee Law* 8(13) (1996): 49–110

Beltran, C., "Going Public: Hannah Arendt, Immigrant Action and the Space of Appearance" in *Political Theory* 37(5) (2009): 595–622

Benhabib, S., "Hannah Arendt and the Redemptive Power of Narrative" in *Social Research* 57(1) (1990): 167–196

Betts, A., "The International Relations of the 'New' Extraterritorial Approaches to Refugee Protection: Explaining the Policy Initiatives of the UK Government and UNHCR" in *Refuge* 22(1) (2004): 58–70

Blencowe, C., "Foucault's and Arendt's 'Insider View' of Biopolitics: A Critique of Agamben" in *History of the Human Sciences* 23(5) (2010): 113–130

Bigo, D., "Security and Immigration: Toward a Critique of the Governmentality of Unease" in *Alternative: Global, Local, Political* 27(1) (2002): 63–92

Bradley, M. "Rethinking Refugeehood: Statelessness, Repatriation, and Refugee Agency" in *Review of International Studies* 40(1) (2013): 101–123

Colatrella, S., "Nothing Exceptional: Against Agamben" in *Journal for Critical Education Policy Studies* 9(1) (2011): 96–125

Darling, J., "Becoming Bare Life: Asylum, Hospitality, and the Politics of Encampment" in *Environment and Planning D: Society and Space* 27(4) (2009): 649–665

Dauvergne, C., "Security and Migration Law in the Less Brave New World" in *Social and Legal Studies* 16(4) (2007): 533–549

Dean, M., *Critical and Effective Histories: Foucault's Methods and Historical Sociology* (London: Routledge, 2002)

Diken, B., "From Refugee Camps to Gated Communities: Biopolitics and the End of the City" in *Citizenship Studies* 8(1) (2004): 83–106

Disch, L., "More Truth than Fact: Storytelling as Critical Understanding in the Writings of Hannah Arendt" in *Political Theory* 21(4) (1993): 665–694

Doná, G., "The *Microphysics* of Participation in Refugee Research" in *Journal of Refugee Studies* 20(2) (2007): 210–229

Dubernet, C., *The International Containment of Displaced Persons: Humanitarian Spaces Without Exit* (Aldershot: Ashgate, 2001)

Edkins, J., "Sovereign Power, Zones of Indistinction, and the Camp" in *Alternatives: Global, Local, Political* 25(1) (2000): 3–25

Edkins, J., and Pin-Fat, V., "Through the Wire: Relations of Power and Relations of Violence" in *Millennium: Journal of International Studies* 34(1) (2005): 1–24

Ek, R., "Giorgio Agamben and the Spatialities of the Camp: An Introduction" in *Geografiska Annaler Series B, Human Geography* 88(4) (2006): 363–386

Ellerman, A., "Undocumented Migrants and Resistance in the Liberal State" in *Politics and Society* 38(3) (2010): 408–429

Fassin, D., and d'Halluin, E., "The Truth from the Body: Medical Certificates as Ultimate Evidence for Asylum Seekers" in *American Anthropologist* 107(4) (2005): 597–608

Fitzpatrick, P., "Bare Sovereignty: *Homo Sacer* and the Insistence of Law" in *Theory & Event* 5(2) (2001)

Foucault, M., "Confronting Governments: Human Rights" [1984a] in Faubion, J. (Ed.), *Essential Works of Foucault, Volume 3: Power* (London: Penguin, 1994): 474–475

Foucault, M., "So, is it Important to Think?" in Faubion, D. (Ed.), *The Essential Works of Foucault 1954–1985, Volume 3: Power* (London: Penguin, 1994): 454–458

Foucault, M., "What is Enlightenment?" in Rabinow, P. (Ed.), *The Essential Works of Foucault 1954–1985, Volume 1: Ethics* (London: Penguin, 1997): 303–319

Foucault, M., "Truth and Power" in Faubion, J. (Ed.), *The Essential Works of Foucault 1954–1985, Volume 3: Power* (London: Penguin, 2000): 111–133

Foucault, M., *The Archaeology of Knowledge* (London: Routledge, 2004)

Geiger, M., and Pécoud, A. (Eds), *The Politics of International Migration Management* (Basingstoke: Palgrave Macmillan, 2010)

Gibney, M., "Liberal Democratic States and Responsibilities to Refugees" in *The American Political Science Review* 93(1) (1999): 169–181

Goodwin-Gill, G., "Asylum 2001 – A Convention and a Purpose" in *International Journal of Refugee Law* 13(1) (2001): 1–15

Goodwin-Gill, G., "The Politics of Refugee Protection" in *Refugee Survey Quarterly* 27(1) (2008): 8–23

Goodwin-Gill, G., "The Right to Seek Asylum: Interception at Sea and the Principle of *Non-Refoulement*" in *International Journal of Refugee Law* 23(2) (2011): 443–457

Gündoğdu, A., *Rightlessness in an Age of Rights: Hannah Arendt and the Contemporary Struggles of Migrants* (Oxford: Oxford University Press, 2015)

Gutting, G., *Michel Foucault's Archaeology of Scientific Reason* (Cambridge: Cambridge University Press, 1989)

Gutting, G., "Foucault and the History of Madness" in Gutting, G. (Ed.), *The Cambridge Companion to Foucault* (Cambridge: Cambridge University Press, 2005): 49–73

Haddad, E., "The External Dimension of EU Refugee Policy: A New Approach to Asylum?" in *Government and Opposition* 43(2) (2008a): 190–205

Haddad, E., *The Refugee in International Society: Between Sovereigns* (Cambridge: Cambridge University Press, 2008b)

Hammerstad, A., "UNHCR and the Securitization of Forced Migration" in Betts, A., and Loescher, G. (Eds), *Refugees in International Relations* (Oxford: Oxford University Press, 2010)

Hardy, C., "Refugee Determination: Power and Resistance in Systems of Foucauldian Power" in *Administration & Society* 35(4) (2003): 462–488

Harrell-Bond, B., *Imposing Aid: Emergency Assistance to Refugees* (Oxford: Oxford University Press, 1986)

Hathaway, J., "Forced Migration Studies – Could We Agree to Date?" in *Journal of Refugee Studies* 20(3) (2007a): 349–369

Hathaway, J., "Refugee Solutions, or Solution to Refugeehood?" in *Refuge* 24(2) (2007b): 3–10

Hayden, P., *Political Evil in a Global Age: Hannah Arendt and International Theory* (London: Routledge, 2009)

Hyndman, J., *Managing Displacement: Refugees and the Politics of Humanitarianism* (Minneapolis: University of Minnesota Press, 2000)

Hyndman, J., and Mountz, A., "Another Brick in the Wall? Neo-*Refoulement* and the Externalization of Asylum by Australia and Europe" in *Government and Opposition* 43(2) (2008): 249–269

Isin, E., and Nielsen, G. (Eds), *Acts of Citizenship* (London: Zed Books, 2008)

Jenkins, F., "Bare Life: Asylum-Seekers, Australian Politics and Agamben's Critique of Violence" in *Australian Journal of Human Rights* 10(2) (2004)

Johns, F., "The Madness of Migration: Disquiet in the International Law Relating to Refugees" in *International Journal of Law and Psychiatry* 27 (2004): 587–607

Johnson, H., "Click to Donate: Visual Images, Constructing Victims and Imagining the Female Refugee" in *Third World Quarterly* 32(6) (2011): 1015–1037

Johnson, H., "Moments of Solidarity, Migrant Activism and (Non)Citizens at Global Borders: Political Agency at Tanzanian Refugee Camps, Australian Detention Centres and European Borders" in Nyers, P., and Rygiel, K. (Eds), *Citizenship, Migrant Activism and the Politics of Movement* (London: Routledge, 2012): 109–128

Johnson, H., *Borders, Asylum, and Global Non-Citizenship: The Other Side of the Fence* (Cambridge: Cambridge University Press, 2014)

Klabbers, J., "Hannah Arendt and the Languages of Global Governance" in Goldoni, M., and McCorkindale, C. (Eds), *Hannah Arendt and the Law* (Oxford: Hart Publishing Ltd, 2012): 229–247

Lang, Jr, A. F., *International Political Theory: An Introduction* (Basingstoke: Palgrave Macmillan, 2015)

Lippert, R., "Rationalities and Refugee Resettlement" in *Economy and Society* 27(4) (1998): 380–406

Lippert, R., "Governing Refugees: The Relevance of Governmentality to Understanding the International Refugee Regime" in *Alternatives: Global, Local, Political* 24(3) (1999): 295–328

Lippert, R., "Sanctuary Practices, Rationalities, and Sovereignties" in *Alternatives: Global, Local, Political* 29(5) (2004): 535–555

Luban, D., "Explaining Dark Times: Hannah Arendt's Theory of Theory" in *Social Research* 50(1) (1983): 215–248

Lui, R., "The International Government of Refugees" in Walters, W., and Larner, W. (Eds), *Global Governmentality: Governing International Spaces* (London, Routledge, 2004): 116–135

Malkki, L., "Refugees and Exile: From 'Refugee Studies' to the National Order of Things" in *Annual Review of Anthropology* 24 (1995): 495–523

Malkki, L., "Speechless Emissaries: Refugees, Humanitarianism and Dehistoricization" in *Cultural Anthropology* 11(3) (1996): 377–404

Marfleet, P., *Refugees in a Global Era* (New York: Palgrave Macmillan, 2006)

McGhee, D., "Accessing Homosexuality: Truth, Evidence and the Legal Practices for Determining Refugee Status – The Case of Ioan Vraciu" in *Body and Society* 6(1) (2000): 29–50

McNevin, A., "Political Belonging in a Neoliberal Era: The Struggle of the Sans-Papiers" in *Citizenship Studies* 10(2) (2006): 135–151

McNevin, A., "Contesting Citizenship: Irregular Migrants and Strategic Possibilities for Political Belonging" in *New Political Science* 31(2) (2009): 163–181

McNevin, A., *Contesting Citizenship: Irregular Migrants and New Frontiers of the Political* (New York: Columbia University Press, 2011)

Monforte, P., and Dufour, P., "Mobilising in Borderline Citizenship Regimes: A Comparative Analysis of Undocumented Migrants' Collective Actions" in *Politics and Society* 39(3) (2011): 203–232

Moulin, C., and Nyers, P., "'We Live in a Country of UNHCR' – Refugee Protests and Global Political Society" in *International Political Sociology* 1(4): 356–372

Muller, B., "Globalization, Security, Paradox: Towards a Refugee Biopolitics" in *Refuge* 22(1) (2004): 49–57

Newman, E., and van Selm, J. (Eds), *Refugees and Forced Displacement: International Security, Human Vulnerability, and the State* (New York: United Nations University Press, 2003)

Nyers, P., "Emergency or Emerging Identities? Refugees and Transformations in World Order" in *Millennium: Journal of International Studies* 28(1) (1999): 1–26

Nyers, P., "Abject Cosmopolitanism: The Politics of Protection in the Anti-Deportation Movement" in *Third World Quarterly* 24(6) (2003): 1069–1093

Nyers, P., *Rethinking Refugees: Beyond States of Emergency* (London: Routledge, 2006a)

Nyers, P., "Taking Rights, Mediating Wrongs: Disagreements over the Political Agency of Non-Status Refugees" in Huysmans, J., Dobson, A., and Prokhovnik, R. (Eds), *The Politics of Protection: Sites of Insecurity and Political Agency* (London: Routledge, 2006b): 48–67

Nyers, P., "No One is Illegal Between City and Nation" in Isin, E., and Nielsen, G. (Eds), *Acts of Citizenship* (London: Zed Books, 2008): 160–181

Nyers, P., and Rygiel, K. (Eds), *Citizenship, Migrant Activism and the Politics of Movement* (London: Routledge, 2012)

Owens, P., "Reclaiming 'Bare Life'? Against Agamben on Refugees" in *International Relations* 23(4) (2010): 567–582

Pew Research Center, "European opinions of the refugee crisis in 5 charts" (16 September 2016) available at: www.pewresearch.org/fact-tank/2016/09/16/european-opinions-of-the-refugee-crisis-in-5-charts/ (last accessed 5 June 2017)

Rajaram, P. K., "Humanitarianism and Representations of the Refugee" in *Journal of Refugee Studies* 15(3) (2002): 247–264

Rajaram, P. K., and Grundy-Warr, C., "The Irregular Migrant as Homo Sacer: Migration and Detention in Australia, Malaysia and Thailand" in *International Migration* 42(1) (2009): 33–64

Redclift, V., "Abjects or Agents? Camps, Contests and the Creation of 'Political Space'" in *Citizenship Studies* 17(3–4) (2013): 308–321

Rousse, J., "Power/Knowledge" in Gutting, G. (Ed.), *The Cambridge Companion to Foucault* (Cambridge: Cambridge University Press, 2005): 95–122

Rygiel, K., "Bordering Solidarities: Migrant Activism and the Politics of Movement and Camps at Calais" in *Citizenship Studies* 15(1) (2011): 1–19

Rygiel, K., "Politicizing Camps: Forging Transgressive Citizenships in and through Transit" in *Citizenship Studies* 16(5–6) (2012): 807–825

Salter, M., "The Global Visa Regime and the Political Technologies of the Self: Borders, Bodies, Biopolitics" in *Alternatives: Global, Local, Political* 31(2) (2006): 167–189

Scheel, S., and Ratfisch, P., "Refugee Protection Meets Migration Management: UNHCR as a Global Police of Populations" in *Journal of Ethnic and Migration Studies* 40(6) (2014): 924–941

Shiner, L., "Reading Foucault: Anti-Method and the Genealogy of Power-Knowledge" in *History and Theory* 21(3) (1982): 382–398

Sigona, N., "Campzenship: Reimagining the Camp as a Social and Political Space" in *Citizenship Studies* 19(1) (2015): 1–15

Soguk, N., *States and Strangers: Refugees and Displacements of Statecraft* (Minneapolis: University of Minnesota Press, 1999)

Squire, V. (Ed.), *The Contested Politics of Mobility: Borderzones and Irregularity* (London: Routledge, 2010)

Squire, V., and Darling, J. "The 'Minor' Politics of Rightful Presence: Justice and Relationality in City of Sanctuary" in *International Political Sociology* 7 (2013): 59–74

UNHCR, "Opening of the high-level meeting to address large movements of refugees and migrants. Remarks by Filippo Grandi, United Nations High Commissioner for Refugees. New York" (19 September 2016), available at: www.unhcr.org/admin/hcspeeches/57dfe7ee4/opening-high-level-meeting-address-large-movements-refugees-migrants-remarks.html (last accessed 5 June 2017)

UNHCR, "Figures at a glance" (2017), available at: www.unhcr.org/uk/figures-at-a-glance.html (last accessed 5 June 2017)

United Nations, *Convention Relating to the Status of Refugees* (1951) United Nations Treaty Series Vol. 189, No. 2545: 138–220

Vollrath, E., "Hannah Arendt and the Method of Political Thinking" in *Social Research* 44(1) (1977): 160–182

Walker, R. B. J., *Inside/Outside: International Relations as Political Theory* (Cambridge: Cambridge University Press, 1993)

Walters, W., "Deportation, Expulsion, and the International Police of Aliens" in *Citizenship Studies* 6(3) (2002): 265–292

Walters, W., "Acts of Demonstration: Mapping the Territory of (Non)-Citizenship" in Isin, E., and Nielsen, G. (Eds), *Acts of Citizenship* (London: Zed Books, 2008): 182–206

Watson, S., *The Securitization of Humanitarian Migration: Digging Moats and Sinking Boats* (New York: Routledge, 2009)

Zivi, K., *Making Rights Claims: A Practice of Democratic Citizenship* (Oxford: Oxford University Press, 2012)

1 On Refugee Problems

The Development of a Problem and a Regime

In July 1951, delegates from 26 states gathered in Geneva to draw up a new Refugee Convention. Their deliberations were observed by representatives from an additional two states, and from 29 non-governmental organisations. As this Conference of Plenipotentiaries drew to a close, a Mr Rees stood up and made the following observation and impassioned plea:

> It [the Conference] had ... to use the popular expression, thrown the baby out with the bath water. Its decisions had at times given the impression that it was a conference for the protection of the helpless sovereign states against the wicked refugee. The draft Convention had been in danger of appearing to the refugee like the menu at an expensive restaurant, with every course crossed out except, perhaps, the soup, and a footnote to the effect that even the soup might not be served in certain circumstances ... He would appeal to the Conference to ensure, at long last, that its deliberations sounded a note of generosity and liberalism, not one of fear and niggardliness.
>
> (United Nations, 1951e: 4–5)

Mr Rees was the Chairman of the Standing Committee of Voluntary Agencies and, as such, represented 32 organisations – national and international – involved in relief work with refugees. He had been present throughout the deliberations of the Conference and, while his remarks were related strictly to these deliberations, they characterise equally well, I contend in this chapter, the development of the refugee regime over the preceding 30 years, as the result of a battle between two competing understandings of the 'problem' in need of a solution: the problems faced by refugees, and the problem of the refugee. The latter understanding of 'the problem' took precedence and has provided the dominant framework for the search for solutions to 'the refugee problem' ever since.

This chapter examines the relationship between 'the refugee problem' and the refugee regime, exploring how a particular understanding of 'the refugee problem' provides the foundation of the international refugee regime that persists to this day: 'the refugee (as) problem'. Understanding how the dominance of the framework of 'the refugee (as) problem' has been present since the very earliest days of international concern with population displacement reveals that the rationale behind contemporary state practices is not novel developments which 'betray' an earlier, humanitarian, guiding conception of 'the refugee problem', but has been present since the very beginning. To do this, the chapter examines the formative years of the international refugee regime, 1921–1951, through the archives of the League of Nations and United Nations, to understand not simply how 'the refugee', 'the refugee problem' and the solutions to this 'problem' have been formally defined, but to examine the characterisations and assumptions upon which these definitions rest, and how, together, they form a distinct discourse governing how the refugee and refugee problem are spoken about; in other words, how they form a 'refugee problem discourse'. To chart the development of this discourse the chapter is structured around three inter-related questions, corresponding to each of the substantive sections of the chapter: How is the refugee characterised? How is the problem understood? What solutions are conceived? In answering each question, attention is first devoted to the formal definitions as given in the Conventions, Agreements and Statutes of the period, before widening the focus to address the assumptions and characterisations contained in meeting minutes, letters, reports, resolutions and conference proceedings of the same period.

While historical inquiry has largely been shunned in scholarship on forced migration – when compared to the fields of law, policy, sociology and anthropology – in favour of the more pressing concern that scholarship be 'of use' to practitioners and policy-makers, a small group of scholars have drawn attention to the importance of inter-war developments in refugee policy. Two studies in particular are noteworthy for my purposes here: Claudena Skran's *Refugees in Inter-War Europe: The Emergence of a Regime*, and Nevzat Soguk's *States and Strangers: Refugees and Displacements of Statecraft*. Skran's study takes a regime theory approach to the inter-war period of refugee protection, arguing that characterisations of early efforts on behalf of refugees as ad hoc and ineffective are based largely on assessments of the League's failure to assist Jewish refugees from Germany in the final two years of the 1930s, when the League of Nations was already disintegrating (Skran, 1995: 9–10). If, however, we take a longer view of League actions on behalf of refugees, then, Skran argues, these ad hoc actions begin to coalesce into a regime, defined by Stephen Krasner as a set of explicit or implicit "principles, norms, rules, and decision-making procedures around which actor expectations converge in a given issue-area" (Krasner, 1982: 185). Skran examines the League of Nations archives to demonstrate how the refugee regime developed around the principles of sovereignty and humanitarianism; the norms of asylum, assistance, and burden-sharing; refugee definitions and the rule of *non-refoulement*; and the decision-making procedures of the various refugee agencies created under the auspices of the League.

As one part of a broader project, Nevzat Soguk also turns to the archives of the League of Nations to analyse refugee protection. The central argument of *States and Strangers* is that the term 'refugee' only makes sense when it is juxtaposed to 'citizen', as its opposite. Refugees are thus defined by what they lack – a state – and this conceptualisation of them in international politics serves to

reinforce the state's centrality. Through examining a series of historical epi-
sodes, Soguk charts the use of the refugee and refugee regime as tools of 'statecraft': practices that posit the state as something "already there", while working
through problematisations in various fields of activity to effect statist identities
and images (Soguk, 1999: 40), and thus reinforcing the predominant position of
the state and citizen in international politics. The central focus of *States and
Strangers* is the (re)construction of the state and of citizenship through the
problem of the foreigner/refugee. The archives of the League of Nations reveal,
on Soguk's account, the integral and instrumental role that the League of Nations
High Commission for Refugees played in the production, stabilisation, and
empowerment of the "contingent images, identities, subjectivities, relations, and
institutions of sovereign statehood in local and global politics" (Soguk, 1999:
111). While we draw on many of the same archival materials, and I largely agree
with his broader analysis, Soguk and I have slightly different concerns in turning
to the inter-war period. Soguk's concern is to demonstrate that the refugee was
portrayed as the citizen's 'other' – thus reinforcing the supremacy of the citizen
subjectivity in international political life – and that the refugee regime serves to
reaffirm the centrality of the sovereign state. My concern is to explore the specifics of this refugee regime, of the 'refugee' as a particular kind of subject, and of
what specific kind of problem 'the refugee problem' was understood to be.

On Refugees

The dissolution of the multi-ethnic empires of Russia, Austria-Hungary, and the
Ottomans, following the end of the First World War, involved massive movements of people. Some fled the new regimes in their home countries, others
were forcibly transferred under international supervision in the attempt to
achieve new ethnically un-mixed nation-states, while others were simply no
longer welcome where they had lived as a result of their ethnic 'incompatibility' with the replacement state. In some of these cases movement was accompanied by formal denationalisation, but whether it was accompanied by
denationalisation or not, many of the new migrants found themselves stranded
abroad with no recognised identification papers and no state willing to claim
them. The traditional story of the development of a regime instituted out of profound concern for the plight of these displaced multitudes, the purpose of which
was to ensure the protection of their rights in the face of persecution, seems to
be given weight by an examination of the international legal accords of the
inter-war period. Throughout the 1920s and 1930s, the League of Nations took
a series of ad hoc measures in response to each new flow of 'refugees'. These
legal accords show a development of the definition of the refugee from group-
based juridical conceptions through to the individualist, persecution-centred
definition that forms the bedrock of the international refugee regime today (for
a detailed examination of these legal developments, see Hathaway, 1984). This
evolution of refugee status mirrors an evolution in international understanding
of the refugee problem from the lack of juridical status manifested in the lack

of recognised identity documents, through to the problem of a fundamental incompatibility between an individual and her state, manifested in persecution or a fear of persecution compelling flight abroad.

The first group of displaced people to come to the attention of the League was a group of roughly 800,000 Russians who had fled the Russian civil war and had since been denationalised by the Bolshevik regime. The International Committee of the Red Cross (ICRC) sent a memorandum to the Council of the League, calling upon it to establish a High Commissioner's office whose primary task would be to define the legal position of the Russians. A Conference on the question of Russian refugees examined the problem of their lack of legal status, and highlighted the role played by the lack of valid identity documents in prolonging their plight. A High Commissioner's office was duly established, with the famed Norwegian explorer, scientist, and philanthropist, Fridtjof Nansen serving as the first High Commissioner, but the formal definition of a refugee was not laid down until 1926 when the competencies of the High Commissioner were extended to Armenian refugees. The *Arrangement of 12 May 1926 relating to the Issue of Identity Certificates to Russian and Armenian Refugees* defines a refugee as any person of Russian or Armenian origin, who no longer enjoyed the protection of either the USSR or the Turkish Republic, and who had not acquired another nationality (League of Nations, 1926a: 48). This same group-based definition of refugees was applied in 1928 to Assyrians, Assyro-Chaldeans and a small group of denationalised Turks (League of Nations, 1928b).

A subtle but fundamental shift occurred in refugee definitions in the 1930s, signalling that one could be a refugee even while formally retaining the nationality of the state from which one had fled. The *Plan for the Issue of a Certificate of Identity to Refugees from the Saar*, of 1935, defined a refugee as a person who, having previously been a resident of the Saar, had "left the territory on the occasion of the plebiscite and are not in possession of national passports" (League of Nations, 1935c: 1681). The plebiscite to which the *Plan* refers concerned the reunification of the Saarland with the rest of Germany, and the decision in favour of reunification prompted an exodus of those opposed to the Nazi regime. A relatively steady stream of people had been leaving Germany since the rise of the Nazis to power in 1933, and the *Provisional Arrangement concerning the Status of Refugees Coming from Germany*, of 1936, and the *Convention concerning the Status of Refugees coming from Germany*, of 1938, expanded the definition of a refugee to include the de facto loss of government protection. These documents defined a refugee as any "person who was settled in that country ... and in respect of whom it is established that in law *or in fact* he or she does not enjoy the protection of the Government of the Reich" (League of Nations, 1936: 77; emphasis added).

The final stage in the development of the refugee definition began with the Constitution of the International Refugee Organisation (IRO) in 1946, when the group-based criterion was dropped (except for persons of German ethnic origin who, as a group, were barred from the protection and assistance of the IRO), and the core of refugeehood was conceptualised as the fundamental incompatibility of an individual with her state of origin (United Nations, 1946c: 18–20). The 1951 *Convention relating to the Status of Refugees* maintains this focus on the individual and persecution in defining a refugee as any person who

> owing to a well-founded fear of being persecuted for reasons of race, religion, nationality, membership of a particular social group or political opinion, is outside the country of his nationality and is unable or, owing to such fear, is unwilling to avail himself of the protection of that country; or who, not having a nationality and being outside the country of his former habitual residence as a result of such events, is unable or, owing to such fear, is unwilling to return to it.
>
> (United Nations, 1951o: Art.1A(2))

These definitions, and the progression from a group-based conception of the refugee to the individualist one of today, are important, not least because they have very real consequences for a person denied Refugee status, but they only tell part of the story. The definitions tell us who a Refugee is in legal terms – they give a formal title/status to the physical and legal realities in which certain persons or groups of persons have found themselves – but the discourse about the refugee was, and still is, larger than simply legal definition. Indeed, the first legal definition of the refugee came five years after the League of Nations first devoted its attention to the displaced. If we widen our focus and look beyond the formal international legal accords of the period, it quickly becomes evident that the refugee is not simply conceived of and spoken about in legal terms.

The Refugee as a Humanitarian Object and Burden

From the very earliest days of League concern with the displaced, the refugee was constructed as a problem figure. The first formal discussion we see in the League of Nations regarding refugees was in response to a letter sent to the Secretary General by Gustav Ador, then President of the ICRC, of 20 February 1921, requesting the assistance of the League in relief efforts on behalf of Russians who had fled the civil war and congregated in the countries bordering the former Russian empire. The memorandum warns that if no effort is made by the international community, then the refugees are "in danger of becoming useless and harmful elements in the Europe of tomorrow" (League of Nations, 1921a: 228). This view of refugees as a pool of potential social unrest and general "uselessness" was shared by the governments invited to provide information for a conference on the Russian refugee question on the numbers and conditions of refugees in their territories, and these discussions are rich in refugee problematisations, among the strongest from the Finnish representative:

> One of the disadvantages due to the presence of the refugees is the demoralising influence exercised on the neighbouring Finnish population by these

multitudes, composed, for the greater part, of persons unaccustomed to discipline and order and used to idleness.

(League of Nations, 1921e: 1010)

The Finnish government, along with many others, had felt it necessary to hold the refugees in concentration camps for "military and political reasons", and placed restrictions on their freedom of movement (League of Nations, 1921e: 1009). The refugees are frequently described as a "burden" on their countries of refuge, and the discussions quickly turn to the concept of "burden sharing". Later that year the League appointed Fridtjof Nansen as the first League of Nations High Commissioner for [Russian] Refugees, and his reports to the League contain similar conceptions of refugees.

This manner of referring to refugees was not confined to the initial discussions in the months preceding formal League action on their behalf but continued throughout the period in question. Nansen continued to speak of the "danger of social and political unrest" engendered by the presence of large numbers of refugees throughout Europe (League of Nations, 1927a: 1337), and the interested governments were at times reluctant to make potentially meaningful reforms to League efforts because of these fears. One notable example comes again from a Finnish representative in a discussion on liberalising the bureaucracy involved in granting and extending entry and transit visas for refugees. The Finnish government was reluctant to liberalise its visa policy for refugees since they "often turn out to be politically and socially undesirable persons" (League of Nations, 1931b: 1009).

Racial and ethnic desirability were also important factors in discussions of refugees, as demonstrated by an Italian representative to the League, Count Tosti di Valminuta:

History will one day recount the effects of the influx of this new blood upon the advancement of the races and their vitality. The time-honoured balance of our social classes is disturbed and the ancient order changed by millions of Russians, Greeks, and Turks, and the hundreds of thousands of Armenians and Macedonians, who are sowing throughout the basin of the Danube and the Balkans the dangerous seeds of strife and unrest.

(Quoted in Soguk, 1999: 113)

This concern with racial and ethnic homogeneity is evident even in the formal legal accords of the period, if perhaps stated in less stark terms than those of the Italian Count. The 1938 conference at Évians-les-Bains, called by US President Roosevelt and resulting in the establishment of the Intergovernmental Committee on Refugees (IGCR), worked from an awareness that

the involuntary emigration of large numbers of people, of different creeds ... is disturbing to the general economy ... [and] that the involuntary emigration of people in large numbers has become so great that it renders racial and religious problems more acute.

(League of Nations, 1938b: 676–677)

A concern with refugees as a potential pool of strife and unrest is also evident in the negotiations surrounding the establishment of international organs to address the refugee problem, with the draft constitution of the International Refugee Organisation of 1946 stressing that refugees should be put to work in order to "avoid the evil and anti-social consequences of continued idleness" (United Nations, 1946a).

In addition to being a burden and a source of potential social danger, refugees are also constructed as apolitical, strictly humanitarian subjects. One does not have to read through many volumes of the League of Nations Official Journal before the words "unfortunate people" come to appear as a synonym for the term "refugee". The information provided by members of the Conference of Enquiry into the Question of Russian Refugees held at Geneva in August 1921 is littered with such references (League of Nations, 1921e: 1006–1028), and the following are a mere handful of examples from the earliest years of League concern alone:

[I]t was impossible for the French Government to ignore the distress of these unfortunate people...

(League of Nations, 1921e: 1010)

Great as is its [the Council of the League] sympathy for the sufferings of these unfortunate people...

(League of Nations, 1921a: 226)

[T]he Government of the Kingdom of the Serbs, Croats and Slovenes has, on many occasions ... signified its willingness to receive still more of these unfortunate people...

(League of Nations, 1923a: 390)

It is not necessary for me to emphasise the deplorable situation of these unfortunate people and the great claim they have on the sympathy of the relief organisations ... I received assurances that everything possible was being done ... to improve the situation of these unfortunate people.

(League of Nations, 1923b: 1041)

If the work which the League is doing for these unfortunate people is to continue...

(League of Nations, 1924b: 963)

Often found alongside these references to "unfortunate people" is an emphasis on the great humanitarian task to be undertaken in providing them with relief. The Council of the League is at first reluctant to coordinate any intergovernmental action on behalf of refugees, taking the opinion that international voluntary organisations, such as the ICRC, Save the Children, Near East Relief and so forth, were best placed to take on such a task (League of Nations, 1921a: 226). That the League did indeed take action does not negate this earlier concern, as is demonstrated both by the organisation and characterisation of such action. In addition to developing an identity certificate to remedy the refugees' lack of recognised legal status, the High Commissioner also had as one of his primary tasks the coordination of the work of relief institutions (League of Nations, 1931a: 309). The majority of resources for such relief came from charitable donations in Europe and North America, rather than from the governments themselves, and when states did take action – even the issuing of identity certificates – such action was always characterised as, in the words of the French representative, "a humanitarian and charitable effort" and "in obedience to purely humanitarian motives" (League of Nations, 1921e: 1010–1012). Each incarnation of the High Commission had its task set out in similar terms, and a central role was consistently given to the great charitable organisations of the time.

Refugees were seen as victims in need of humanitarian aid, not as politically able subjects who may have some sort of formal political claim on the international community and worthy of recognition as anything other than hapless victims. There is no starker manifestation of this than the relative exclusion of refugees from any significant role in the solution to their own problems. The international conferences called throughout the period to discuss the refugee problem and to develop and coordinate solutions were attended by governments, and in some cases, but only in a strictly advisory capacity, by charities. On the rare occasions in the sources where any reference is made to consultation with refugees themselves, such consultation is for the purposes of ascertaining census information (League of Nations, 1921d: 900). Where they are included at all in the governance structures of international organisations (which does improve through the 1930s) their role was minimal: it is only in the 1930s that two of the 12 places on the Governing Body of the Nansen International Office (NIO) were reserved for refugees (Skran, 1995: 84). The political nature of the decision to restrict the input of refugees themselves into the search for solutions is particularly obvious in the case of Russian refugees: Nansen had employed, at a minimal salary, a handful of Russian refugees as delegates of the High Commission in host countries, who would communicate information back to Geneva on local conditions, but these were all dismissed when the Soviet Union joined the League (Skran, 1988: 280). In discussing the future of the High Commission in 1929 (prior to the establishment of the NIO), the question of the inclusion/ employment of refugees was addressed, and it was decided that:

> refugees should not be employed in the services of the High Commissariat. The High Commissioner and certain members of the Commission pointed out, however, that, in certain exceptional circumstances, recourse by the High Commissariat to the technical collaboration of refugees in his external services would present important advantages.
>
> (League of Nations, 1929: 1080)

The inclusion of the refugees on the Governing Body of the NIO was an example of this "technical collaboration" and was agreed upon primarily because the funds for the humanitarian work of the League were provided mainly by the sale of stamps affixed to the refugees' identity documents – and was thus a kind of tax paid by refugees (Hope-Simpson, 1939: 210). Even this minimal inclusion was not taken in the best grace by governments. When the NIO was to be disbanded, and its responsibilities combined with those of the separate High Commissioner for Refugees Coming from Germany into a single High Commissioner for Refugees, it was written into the Statute of the Office that "neither members of the High Commissioner's staff nor the aforesaid representatives or their assistants may be refugees or former refugees" (Hope-Simpson, 1939: 596–597).

Finally, the technocratic language often used to describe what needed to be done about the presence of refugees in Europe paints a picture of the refugee as an object of intervention – a problem to be solved by being acted upon rather than a person to be engaged with in any meaningful sense. Words and phrases which one does not expect to encounter when discussing human beings, such as "liquidation", "equitable distribution", "allocation", and "disposal" are employed throughout the earliest years of League involvement with the refugee question, and not only by government representatives but also by the High Commissioner and his deputies in their reports and recommendations. One notable example of this is in reference to a group of 1,000 Russian refugees, who also happened to be invalids, describing them as "the most difficult category of refugees to dispose of" (League of Nations, 1922e: 924). This kind of instrumental language, when combined with representations of refugees as "unfortunate people" who are a "burden" to those countries in which they seek refuge, who pose a "danger of social and political unrest" and a threat to ethnic harmony, and who require the assistance of a "great humanitarian effort", constructs refugees as far more (or less, depending on one's point of view) than individuals lacking legal status and outside their countries of origin.

On Problems

As with the question of what a refugee is, the international agreements and conventions of the period seem to be the most logical places to begin the search for an understanding of how 'the refugee problem' has been conceived. In its simplest terms, the conventional wisdom surrounding the refugee problem is that it is one of the international protection of displaced persons. When the attention of the League of Nations was first brought to the issue of the Russian refugees, the obstacle of their lack of legal status was immediately highlighted. In his letter to the Secretary General, Gustav Ador characterised as an obligation of international justice the necessity of addressing the "eight hundred thousand Russian refugees scattered throughout Europe without legal protection or representation" (League of Nations, 1921a: 227). The memorandum drafted by the ICRC attached to the same letter calls upon the Council of the League to establish a High Commissioner's office whose primary task would be to "define the legal

position of the Russian refugees, wherever they may be ... because it is impossible that, in the twentieth century there could be 800,000 men in Europe unpro-
tected by *any legal organisation recognised by international law*" (League of
Nations, 1921a: 228; emphasis in original).

This concern with international legal status formed the centrepiece of early
League action on behalf of refugees, alongside the distribution of relief by private
organisations and coordinated by the High Commissioner. Most of the Russian
refugees had been denationalised in 1921, and the Conference on the Question of
the Russian Refugees, which established the first High Commission, examined the
problems that this lack of status, and corresponding lack of valid identity documents, posed (League of Nations, 1921d: 900). After consultation with these governments, Nansen developed an identity certificate for Russian refugees, certifying
that the bearer was a former Russian national in possession of no other nationality.
The certificate contained a description and photograph of the bearer, personal
details such as occupation, date and place of birth, and spaces for the issuing government to place a visa, and other governments to place transit visas (League of
Nations, 1922d: 241). This was the basic form of identity certificate extended to all
other groups of refugees who became the concern of the League, and was the tem-
plate for the identity documents developed by the IGCR during the Second World
War (United Nations, 1946b: 74–105), those used by the IRO in the aftermath of
the war, and the refugee travel document issued by UNHCR today. The concern
with the international status of refugees as integral to the refugee problem facing
Europe was further evidenced in the late 1920s when, in addition to extending the
identity certificate system to other categories of refugees, it was also considered
necessary to conclude an agreement providing consular services to refugees. The
Agreement [of 30 June 1928] *Concerning the Function of the Representatives of
the League of Nations High Commissioner for Refugees* allows for representatives
of the High Commissioner, with the consent of the government concerned, to
render consular services to refugees, including certifying their identity, testifying
to the validity of documents issued by their country of origin, and certifying signa-
tures and translation of documents (League of Nations, 1928c: 379).

At the same time as we see a shift in the conception of the refugee from a
purely juridical subject – or, perhaps more accurately, a 'de-juridical' subject in
need of formal status – to an individual fleeing persecution, we also see a shift in
the surface-level conception of the refugee problem. The League no longer considers the problem to be purely one of legal status, but also of ensuring the protection of certain rights for those granted the legal status of Refugee. The 1933
Convention Relating to the International Status of Refugees is the first international protocol to list the rights and privileges to which Refugees will be entitled. This concern with the rights of refugees is strengthened by the experiences
of the Second World War, and the development of the Universal Declaration of
Human Rights, and is carried through to the 1951 Convention:

[C]onsidering that the United Nations has ... manifested its profound
concern for refugees and endeavoured to assure refugees the widest possible

exercise of [these] fundamental rights and freedoms; Considering that, in the light of experience, the adoption of an international convention would appear to be one of the most effective ways of guaranteeing the exercise of such rights...

(United Nations, 1951o)

At first glance, then, the various agreements and conventions of the period would appear to provide a clear and unproblematic understanding of what 'the refugee problem' is. The refugee problem was originally one of legal status – the lack of legal protection by the government of the refugee's country of origin, as evidenced by the lack of valid identity documents, thus inhibiting freedom of movement. As the definition of the refugee expanded, and conditions other than her *de jure* lack of status were taken into consideration, so too did the scope of the problem grow. The problem to be solved became the consequences of persecution and the relationship of the individual to her state and the rights to which she would ordinarily be entitled. The concern then becomes establishing a system by which these rights can be guaranteed to the refugee in the country to which she has fled. This reading of the sources has been sufficient for many scholars researching the refugee problem. However, as with the question of what the refugee is, as soon as we widen our focus and look beyond formal legal agreements a more nuanced picture emerges; a picture in which these problems that refugees face (lack of status and protection) present considerable problems (primarily economic but with racial and ethnic side-effects and undertones) for the states in which refugees found themselves. The very existence and *presence* of these non-status individuals placed a burden on states that needed to be relieved.

The Refugee as Problem

From the very beginning, League concern about refugees was expressed in economic terms. French statesman Gabriel Hanotaux submitted one of the first reports on the Russian refugee question, stating that

> The Russian refugee question is not merely a political, social and humanitarian question, it is mainly a financial problem ... the fugitives, unemployed through no fault of their own, constitute a very heavy charge upon several governments, either because they have taken refuge on their territory, or because they are still in receipt of assistance in the form of food subsidies.
>
> (League of Nations, 1921c: 757)

Concerted action on the part of the League was necessary "in order to relieve the countries concerned of their responsibilities in regard to these refugees" (League of Nations, 1921c: 757). This concern with the financial realities of the existence of large groups of displaced persons in a Europe struggling to recover from a devastating four years of total war, and the need to relieve countries of the burdens they faced in providing for them, underpins League concern with rectifying the anomaly of the refugee's legal status. Recalling the concern surrounding the difficulties faced by refugees due to their lack of identification papers highlighted above, the decision to appoint a High Commissioner who would develop a valid form of identity certificate takes on a slightly altered dimension when we consider the concern expressed, from the beginning, about the economic nature of the problem. Many of the memoranda submitted by the states attending the Conference of Enquiry highlight the economic burdens placed on them by hosting large numbers of unemployed refugees. The French government spoke of the "very heavy burden of their food supply, their support and their housing" (League of Nations, 1921e: 1010), while the British government included an extensive summary of the monies spent in various territories in caring for the refugees (League of Nations, 1921e: 1015–1018), noting that "the Russian refugees at present being maintained by His Majesty's Government originally became a *charge on the public funds* at the beginning of 1920" (League of Nations, 1921e: 1012; emphasis added). The Finnish memorandum drew attention to the potential social problems presented by situations of unemployment in their territories due to the presence of refugees, highlighting that efforts by the Ministry of Home Affairs to organise employment for the refugees caused increased unemployment among Finns and had become a source of discontent (League of Nations, 1921e: 1009).

This concern on the part of governments to relieve themselves of the financial burden of caring for destitute refugees was carried through into the functions of the High Commissioner's office. Nansen saw his primary object as High Commissioner as "the dispersal of the refugees ... to places where they could obtain employment" (League of Nations, 1922a: 386), recognising that "the number for whom inter-governmental action is necessary, with a view to securing them employment, is still very large" (League of Nations, 1922a: 393). It had quickly become evident to Nansen that the most significant obstacle to achieving this 'dispersal' was the refugees' lack of valid identity documents which would allow them to travel in search of employment (League of Nations, 1922b: 396). In his request to the governments of the Members of the League to help him develop a solution to this problem he was keen to frame it in state-centric terms, highlighting the "importance ... of securing the movement of refugees to countries where they will not be a charge on the public funds" (League of Nations, 1922b: 398).

We can thus see from this brief survey that the decision to develop an identity document for Russian refugees was not taken for "purely humanitarian" reasons, and out of profound concern with the refugee's lack of legal status in and of itself. It appears, rather, that the concern on the part of the League to remedy this lack of status was based primarily on the desire of states to relieve themselves of an economic burden that the presence of refugees placed on their public funds. Not possessing valid identity documents was indeed difficult for the refugee, but state concern with this issue was primarily because without valid identity papers the refugees had no freedom of movement, which meant that they had to remain where they were, and without work became charges on the public funds. It was *this problem* that the Members of the League were keen to address. Further evidence in support of this interpretation can be found in the process of, and reaction to, reforming the identity certificates to allow refugees to obtain return visas. Prior to 1924 the Nansen certificates contained no authorisation for the refugee to return to the issuing country. In his report to the League in June 1924, Nansen suggested that, in addition to extending the certificate system to Armenian refugees, governments also grant return authorisation to the refugees who are issued these documents. He did so, however, because

> It has been found that if the refugee certificate authorises return to the issuing country the economic position of the holder is improved by the facilities which he thus obtains for visiting temporarily other countries which may offer him opportunities for employment or business, and his definitive emigration to another country is, in fact, encouraged.
>
> (League of Nations, 1924c: 968)

Further lobbying of governments on the part of Nansen and the private voluntary organisations working with refugees was necessary before an agreement on return visas was finally struck, but the rationale offered by this same agreement is telling. The *Arrangement of 12 May 1926*, which affirmed the principle of affixing return visas to Nansen certificates, would confer benefits not only upon refugees, but "also on the countries for whom the unemployed refugees represent a heavy expense, and on the immigration countries anxious to increase their productive populations" (League of Nations, 1926b: 984). Whereas the initial Arrangement in 1922 establishing the Nansen certificate was ratified by 52 states, the 1926 Arrangement retained only 22 of those states as signatories. The earlier form of the certificate offered the bearer no guarantee of readmission to the issuing country, and so states were arguably keen to issue them to refugees to facilitate their departure. But once the certificates were amended to allow the refugee to return to the issuing state there was a marked decline in overall support for the certificate system (for a table of signatories to each agreement, see Skran, 1995: 106).

Countries of immigration – Canada, Australia, the United States, and the countries of South America – would, it was hoped, play an important role throughout the 1920s and into the 1930s in 'solving' the refugee problem, and highlight another important episode which demonstrates the underlying economic nature of the refugee problem. In the first three years of League action only France acted as a country of immigration. As France had lost a significant proportion of its male working population during the First World War, French industry needed workers, and the French government turned to the Russian refugees. However, by 1924, Nansen reported to the League that "no other country in Europe is capable of absorbing foreign labour, and efforts must be redirected towards the large immigration countries" (League of Nations, 1924b: 962). When the Council met to discuss the issue, it was decided that as the question was mainly one of employment, it could usefully be dealt with by the International Labour Office (League of Nations, 1924a: 905). This expression of concern with the employment opportunities for refugees was also oriented towards the states: such efforts should be made "to secure substantial relief *for the countries overburdened with refugees*" (League of Nations, 1924a: 905; emphasis added). From 1925 to 1929 the ILO took over a substantial amount of the work on the refugee problem. The High Commissioner's office would still coordinate relief and provide consular services, but these measures were considered to be temporary expedients which would only continue until such time as the primary problem, that of the dispersal of the refugees in countries of immigration, could be accomplished by the ILO.

Even though the ILO returned its work to the High Commissioner in 1929, the League still understood the refugee problem in economic terms. As Europe and North America plunged into depression as a result of the stock market crash of 1929, governments adopted ever more protectionist attitudes towards labour markets, making even the possibility of overseas emigration difficult, and so renewed focus was placed on addressing the problems associated with lack of legal status for refugees remaining in Europe. The first convention to list the rights and privileges of the so-called "Nansen" refugees was concluded in 1933. Despite the enumeration of specific rights and privileges, the way in which these measures are discussed demonstrate clearly not only an economic side of the problem that needed to be addressed, but that 'the problem' was the refugee herself:

> [C]onsidering that *their presence* in those countries *constitutes an economic, financial and social problem* which can only be solved by international collaboration...
>
> (League of Nations, 1933b: 1617; emphasis added)

> Appreciating the *difficulty experienced by Governments* in continuing to support the direct and indirect *charges imposed upon them by the presence* of large numbers of unemployed refugees in their territories...
>
> (League of Nations, 1935b: 657; emphasis added)

> [I]nvoluntary emigration ... is *disturbing to the general economy*, since these persons obliged to seek refuge ... in other countries at a time when there is serious unemployment; that, in consequence, *countries of refuge and settlement are faced with problems*, not only of an economic and social nature, but also of public order
>
> (League of Nations, 1938b: 676–677; emphasis added)

For a five-year period during the 1920s the relief functions and the search for durable solutions in the form of employment programmes were separated between the ILO and the High Commissioner, but in the aftermath of the Second World War they were combined in the IRO. It was the opinion of the states that drew up the Constitution of the IRO that refugees needed to be "put to useful employment in order to avoid the evil and anti-social consequences of continued idleness" (United Nations, 1946a). Perhaps the most telling expression of the economic aspect of 'the refugee problem' in the immediate post-war period, however, is to be found in the first annual report of the IRO to the UN. The report gives an overview of repatriation and resettlement efforts undertaken and details the difficulties faced by the IRO regarding the following groups of people:

1   Unemployable individuals and families without a wage-earner;
2   Individuals in families who have been rejected by country selection commissions because of social or health problems;
3   Unaccompanied children; and
4   Families with a seriously ill member.

(United Nations, 1949a: 23)

Each of these groups of refugees would be considered charges on the public funds, and it was precisely these groups who made up the 'hard core' of the remaining refugees who could not be repatriated or resettled by the IRO, because they were too undesirable for other countries, that the UNHCR was created to assist.

What becomes clear by recognising the role of economics in the construction of a distinct 'refugee problem' is that the problem is the refugee herself. Her presence in the country of refuge places an economic burden on the state, for which a solution needs to be found. Regularising her status, negotiating the retention of her property when she flees her home, and providing some measure of employment rights, all appear to be much less humanitarian and much more self-interested on the part of states when we examine a wider selection of sources a little more closely. It is true that the League of Nations and the United Nations were both concerned with the problem of legal status, and of giving content to that status, and with the international protection of refugees. But while these were problems *for* the refugee, they required solutions because without them the refugee would continue to be a burden on her country of refuge. This problem *of* the refugee is what 'the refugee problem' was understood to be.

On Solutions

International action to 'solve' the refugee problem revolves around establishing a distinct legal status and specifying the content of that status – the rights and protections to be provided to individuals with that status – and assisting them to access one of the three so-called 'durable solutions': voluntary repatriation of refugees to their countries of origin, resettlement in safe third countries, or assimilation/local integration in their countries of refuge. As with our understanding of the refugee and the nature of the refugee problem, these solutions have their roots in the period under consideration.

From the very earliest days of international action on the refugee problem, repatriation of the refugees to their country of origin was considered the best and most durable solution, but the lack of diplomatic relations and the presence of political animosity between the League Members and the newly formed USSR made repatriation the least practical of options (for a detailed discussion of efforts to repatriate Russian refugees, see Long, 2009). The Members of the League therefore felt that a High Commissioner would also need to facilitate the movement of refugees to other countries where they might obtain employment should they not wish to return to Russia (League of Nations, 1921b: 488). Sir Samuel Hoare, one of Nansen's deputies stationed in Constantinople, offered one of the first expressions of the principle now known as *non-refoulement* in March of 1922, when he stated in his report to the League that it should be constantly exploring the possibilities of repatriation, but that no Russian would be compelled to return against his will (League of Nations, 1922c: 403).

If recognition that many Russian refugees had no desire to return to Russia while the Bolshevik regime remained in power made repatriation efforts difficult, repatriation of Armenian refugees would prove to be an even greater problem given the lack of an Armenian national home and the rejection of Armenians as citizens by the new Turkish Republic. Resettlement was deemed the best option for Armenian refugees and Nansen devoted significant time and effort on numerous schemes for Armenian resettlement, including the establishment of an Armenian national home rather than the "distribution" of Armenians to other states, all of which ultimately failed primarily due to lack of adequate financing and political will on the part of other states (Skran, 1995: 147–184). Despite the failure of these grand resettlement plans the League still placed great emphasis on the desirability of resettlement out of Europe as a solution where repatriation was deemed impossible, as demonstrated by the decision in 1924 to transfer "technical services" – all issues involved in the search for employment and resettlement – to the ILO, deemed to possess the necessary expertise to carry out this work successfully.

Agreement that refugees should not be compelled to return to their countries of origin is present in the sources from the beginning of League concern with refugees, but prohibitions on the expulsion of refugees came much later. The first formal recommendations against, not yet prohibitions of, expulsion are found in the *Arrangement* [of June 1928] *Relating to the Legal Status of Russian and Armenian Refugees*:

> It is recommended that measures for expelling foreigners or for taking other such action against them be avoided or suspended in regard to Russian and Armenian refugees in cases where the person concerned is not in a position to enter a neighbouring country in a regular manner.
>
> (League of Nations, 1928a: 57)

The first legal prohibition of expulsion does not appear until five years later with the 1933 Convention, in Article 3.

The final durable solution, assimilation/local integration in the host country (read, European country), does not appear to have been considered until the late 1920s, and was quickly deemed to be an unrealistic solution given the ever-increasing number of refugees for whom the League was taking responsibility. One of the earliest documents mentioning assimilation as a possible solution is an Assembly resolution issued during its ninth ordinary session, and quoted in one of Nansen's reports to the League on 14 December 1928: "a complete solution to the problem can only be provided by the return of the refugees to their country of origin or their assimilation by the countries at present giving them shelter" (League of Nations, 1928d: 175). But no less than six months later when the Advisory Commission issued their report on the possible ways and means of securing a definite solution of the refugee problem within the shortest possible time, the "radical solution" of naturalisation was deemed impractical given that naturalisation is a privilege that "cannot be granted without distinction to every person who requests it" (League of Nations, 1929: 1078). It was recommended that the High Commission be maintained along with the Nansen certificate system, and the High Commissioner should continue to pursue resettlement (League of Nations, 1929: 1079). By the time of the establishment of the IRO, naturalisation of the refugee in her country of refuge was considered "the only radical solution to the problem of the refugee who cannot be repatriated" (United Nations, 1949a: 65), and can thus be understood as occupying the lowest position in the hierarchy of durable solutions. Assimilation in the (usually European) country of refuge was the last remaining option after repatriation and resettlement prove impossible.

Calculating the Cost of Profound Concern

When we delve a little deeper into the sources once more, we do not find different solutions per se. What comes into relief are the calculations, the assumptions, the concerns, and the logics at work that frame how these solutions would be understood and implemented. To do justice to a proper examination of these frames of reference would require more space than I have available to devote to them, but by organising them into two overriding logics – of burden-limiting/shifting and self-interest – I hope to provide a sufficiently detailed exposition.

The overriding concern when it came to developing the solutions and measures to implement them highlighted above was not humanitarianism, as may be supposed, but rather to limit the burden placed by refugees on sovereign states. We can see this principle of burden-limiting most clearly in the abdication of formal financial responsibility evident in the funding (or lack thereof) of the various High Commissioners – a problem which plagues UNHCR to this day – and through the constant invocation of national security. In creating the High Commission, it was stipulated that the High Commissioner could not make himself in any way directly responsible for the relief of refugees, but would instead coordinate relief efforts undertaken by voluntary organisations (League of Nations, 1922a: 385). In March 1922 Nansen delivered a report in which he complained of inadequate funds placed at his disposal by the League and how this had hindered his ability to "solve the problem" as quickly as he could have if even a fraction of the monies that states had spent on their own relief efforts had been made available to the High Commission (League of Nations, 1922a: 385–386). What is interesting about this report is not so much the fact that adequate funds for the service of refugees were not available, but that they were not made available *to Nansen*. Inadequate funding for the High Commission's work was a recurring refrain through the League of Nations years, and private voluntary organisations frequently stepped in to close vital funding gaps. In this same report Nansen spoke of the "invaluable" services rendered by the Advisory Committee of Private Organisations, attached to the High Commission, most notably in the case of raising the necessary funds to continue to feed 25,000 starving Russian refugees in Constantinople after the French government announced it would no longer take on the responsibility of their maintenance (League of Nations, 1922a: 387–388). In another report of the same year, Nansen highlighted the role played by the Russian Red Cross in striking an agreement with the Bulgarian government for the evacuation of 1,000 invalids and their families to Bulgaria. Under the terms of the agreement the Bulgarian government would be relieved of financial responsibility of caring for the refugees, and this burden would be taken on by the Red Cross, which would, in fact, not only pay for the upkeep of the refugees, but also pay the Bulgarian government for allowing them access to its territory in the first place (League of Nations, 1922g: 1226).

In 1929, in its report on the re-organisation of the work of the League, the Advisory Commission to the High Commissioner for Refugees recommended a prolongation of the Office but stipulated once again that the League would only be responsible for funding its administrative expenses. They further stated that the cost of relief for refugees unable to work should come from the sale, to refugees, of the stamps validating their identity certificates, and any private donations made by charitable organisations (League of Nations, 1929: 1079). This recommendation was formalised in the statute of the Nansen International Office. Using money obtained through the compulsory purchase of stamps by refugees for relief purposes, thereby relieving the states of any formal financial responsibility for financing such work, was first suggested formally in 1926 when the money was put into a revolving fund to provide for the cost of transportation and settlement of resettled refugees – another expense for which states refused to make themselves liable (League of Nations, 1926a). We encounter the same abdication of formal financial responsibility by states with each incarnation of the High Commissioner's office, in 1931, 1933, 1938, and 1950. Even the comparatively well-financed IRO had state-imposed restrictions placed on its resources. The mandate of the IRO was to facilitate resettlement and repatriation, and this could include large-scale resettlement projects. The draft constitution of the IRO had stipulated that *all* expenditure, including resettlement projects, would be financed by mandatory contributions from Member Governments (United Nations, 1946a: Art.10.4). When the Constitution was finalised by the States Members this mandatory contribution was watered down to contributions on a voluntary basis and subject to the requirements of each state's constitutional procedure (United Nations, 1946c: Art.2.2i). Much as with the funding of Dr Nansen's work in the 1920s, what states appeared to be resistant to was agreeing to formal and mandated contributions for refugee relief or resettlement work, rather than being resistant to spending any money whatsoever. The general attitude governing the financing of the search for and implementation of solutions can best be summarised by the following statement from the Minutes of a League of Nations Council meeting in October 1927:

> Every member of the Council was filled with the most humanitarian feelings, and if it were in the Council's power to help all those who stood in need, he would be the first to propose that such assistance be given. After a decision had been taken, however, the states were called upon to pay the bill. When that moment came, the general attitude became somewhat more stringent.
>
> (League of Nations, 1927b: 1138)

Just as the term "unfortunate people" could easily be taken as a synonym for "refugee" by even the most cursory examination of the sources, so too does "national security" appear as the supreme burden-limiter, built into international agreements and conventions. The very first agreement regarding League action for refugees, of 5 July 1922, was, by comparison with later accords, severely limited in its actions, providing simply for the issue of a certificate of identity to Russian refugees. However, it was still subject to reservations on the grounds of national security. The Spanish attached the following reservation to their signature:

> Granting of the certificate and visa in no way infringes on the right of the Government, where national interest requires, to expel the refugee; and that the Government from whence the refugee came is obliged to readmit him to their territory.
>
> (League of Nations, 1922d: 240; translated from the French original)

Throughout the League of Nations period we see qualifications attached to the issuance of the identity certificate intended to enable the refugees to travel in search of work, that such issue shall in no way infringe on the right of the state to "supervise and control foreigners" (League of Nations, 1935c: 1681). The exact phrasing of these qualifications implies that this supervision and control extended not simply to the entry of other nationals but also to their movements within the state once admitted.

This reluctance to take a liberal approach to the admission of refugees is further evidenced by the practice of expulsion of refugees. Despite the efforts made by voluntary organisations and the High Commissioner to develop a travel document allowing legal border-crossing, they had noted on several occasions throughout the late 1920s and early 1930s that states were making increased use of their powers of expulsion of foreigners, particularly with regard to refugees (League of Nations, 1933a: 855). A report of the Inter-Governmental Advisory Commission for Refugees in 1933 noted that despite its repeated recommendations, state practice of expelling refugees continued, and while recognising that states had the right to regulate entry and expulsion, the Commission recommended the use of "internal measures" of a security nature to deal with refugees who had unlawfully entered a state's territory (League of Nations, 1933a: 855). The Commission further noted that states had been attempting to circumvent their obligations under previous arrangements to allow for the return of a refugee to the country which issued the certificate and where the refugee was thus deemed lawfully to reside. In many cases, states had been submitting such applications for return to lengthy bureaucratic and administrative procedures, "depriving the [re-entry] clause of all value" (League of Nations, 1933a: 855). Jacques Rubinstein, a prominent legal figure and Russian refugee, noted that the Assembly of the League still had to issue repeated resolutions – in 1933, 1934, and 1935 – condemning the practice of expelling refugees, indicating that state practice was not becoming more liberal but, in fact, more and more restrictive (Rubinstein, 1936: 724).

Even the 1951 Convention is qualified by state concerns for national security. The Ad hoc Committee on Statelessness and Related Problems, which prepared the draft convention, discussed the issue of expulsion, and concluded that the "sovereign right of a State to remove or keep from its territory foreigners regarded as undesirable cannot be challenged", but they recommended that expulsion should be dictated by reasons of national security and public order (United Nations, 1950a: 22). The discussion of a national security qualification to the prohibition of expulsion of refugees continued throughout the 1951 Conference of Plenipotentiaries, by way of amendments submitted by the United Kingdom (United Nations, 1951i) and Sweden (United Nations, 1951j). A new paragraph was inserted into Article 33 (*non-refoulement*) stating that "the benefit of the present provision may not, however, be claimed by a refugee who there are reasonable grounds for regarding as a danger to the security of the country in which he is" (United Nations, 1951o: Art.33.2). Article 32 of the Convention, on expulsion (the practice rather than its prohibition), contains a similar national security qualifier, but goes so far as to insert it into the subsection allowing the refugee to appeal an expulsion order. The Italian delegation had submitted an amendment calling for the removal of any right of appeal by the refugee (United Nations, 1951f), and by way of a compromise with the Belgian (United Nations, 1951h) and French amendments (United Nations, 1951g), the right to appeal was retained, but the ability of the refugee to submit evidence to clear her name would be subject to the exigencies of national security. The individual state in question would, of course, be the party to decide whether a refugee represented such a threat and could therefore be expelled, thereby relieving itself of the responsibility of guaranteeing to the refugee all the other rights enumerated in the Convention.

Self-Interest

The concept of self-interest is intimately linked with each of the above considerations, but there is a sense in which economic considerations dictated not only the limiting of state responsibility, but also their offers of sanctuary. As detailed above, the League of Nations addressed the refugee problem from an economic perspective from its earliest days. This led to a system whereby refugees were 'selected' for resettlement to fill the labour needs of states. One early example of this, in the years immediately following the First World War, is the French policy of relying on Russian refugees to replenish a workforce depleted by the war, and then promptly reversing this policy and embracing protectionism in the latter half of the 1920s (Skran, 1995: 24). Indeed, the economic depression caused by the stock market crash of 1929 saw increased protectionism on the part of states regarding access to employment opportunities for non-nationals, but also with regard to their borders. Gaining lawful entry became increasingly difficult for refugees throughout the 1930s, and this is nowhere more evident than in policies towards Jewish refugees from Germany who had been stripped of their property by the Nazi regime. Visa restrictions were redoubled to prevent arrivals at the border, and Jews were often turned away when they did arrive (Long, 2013: 11–12).

The policies pursued by the IRO during its three years of operations after the end of the Second World War are further examples of this logic of economic self-interest. The IRO was permitted to enter into resettlement agreements with governments, whereby the IRO would determine the eligibility for Refugee status of those applying for its assistance, and governments could then send 'selection missions' to the refugee camps administered by the IRO in order to select refugees with the required skills to fill labour shortages. Once the refugees had been through the selection process, the IRO would arrange for their travel to the country in question, where the refugee would be required to work in the pre-determined industry for a pre-determined period of time (United Nations, 1949a: 9; also Long, 2013: 14). The following excerpt is from the agreement the IRO concluded with the Australian government:

> The Commonwealth will submit ... particulars of the numbers and qualifications of desired immigrants.... The Commonwealth estimates that during the balance of 1947 the number of workers and dependents desired will approximate a total of 4000 persons. The Commonwealth shall have the full right of selection by officers of the Department for Immigration ... The PCIRO will be responsible for instituting such preliminary selection as may be required by the Commonwealth....
>
> (Holborn, 1956: 676)

The IRO resettled over one million refugees under such arrangements in just five years, but it drew sharp, often politically motivated criticism from Communist states. As a bloc, they had refused to become Parties to the IRO, and accused

Western states of using it as little more than an employment agency, saying that by doing so they had politicised what was an inherently humanitarian issue. There is no doubt a degree of political posturing involved in these accusations, which take up a significant proportion of the contributions by the Communist states to the discussions of how to replace the IRO when its mandate expired (United Nations, 1949b and c), but there also appears to be some degree of truth in this characterisation of the IRO. Refugees were not only resettled via employment programmes in Australia, Canada and the United States, but also in other European countries, including the UK. The UK instituted a European Voluntary Workers Programme (the EVW) and recruited workers from the camps run by the IRO. Under this scheme, the refugees were refused access to a travel document during their first year of residency, for fear that the best recruits might travel on to the land of their choice (Long, 2013: 14). The bargain of the EVW was explicit, Long claims: refugees were to work for their eventual right to settlement, and where they could no longer work – for medical reasons, including pregnancy, for example – they were returned to the camps on the continent (Long, 2013: 15).

The IRO had perhaps the largest budget of any intergovernmental organisation created to assist refugees, but therein lay the roots of its demise. As its mandate drew to a close, plans were drawn up for a replacement organisation. The United States had been its primary funder and, as disagreements and divisions between the US and its wartime ally, the USSR, grew, political and economic considerations in the US took over, manifesting in Congressional refusal to fund any organisation whose membership might include Communist countries (Karatani, 2005), and in the insistence that the new organisation have a greatly reduced budget and mandate, leaving the ultimate power to negotiate and facilitate resettlement of refugees with governments. It was clear from these discussions that, just as with each incarnation of formal refugee relief and protection in preceding years, the control of the cost of refugee assistance activities was to remain with the states themselves (Loescher and Scanlan, 1986: 40–42). UNHCR, with a greatly reduced budget and severely limited mandate, was thus founded to address the problem posed by the continued displacement of refugees who could not be repatriated or resettled because they were too old, too young, invalids, or in some other way incapable of skilled or unskilled labour. They were of no value to country selection commissions and so were left behind, languishing in refugee camps in a Europe struggling to recover from the ravages of war.

Private Voluntary Organisations and Refugees' Problems

It was not lost on Mr Rees, the gentleman with whom we began this chapter, that perhaps the private voluntary organisations that he, and others, represented were engaged in a different battle to that of the states attempting to 'solve' 'the refugee problem'. The identity certificate system, its reform to enable the refugee to return to the issuing country, and a convention listing specific rights and protections from expulsion, were all lobbied for persistently by private voluntary organisations that were also doing most of the leg-work on the ground in providing relief and assistance to refugees. While they won key victories, their work was also frequently frustrated by states that appeared to have a fundamentally different understanding of what the problem was that they were addressing. For example, refugee advocacy groups played a central role in the early 1930s in the discussions held by the Intergovernmental Advisory Commission for Refugees on the issue of expulsion. Largely as a result of persistent lobbying, the Commission recommended that refugees should only be expelled under serious circumstances, and not simply for the violation of police regulations (Skran, 1995: 134–135). As we saw above, however, states made increasing use of their powers of expulsion throughout the 1930s, in the face of repeated condemnation by the Assembly of the League. Private voluntary organisations also consistently intervened on behalf of refugees throughout the inter-war period. At the end of 1922 the Polish government threatened the expulsion of 6,000 Jews. At the urging of the Jewish Colonisation Association the League intervened and negotiated a reprieve until the refugees could gain visas to the US and elsewhere (Skran, 1995: 138). Jewish organisations played a vital role in securing orderly emigration of Jews from Germany, undoubtedly saving scores from the fate that eventually awaited their trapped compatriots. British Jewish organisations spent £3 million between 1933 and 1939 on assistance to Jews in Europe, and the American Joint Distribution Committee spent £4 million in the same period. These organisations, along with others, also managed to assist 40,000 refugees to leave Germany through obtaining visas and helping finance transportation costs (Skran, 1995: 202). The charitable organisations assisting refugees in this period were a diverse group, and certainly not all of them were immune to the more unsavoury characterisations of refugees, or paternalistic approaches to assistance, often exhibited by state representatives. It was not uncommon, for instance, for Christian charities to take an interest in assisting women and child refugees out of a desire to save them from 'moral threats' posed to them by Islam (Gatrell, 2013: 61). Other organisations also exhibited a concern, lying behind their offers of assistance, for protecting 'Western civilisation' from the potential dangers to be posed by states struggling to cope with hordes of uneducated or unemployed refugees (Gatrell, 2013: 54).

These problems aside, however, it is undeniable that without the assistance and advocacy of private voluntary organisations, much less progress would have been made on behalf of refugees. Perhaps the most telling evidence that these voluntary organisations had quite a different idea of the problem that needed to be addressed than did the states concerned lies in the victories they were unable to secure. At the same Conference of Plenipotentiaries at which Mr Rees made his impassioned plea for a spirit of liberalism and generosity, non-governmental organisations that were invited to observe the Conference were permitted to submit memoranda on the draft convention that had been circulated prior to the start of the deliberations. In many of these memoranda, the interested organisations drew attention to serious flaws and omissions in the draft convention relating to concrete problems that refugees faced, and made a series of concrete suggestions to address them, many of which were not taken on board by state representatives. The International Union of Catholic Women's Leagues highlighted the lack of formal protection for the family unity of refugees, noting that "in the life of refugees, this unity is constantly threatened by various measures relating to their admission to countries, to permission for them to work, etc." (United Nations, 1951n), and recommended that a new article be included in the convention which would protect refugees' right to a family life. The non-binding Recommendations of the Conference mention the importance of family unity, but no formal, legal guarantee was forthcoming. The World University Service and the World Jewish Congress both drew attention to the differential importance placed on elementary education and post-elementary education for refugees in the draft convention, and lobbied for the right to access post-elementary education on the same level as nationals of the country in which the refugee resided (United Nations, 1951m). The memorandum of the World Jewish Congress stated that the children of refugees are "future citizens of the country of residence which ought to be interested in their proper education. It is therefore suggested to extend 'national treatment' also to education dealt with in art. 17(2) [post-elementary education]" (United Nations, 1951k). But no changes to the draft articles on education materialised. The submission of the World Jewish Congress also noted two other key omissions in the draft convention, relating to the right to work and to the lack of provisions relating to refugee status determination, both of which are worth quoting at length:

> [T]he position of refugees is generally difficult indeed: they have lost their former positions, all their property; they have suffered physical and moral deprivations. All this puts them in an inferior position compared with other foreigners, let alone nationals of the country of their residence. Particularly difficult is the situation of self-employed persons and persons in liberal professions. For these reasons it would seem that Art. 13 and 14 are unnecessarily harsh and ought to be replaced by the same rule which governs wage-earning employment.
>
> (United Nations, 1951k)

> A definition does not by itself create rights for the person involved; the person must be declared to fall within one of the categories by a competent authority.... If there is no specific provision in the Convention, the determination would be within the competence of every contracting State. Under these circumstances, it would be perfectly possible for the same person to be regarded as a refugee in one contracting State and not to be recognised as such in another. To solve this difficulty it is suggested that the parties to the Convention agree that the determination made by the High Commissioner will be recognised by them.
>
> (United Nations, 1951k)

Neither of these suggestions, the latter deriving from a particularly prescient observation in light of contemporary approaches to asylum, was heeded by the states. One final example worth noting is the submission by the Confederation of Free Trade Unions, which criticised the financial straitjacket that the UNHCR had been put in, noting that "it is hard to see how the High Commissioner's work could be effective without some international financial assistance; it is, therefore, difficult to understand why he is directed not to approach governments with a request for voluntary contributions" (United Nations, 1951*l*). The preceding discussion in this chapter has shown that if we do not assume that all actors involved had alleviation of the same problems in mind it is easy to understand these restrictions placed on the competencies of the High Commissioner for Refugees.

Conclusion

Examining a wider range of sources beyond the specific legal agreements that give the formal contours of the international refugee regime demonstrates that 'the refugee problem' in need of a solution should be understood, primarily, as 'the refugee (as) problem'. In their essentials, the refugee regime, and the underlying 'refugee problem' that this regime was intended to 'solve', have remained largely unchanged. In 1967, a Protocol to the 1951 Convention was signed which removed the temporal and geographic qualifications of the original definition of a refugee; and regional agreements in the Americas – the *Cartagena Declaration* – and Africa – the *OAU Convention Governing the Specific Aspects of Refugee Problems in Africa* – have expanded the definition of the Refugee to include those who flee 'generalised violence', foreign domination, or events seriously disturbing public order, extending protection, at least on paper, to larger groups of displaced persons. The international refugee regime functions alongside, and often overlaps with, other international regimes such as that governing human rights, leading Alexander Betts to rename it the "refugee regime complex" (Betts, 2010). And yet, as promising as these developments may appear to be, in many ways access to any of the three durable solutions – themselves also oriented towards the problem of reinserting individuals into the state-based system, and thus preserving its integrity – has become even more elusive in recent decades.

Repatriation now tops the hierarchy of durable solutions, indeed being conceived by states – and often also by UNHCR – as the only viable solution to forced displacement, regardless of whether this repatriation is desired by the refugees themselves and thus voluntary, or whether such repatriation would be safe and successful (Chimni, 2004). The logic of burden-shifting has become ever more pronounced, particularly in the states of the global North. The Common European Asylum Policy functions, essentially, on an underlying logic of prevention: preventing asylum seekers from reaching European territory and thus accessing the harmonised procedures (Hyndman and Mountz, 2008). For those who do manage to make it to Europe, the burden of examining an asylum claim and providing protection is shifted on to the border states of the Union and, if at all possible, on to 'safe third countries' beyond the EU. Australia, while regularly offering the second highest number of resettlement places in the global North (although still a paltry figure when compared with the number of refugees UNHCR claims need to be resettled), has one of the harshest asylum regimes in the world, outsourcing the imprisonment of asylum seekers to neighbouring south-east Asian states, many of which are signatories of the 1951 Refugee Convention, but whose treatment of asylum seekers and refugees falls well below even the most basic protection standards.[1] The UNHCR itself has opened the door to many of these restrictive policies, and more. 'Temporary Protection' – the provision of reduced and time-limited protection – was the brainchild of High Commissioner Ogata in the wake of the breakdown of the former Yugoslavia, as were the 'right to remain' and 'preventive protection' – whereby UNHCR and other actors intervene during a potential refugee-producing situation to prevent displacements over the borders that would be 'destabilising' for surrounding states (Loescher, 2001: 295–301). It is no coincidence, perhaps, that these policies were ushered in at the same time as increasing numbers of asylum seekers from the global South began to make their way north. As Northern states began to shut off avenues for refugee resettlement and restrict access to asylum, Southern states began to restrict access to local integration. Enforced encampment policies, such as those pursued by the Kenyan government, host of the largest refugee camp complex in the world, are rationalised by national security concerns and the perceived need to avoid over-burdening fragile social services and employment markets (Lindley, 2011). The financial needs of UNHCR and other actors involved in camp management regularly fail to be met by donors, resulting in situations where even the most basic rights of refugees – such as the right to elementary education – cannot be fulfilled, let alone the right to work, to embark on vocational training, rights of association, family reunification, and so on. An increasing number of refugees now seek to 'self-settle' in urban environments, rather than be encamped, but in doing so face the risks and obstacles of a clandestine existence without papers or formal legal status.

It is, thus, difficult to imagine that these policy priorities would prevail if the driving force behind them was the desire to address the problems faced by refugees. But, rather than a betrayal of earlier efforts to solve the refugee problem', this chapter has shown that these policies are in fact an extension of, and consistent with, a fundamental underlying assumption of the problem in need of a solution: while aid workers, rights advocates, doctors, lawyers, and many thousands of others who work within the international refugee regime attempt to solve, or at least alleviate, problems *for* refugees, the international refugee regime itself was created to solve the problem *of* the refugee. The next two chapters will examine why 'the refugee (as) problem' emerges when it does – in the early decades of the twentieth century – and examine how 'the refugee problem' is managed and the consequences of this management.

Note

1 In August 2016, the *Guardian* newspaper in the UK received a cache of over 2,000 leaked documents, now known as the Nauru Files, detailing appalling living conditions in the detention camps and allegations of widespread abuse, including of children, by authorities.

References

Betts, A., "The Refugee Regime Complex" *Refugee Survey Quarterly* 29(1) (2010): 12–37

Chimni, B. S., "From Resettlement to Involuntary Repatriation: Towards a Critical History of Durable Solutions to Refugee Problems" in *Refugee Survey Quarterly* 23(3) (2004): 56–73

Gatrell, P., *The Making of the Modern Refugee* (Oxford: Oxford University Press, 2013)

Hathaway, J., "The Evolution of Refugee Status in International Law: 1920–1950" *International and Comparative Law Quarterly* 33(2) (1984): 348–380

Holborn, L., *The International Refugee Organisation: A Specialised Agency of the United Nations: Its History and Work 1946–1952* (London: Oxford University Press, 1956)

Hope-Simpson, Sir J., *The Refugee Problem: A Report of a Survey* (Oxford: Oxford University Press, 1939)

Hyndman, J., and Mountz, A., "Another Brick in the Wall? Neo-*Refoulement* and the Externalization of Asylum by Australia and Europe", *Government and Opposition* 43(2) (2008): 249–269

Karatani, R., "How History Separated Refugee and Migrant Regimes: In Search of Their Institutional Origins" *International Journal of Refugee Law* 17(3) (2005): 517–541

Krasner, S., "Structural Causes and Regime Consequences: Regimes as Intervening Variables" in *International Organization* 36(2) (1982): 185–205

League of Nations, "The Question of the Russian Refugees – Covering Letter and Memorandum by the Secretary General, and Annexes" in *League of Nations Official Journal* 2(3–4) (1921a): 225–230

League of Nations, "The Question of the Russian Refugees – Circular Letter by the Secretary General to All States Concerned with the Question, and Documents Received" in *League of Nations Official Journal* 2(7–8) (1921b): 485–509

League of Nations, "The Question of the Russian Refugees – Report by M. Hanotaux" in *League of Nations Official Journal* 2(9) (1921c): 755–758

League of Nations, "Resolutions Adopted by the Conference on the Question of the Russian Refugees" in *League of Nations Official Journal* 2(10) (1921d): 899–902

League of Nations, "Information Provided by Members of the Conference of Enquiry Held at Geneva, August 22nd–24th, 1921, and Memoranda Submitted to That Conference" in *League of Nations Official Journal* 2(11) (1921e): 1006–1028

League of Nations, "Annex 321 – General Report on the Work Accomplished up to March 15th 1922, by Dr Fridtjof Nansen, High Commissioner of the League" in *League of Nations Official Journal* 3(5) (1922a): 385–395

League of Nations, "Annex 321a – Special Report by the High Commissioner of the League Requesting the Assistance of the Governments of Members of the League in the Accomplishment of His Work" in *League of Nations Official Journal* 3(5) (1922b): 396–400

League of Nations, "Annex 321b – The Russian Refugees in Constantinople – Report by Sir Samuel Hoare" in *League of Nations Official Journal* 3(5) (1922c): 401–403

League of Nations, *Arrangement with Respect to the Issue of Certificates of Identity to Russian Refugees* (League of Nations Treaty Series Vol. 13, No. 355) (1922d): 238–242

League of Nations, "Annex 384 – Russian Refugees – Report by Dr Nansen, Submitted to the Council" in *League of Nations Official Journal* 3(8) (1922e): 923–928

League of Nations, "Russian Refugees – Report by Dr Fridtjof Nansen, High Commissioner of the League of Nations, to the Fifth Committee of the Assembly" in *League of Nations Official Journal* 3(11) (1922f): 1134–1139

League of Nations, "Annex 401 – Russian Refugees – Report by Dr Nansen Submitted to the Council on September 1st, 1922" in *League of Nations Official Journal* 3(11) (1922g): 1225–1227

League of Nations, "Annex 472: Report by Dr Nansen, High Commissioner of the League for Refugees, Submitted to the Council" in *League of Nations Official Journal* 4(3) (1923a): 389–393

League of Nations, "Annex 542: Report by Dr Nansen, submitted to the Council" in *League of Nations Official Journal* 4(8) (1923b): 1040–1045

League of Nations, "Minutes: Second Meeting (Public) Thursday June 12th 10:30am" in *League of Nations Official Journal* 5(7) (1924a): 904–908

League of Nations, "Annex 635: Report by Dr Fridtjof Nansen, High Commissioner for Refugees, Presented to the Council" in *League of Nations Official Journal* 5(7) (1924b): 958–963

League of Nations, "Annex 637 – Armenian Refugees – Report by Dr Nansen, High Commissioner for Refugees" in *League of Nations Official Journal* 5(7) (1924c): 967–971

League of Nations, *Arrangement Relating to the Issue of Identity Certificates to Russian and Armenian Refugees, Supplementing and Amending the Previous Arrangements Dated 5 July, 1922 and 31 May, 1924* (League of Nations Treaty Series Vol. 89, No. 2004) (1926a): 48–52

League of Nations, "Annex 884 – Conference on Russian and Armenian Refugee Questions – Report by Dr Nansen, High Commissioner of the League of Nations for Refugees" in *League of Nations Official Journal* 7(7) (1926b): 983–986

League of Nations, "Annex 990 – Letter from the Director of the International Labour Office to the Secretary General, and Report by the High Commissioner" in *League of Nations Official Journal* 8(10) (1927a): 1336–1338

League of Nations, "Extension to Other Categories of Refugees of the Measures Taken to Assist Russian and Armenian Refugees" in *League of Nations Official Journal* 8(10) (1927b): 1137–1139

League of Nations, *Arrangement Relating to the Legal Status of Russian and Armenian Refugees* (League of Nations Treaty Series Vol. 89 No. 2005) (1928a): 55–61

League of Nations, *Arrangement Concerning the Extension to Other Categories of Refugees of Certain Measures Taken in Favour of Russian and Armenian Refugees* (League of Nations Treaty Series Vol. 89, No. 2006) (1928b): 65–67

League of Nations, *Agreement Concerning the Function of the Representatives of the League of Nations' High Commissioner for Refugees* (League of Nations Treaty Series Vol. 92 No. 2126) (1928c): 378–380

League of Nations, "Annex 1092 – Russian, Armenian, Assyrian, Assyro-Chaldean and Turkish Refugees – Memorandum by Dr Nansen, High Commissioner for Refugees" in *League of Nations Official Journal* 10(1) (1928d): 174–176

League of Nations, "Annex 1131 – Report of the Advisory Commission to the High Commissioner for Refugees, Submitted to the Council" in *League of Nations Official Journal* 10(7) (1929): 1077–1080

League of Nations, "Constitution of the Nansen International Office for Refugees" in *League of Nations Official Journal* 12(2) (1931a): 308–311

League of Nations, "Work of the Governing Body of the Nansen International Office for Refugees During Its First and Second Session" in *League of Nations Official Journal* 12(6) (1931b): 1004–1011

League of Nations, "Annex 1440 – "Work of the Intergovernmental Advisory Commission for Refugees During its Fifth Session, and Communication from the Nansen International Office for Refugees" in *League of Nations Official Journal* 14(7) (1933a): 854–858

League of Nations, "Organisation on an International Basis of Assistance to Refugees (Jewish and Other) Coming from Germany – Resolution Adopted by the Assembly" in *League of Nations Official Journal* 14(12) (1933b): 1616–1618

League of Nations, *Convention Relating to the International Status of Refugees* (League of Nations Treaty Series Vol. 159, No. 3663) (1933c): 201–217

League of Nations, "Annex 1537 – Resignation of Mr James G. McDonald, High Commissioner for Refugees (Jewish and Other) Coming from Germany" in *League of Nations Official Journal* 17(2) (1935a): 160–163

League of Nations, "Annex 1541 – Work of the Inter-Governmental Advisory Commission for Refugees during its Seventh Session" in *League of Nations Official Journal* 16(6) (1935b): 656–659

League of Nations, "Plan for the Issue of a Certificate of Identity to Refugees from the Saar" in *League of Nations Official Journal* 16 (1935c): 1681–1683

League of Nations, *Provisional Arrangement Concerning the Status of Refugees Coming from Germany* (League of Nations Treaty Series Vol. 171, No. 3952) (1936): 77–87

League of Nations, *Convention Concerning the Status of Refugees Coming from Germany* (League of Nations Treaty Series, Vol. 192, No. 4461) (1938a): 61–81

League of Nations, "International Assistance to Refugees: Action Taken on the Initiative of the President of the United States of America" in *League of Nations Official Journal* 19(8–9) (1938b): 676–677

Lindley, A., "Between a Protracted and a Crisis Situation: Policy Responses to Somali Refugees in Kenya" in *Refugee Survey Quarterly* 30(4) (2011): 14–49

Loescher, G., *The UNHCR and World Politics: A Perilous Path* (Oxford: Oxford University Press, 2001)

Loescher, G., and Scanlan, J. A., *Calculated Kindness: Refugees and America's Half-Open Door, 1945–Present* (New York: The Free Press, 1986)

Long, K., "Early Repatriation Policy: Russian Refugee Return 1922–1924" in *Journal of Refugee Studies* 22(2) (2009): 133–154

Long, K., "When Refugees Stopped Being Migrants: Movement, Labour and Humanitarian Protection" in *Migration Studies* 1(1) (2013): 4–26

Rubinstein, J. L., "The Refugee Problem" in *International Affairs (Royal Institute of International Affairs 1931–1939)* 15(5) (1936): 716–734

Saunders, N., "Paradigm Shift or Business as Usual? A Historical Reappraisal of the 'Shift' to Securitisation of Refugee Protection" in *Refugee Survey Quarterly* 33(3) (2014): 69–92

Skran, C., "Profiles of the First Two High Commissioners" *Journal of Refugee Studies* 1(3–4) (1988): 277–296

Skran, C., *Refugees in Inter-War Europe: The Emergence of a Regime* (Oxford: Oxford University Press, 1995)

Soguk, N., *States and Strangers: Refugees and Displacements of Statecraft* (Minneapolis: University of Minnesota Press, 1999)

United Nations, "Refugees and Displaced Persons" *Economic and Social Council*, E/RES/18 (III) (1946a)

United Nations, *Final Act of the Intergovernmental Conference on the Adoption of a Travel Document for Refugees and Agreement Relating to the Issue of a Travel Document to Refugees Who Are the Concern of the Intergovernmental Committee on Refugees* (United Nations Treaty Series Vol. 11, No. 150) (1946b): 74–105

United Nations, *The Constitution of the International Refugee Organisation* (United Nations Treaty Series Vol. 18, No. 283) (1946c): 3–24

United Nations, *Universal Declaration of Human Rights* (1948)

United Nations, "First Annual Report of the International Refugee Organisation to the United Nations" *Economic and Social Council*, E/1334 (1949a)

United Nations, "Summary Record of the Two Hundred and Twenty-Eighth Meeting" *General Assembly (Third Committee)*, A/C.3/SR.228 (1949b)

United Nations, "Summary Record of the Two Hundred and Twenty-Ninth Meeting" *General Assembly (Third Committee)*, A/C.3/SR.229 (1949c)

United Nations, "Provisional Summary Record of the 257th Meeting" *General Assembly (Third Committee)*, A/C.3/SR.257 (1949d)

United Nations, "Provisional Summary Record of the Two-Hundred and Sixty-Third Meeting" *General Assembly (Third Committee)*, A/C.3/SR.263 (1949e)

United Nations, "Status of Refugees and Stateless Persons – Memorandum by the Secretary General" Ad hoc *Committee on Statelessness and Related Problems*, E/AC.32/2 (1950a)

United Nations, "Report of the Ad hoc Committee on Statelessness and Related Problems" Ad hoc *Committee on Statelessness and Related Problems*, E/AC.32/5 (1950b)

United Nations, "Statute of the Office of the United Nations High Commissioner for Refugees, Established by UNGA Res.428(V)" *General Assembly*, A/Res/428(V) (1950c)

United Nations, "Texts of the Draft Convention and the Draft Protocol to Be Considered by the Conference" *Conference of Plenipotentiaries on the Status of Refugees and Stateless Persons*, A/CONF.2/1 (1951a)

United Nations, "Summary Record of the Third Meeting" *Conference of Plenipotentiaries on the Status of Refugees and Stateless Persons*, A/CONF.2/SR.3 (1951b)

United Nations, "Draft Convention Relating to the Status of Refugees, Switzerland: Amendment to Article 10" *Conference of Plenipotentiaries on the Status of Refugees and Stateless Persons*, A/CONF.2/35 (1951c)

United Nations, "Summary Record of the Eighth Meeting" *Conference of Plenipotentiaries on the Status of Refugees and Stateless Persons*, A/CONF.2/SR.8 (1951d)

United Nations, "Summary Record of the Nineteenth Meeting" *Conference of Plenipotentiaries on the Status of Refugees and Stateless Persons*, A/CONF.2/SR.19 (1951e)

United Nations, "Draft Convention Relating to the Status of Refugees, Italy: Amendment to Article 27" *Conference of Plenipotentiaries on the Status of Refugees and Stateless Persons*, A/CONF.2/57 (1951f)

United Nations, "Draft Convention Relating to the Status of Refugees, France: Amendment to Article 27" *Conference of Plenipotentiaries on the Status of Refugees and Stateless Persons*, A/CONF.2/63 (1951g)

United Nations, "Draft Convention Relating to the Status of Refugees, Belgium: Amendment to Article 27" *Conference of Plenipotentiaries on the Status of Refugees and Stateless Persons*, A/CONF.2/68 (1951h)

United Nations, "Draft Convention Relating to the Status of Refugees, United Kingdom: Amendment to Article 28" *Conference of Plenipotentiaries on the Status of Refugees and Stateless Persons*, A/CONF.2/69 (1951i)

United Nations, "Draft Convention Relating to the Status of Refugees, Sweden: Amendment to Article 28" *Conference of Plenipotentiaries on the Status of Refugees and Stateless Persons*, A/CONF.2/70 (1951j)

United Nations, "Memorandum Concerning the Draft Convention Relating to the Status of Refugees and the Draft Protocol Relating to the Status of Stateless Persons: Statement Submitted by the World Jewish Congress" *Conference of Plenipotentiaries on the Status of Refugees and Stateless Persons*, A/CONF.2/NGO.1 (1951k)

United Nations, "Proposals Concerning the Draft Convention Relating to the Status of Refugees: Statement Submitted by the International Confederation of Free Trade Unions" *Conference of Plenipotentiaries on the Status of Refugees and Stateless Persons*, A/CONF.2/NGO/5 (1951l)

United Nations, "Memorandum Concerning Article 17 the Draft Convention Relating to the Status of Refugees: Statement Submitted by World University Service" *Conference of Plenipotentiaries on the Status of Refugees and Stateless Persons*, A/CONF.2/NGO/9 (1951m)

United Nations, "Observations Concerning the Draft Convention and Draft Protocol: Statement Submitted by the International Union of Catholic Women's Leagues" *Conference of Plenipotentiaries on the Status of Refugees and Stateless Persons*, A/CONF.2/NGO/12 (1951n)

United Nations, *Convention Relating to the Status of Refugees* (United Nations Treaty Series Vol. 189, No. 2545): 138–220 (1951o)

United Nations, *Protocol Relating to the Status of Refugees* (United Nations Treaty Series Vol. 606, No. 8791): 268–276 (1967)

2 Michel Foucault, Governmentality, and the State

The Emergence of the Refugee (as) Problem

Refugees have existed throughout recorded history and probably since the dawn of the human community.

(Smyser, 1985: 154)

[I]t is the genealogy of problems that concerns me. Why a problem and why such a kind of problem, why a certain way of problematizing appears at a given point in time.

(Foucault in Lotringer, 2007: 141)

On 20 February 1921, the International Committee of the Red Cross sent a memorandum to the Council of the League of Nations. The League had recently completed an ambitious effort to repatriate prisoners of war from the Great War, and the successful coordination of these efforts led the ICRC to believe that the League was best placed to undertake a new commission, on behalf of Russian refugees. The memorandum sought to draw the attention of the League to:

More than 800,000 Russian refugees ... at present dispersed in all the countries of Europe, especially in the Baltic States, in Poland, in Turkey, in Bulgaria, and in Jugo-Slavia. These people are without legal protection, and without any well-defined legal status. The majority of them are without means of subsistence, and one must particularly draw attention to the position of the children and the youths amongst them who are growing up in an ever-increasing misery, without adequate means of education, and who are in danger of becoming useless and harmful elements in the Europe of tomorrow.

(League of Nations, 1921: 228)

In the previous chapter, we saw how the League did indeed respond to the ICRC's call and an international regime was created to address 'the problem' of the appearance of these Russians in countries surrounding the former Russian Empire. And yet, this was by no means the first mass displacement episode in human history. In 1985, then-Deputy United Nations High Commissioner for

Refugees, W. D. Smyser, characterised such forced migration as a phenomenon as old as human history. Why, then, was it not until the early years of the twentieth century that a distinct 'refugee problem' was recognised, and that coordinated, international efforts were made to address it? This chapter seeks to answer this question. Why, despite the arguably age-old phenomenon of forced migration, did it become a problem in need of a solution only in the early years of the twentieth century? Why did 'the refugee (as) problem' appear at this "given point in time"?

I am certainly not the first to address the emergence of the refugee problem, and in what follows I do not seek to contradict or disagree with previous analyses but, rather, to supplement them. Previous accounts, such as those by Nevzat Soguk and Emma Haddad, have done a great deal to explain the emergence of the 'refugee' as a distinctly modern subject, noting the centrality of the identity of the state as *nation*-state in this process. Both Haddad (2008) and Soguk (1999) argue that as states became nation-states, the foreign 'other' became necessary for the consolidation of the national citizen as the rightful subject of political life. As the state nationalised, the expulsion of individuals who came to be understood as 'foreign' served what Soguk calls the "task of statecraft", helping to artificially produce the cultural/religious/national homogeneity deemed necessary for modern territorial governance (Soguk, 1999: 85–86). Once they have been expelled, conceptualising such foreigners as refugees – as figures lacking the fundamental characteristics of citizenship – serves the task of statecraft both for those states to which refugees seek admittance and to the territorial order in general, providing the concrete 'other' against which citizenship as the modern political subjectivity can be constructed and empowered, and which, in turn, justifies the continued existence of the state as nation-state. These are analyses with which I largely agree. And yet, there is still a question left unanswered, perhaps due to the implicit focus of these analyses on the emergence of the *refugee* rather than the refugee *problem*. The emergence of the first nation-state, France, preceded international recognition of a refugee problem by well over a century, and the history of this intervening century is arguably one of the messy process of attempted nationalisation of the states of Europe, similarly accompanied by population displacements. And so why was this displacement, of those who did not 'belong', not conceptualised as a problem in need of coordinated international action at the time? Michael Marrus argues that the numbers of displaced people prior to the early twentieth century were simply not high enough to become a cause of concern to governments. Even as numbers began to rise through the nineteenth century, particularly in response to the revolutions sweeping Europe from 1848, this increase was too insubstantial to worry host governments (Marrus, 1985: 22–25). While there may be some element of truth to this diagnosis, I suggest that it is but a partial diagnosis. I posit, rather, that refugees did not represent any drastic disruptions, either for host societies or for the international community in general, prior to the twentieth century, because, in important ways, neither these host societies nor the international system yet existed in such a way as to be disrupted by the emergence and presence of such persons. Neither 'the state' nor the 'international system' existed in such a way as to enable the conceptualisation of mass population displacement as a distinct 'problem' in need of international coordination. The nationalisation of the state is an important part of the development of the modern state and state system, but we also need to attend to the *state* partner of the nation-state coupling. Essentially, this chapter asserts that it is helpful to look beyond the nationalisation of the state, and international (or inter-state) system, to understand why forced displacement comes to be understood as a distinct 'problem'; not because such an explanation is mistaken, but because it is incomplete. Attending to other important dynamics at work in the development of the modern state and state system will not only deepen our understanding of the emergence of the refugee (as) *problem*, but will also shed light on why this problem comes to be managed in the way that it does, a task to which I will turn in the next chapter. Ultimately, this chapter argues that while people have always moved between communities and attempted to escape from violence and persecution, it was only with the development of the political rationality underpinning, and indeed enabling, the rise of the modern state and inter-state system that it was possible for the 'refugee (as) problem' to emerge as a distinct problem in need of sustained attention. With the emergence of population as a distinct entity, the management of which became the responsibility of government, migration became a phenomenon in need of regulation, necessitating the development of a nascent migration regime. When groups of people emerged, *en masse*, on to the international scene unable to conform to the newly systematised rules of the game, a new 'problem' was conceptualised, and a new regime needed to attempt to manage it.

To make this argument I turn, primarily, to the lectures given by Michel Foucault at the Collège de France between 1975 and 1979, as it is in these lectures that Foucault turns his attention to the state. Employing the Collège de France lectures is not without its problems. Unlike Foucault's studies of madness, discourse, discipline, social medicine, and sexuality, the lecture courses were never intended to be published. The lectures that Foucault gave while holding the Chair in the History of Systems of Thought are accounts of work in progress, and as such are characterised by stops and starts, by the exploration of trains of thought that lead to dead-ends, by positing new directions which had opened where he least expected, and of questions still left unexplored. Nevertheless, the posthumous publication of the lectures has led to an upsurge of interest in Foucault's work and has given much-needed additional detail to some of his most influential concepts, such as governmentality, and improved our understanding of Foucault's views on the state. When employed with due attention to the nature of the material, and supplemented by the work of others, these lectures provide several useful insights into the way in which the modern state and state system developed, focusing on the underlying rationality – or modes of thought and practice – supporting, and indeed enabling, this process. To put it another way, Foucault's reflections in these lectures can provide a 'grid of intelligibility' upon which a series of events and emerging practices, important to understanding the emergence of the refugee (as) *problem*, can be mapped. The nationalisation of the state so central to Soguk and Haddad's analyses occurred contemporaneously with a series of other events and processes including: the rise of humanitarianism; the birth of the welfare state; the emergence of health as a 'global' area of concern; and the utilisation of international conferences as a mechanism to address collective problems and facilitate international interaction – arguably a key step in the emergence of an international *system*. To be clear, in what follows I do not seek to locate 'the cause' of 'the refugee (as) problem'. Rather, I seek to explore how the emergence, or conceptualisation, of such a problem is made possible. These developments will be analysed first at the level of the state, demonstrating that as the rationality and practices of governing change, migration as a phenomenon becomes problematised in different ways: where population is understood simply as an aggregate of productive subjects and key to the state's strength, it is emigration and the 'internal' distribution of population, rather than immigration which is problematised. As practices and rationalities of government changed from the late eighteenth century, and population came to be understood as a kind of quasi-natural being, whose processes government must manage, migration was problematised differently: as a phenomenon in need of regulation and management rather than strict prohibition or permission. The third section of the chapter addresses how these same developments in the rationality and practice of governing, at the level of the state, also reveal shifting understandings of inter-state relations, and, thus, how migration can come to be understood as a process, or phenomenon, in need of *international* cooperation to be effectively managed. The final section will then revisit the immediate population/migration management concerns contemporaneous with the appearance of 'the refugee problem', in the aftermath of the First World War.

The State: Governmentality and Population

As a thinker who came to be more and more concerned with overtly 'political' matters, Foucault takes an unconventional approach to the study of the state. In line with the method he had employed in his earlier studies on madness, Foucault refused to grant a privileged place to 'the state', refusing to develop a 'theory of the state' on the basis of its supposed 'essence', or fundamental properties or propensities. He instead approaches the question of the development of the state from the perspective of the practice of governing. An analysis of government

> studies the practical conditions under which forms of statehood emerge, stabilise and change, how they combine and connect different and diverse 'elements' in a way that, retrospectively, an 'object' – the state – appears that seems to have existed prior to the historical and political process, presumably guiding and directing it.
>
> (Lemke, 2007: 47)

Foucault's focus is not, therefore, on the state 'itself' but on the practices and rationalities of governing/government. Approaching the state, and its development, from the perspective of the problematique of government sheds light not only on the emergence of forms of national government, administration, and its techniques, but also on the emergence of "forms of rational knowledge taking the direction of public policy as their objective – principally, political economy, political arithmetic, vital and social statistics, and the social sciences and economics" (Dean, 2003: 179). Foucault thus understands 'the state' as both an object and product of developments in the reflective practices of government, or governmentality. Three broad stages of the historical development of this governmentality are evident in his lectures delivered between 1975 and 1979, relating to three broad situations in which government becomes a problem (Leira, 2011: 119): the period of the 'administrative state', from roughly the mid-sixteenth to the mid-eighteenth centuries, characterised by *raison d'état*, mercantilism and police; the period of the 'governmentalising state', from the late eighteenth to the mid-twentieth centuries, characterised by the development of a liberal art of government, political economy, biopolitics, and mechanisms of security; and the current period of neoliberal 'governmentalisation of government', in which individuals and groups increasingly take upon themselves responsibility for their own government. These different 'problematisations' of government should not be understood as strictly separate periods, with single, easily identifiable ruptures, and in which one art of government is completely and permanently replaced by another. Rather, they are schematic, where "residues of past rationalities intersect with the phantasms that prefigure the future" (Rose, 1993: 285). Of these three stages, only the first two will be of concern here, and each will be addressed in turn, both on their own terms, and in their implications for conceptualising migration and displacement. Understanding these developments is central to understanding how certain kinds of migration become problematised at certain points in time, and thus how a 'refugee problem' emerges only in the late nineteenth/early twentieth century, rather than before.

From Administrative State to Governmentalising State

Foucault locates the emergence of the state as an object of reflected practice in the mid-sixteenth century, when the confluence of two events provoked a general crisis of, and explosion of interest in, 'government'. These two events were the decline of feudalism, and the religious upheavals of the Reformation and Counter-Reformation. Whole bodies of thought emerged which took 'government' – the conduct of conduct (Foucault, EWP: 381) – as their central problematique: the revival of Stoicism and the problem of the government of oneself, the emergence of pedagogy and the problem of the government of children, theological battles over the proper government of souls, and, in the political realm, the problem of the government of the state (Foucault, STP: 88). Foucault calls these reflections on the problem of governing the state, reflections on the "art of government". He takes Machiavelli's *The Prince* as a point of comparison to explain what was unique about this new type of political reflection. Treatises such as *The Prince* were primarily concerned with the ways in which the sovereign can maintain control over his territory and rule in accordance with natural or divine laws, or with due regard to the vagaries of fortune (Foucault, STP: 91–92). The knowledge required of the prince, if he was to maintain control over his territory, was of natural and divine laws, and he must also know when, how, and to what degree to apply this "wisdom" (Foucault, STP: 273). With the treatises on the art of government there is a shift from sovereignty as command to government as conduct, via a very different kind of knowledge. To be able to hold on to one's territory was not considered to be the same as possessing the art of governing. In order to govern one had to understand the 'things' to be governed, to be conducted or arranged. In much the same way as the head of the family must know the proper way to manage his wife, his children and his servants – known at the time as "economy" – the prince, if he is to govern properly, must know how to introduce economy – the proper management of individuals, goods and wealth – in his territory:

> To govern a state will thus mean the application of economy, the establishment of an economy, at the level of the state as a whole, that is to say, exercising supervision and control over its inhabitants, wealth, and the conduct of all and each, as attentive as that of a father's over his household and goods.
>
> (Foucault, STP: 95)

The idea that the aim of the sovereign – the aim of government – is to strengthen the state itself, rather than strengthening the sovereign, was known at the time as *raison d'état*. We are used to thinking of *raison d'état* in terms of arbitrariness, or violence, but in this period it was understood as a rationality specific to the art of governing states. At the end of the sixteenth century, Italian jurist Giovanni Botero defined *raison d'état* as "a perfect knowledge of the means through which states form, strengthen themselves, endure and grow" (Foucault, EWP: 406). Chemnitz, in the mid-seventeenth century, similarly defined *raison d'état* as "a certain political consideration required for all public matters, councils and projects, whose only aim is the state's preservation, expansion and felicity" (Foucault, EWP: 406). The strength, expansion, and endurance of the state was to be assured through the introduction of economy. The supervision and control over the inhabitants, wealth, and conduct "of all and each" that this required is only possible, however, if one possesses sufficient knowledge of what is to be supervised and controlled. Such knowledge went by the name of "statistics" – knowledge of the state in its different elements, dimensions and factors of its strength (Foucault, STP: 100). The collection of this knowledge, however, necessitated the development of an administrative apparatus – an apparatus that could both collect the necessary knowledge and use that knowledge in the effective regulation of the state. This apparatus went by the name of "police", or

Polizei, which, in the seventeenth and eighteenth centuries, meant something quite different, and much broader, than what it means today. It was not simply an institution of law enforcement, but a technology of government which intervened in the behaviour of individuals in specific, minute detail, in permanent and positive ways, in order to preserve and enhance the lives of individuals so that they may be of most use to the state (Foucault, EWP: 413). The police's purview covered such broad areas as religion and morals, public health, roads and highways, public safety, trade, factory workers, liberal arts, and the poor. The police were, thus, the internal array of forces intended to modulate and enhance the conduct of domestic populations (Johnson, 2014: 12), in order to align the welfare of the people with the concern to preserve and enhance state power (Valverde, 2007: 170).

The establishment of police was inseparable from mercantilism. Not simply an economic ideology, and the dominant one between the sixteenth and eighteenth centuries, mercantilism was an effort to rationalise the exercise of power – through the police – in terms of the knowledge acquired through statistics, and simultaneously was a set of doctrinal principles concerning how to increase the power and wealth of the state (Foucault, STP: 101). Mercantilism was, in other words, concerned with population as a productive force; as a source of the strength of the state. In providing manpower for agriculture, the population guarantees abundant harvests and extensive cultivated land, leading to a low price for grain and agricultural products. In providing manpower for manufacturing, it enables the state, as far as possible, to do without imports, ensuring that steady levels of bullion remain in the territory and treasury. A strong and productive population also ensures competition within the workforce, which ensures low wages. Low wages, in turn, meant low prices of products, and, therefore, a greater possibility of export, further enriching the state treasury (Foucault, STP: 68–69). This wealth can then be used to equip large armies, as a visible sign of the strength of the state. This 'population-wealth' couple was, thus, the privileged object of governmental reason (Foucault, STP: 365): the way to increase the wealth of the state is to increase its population. However, the population can only be the basis of the state's wealth, and therefore strength, in this way if it is framed on the one hand by a regulatory apparatus that ensures the continual growth of the population – i.e. that prevents emigration, encourages immigration, and promotes the birth rate – and framed on the other hand by a regulatory apparatus that ensures the continued productivity of that population – i.e. that defines useful and exportable products, fixes the products to be produced, the means of their production, and the wages to be paid for their production, and which prevents idleness and vagrancy (Foucault, STP: 69). The police, in its meticulous, constant, and detailed regulation of the daily lives of the population, provide this regulatory apparatus.

The administrative state – the state of police and mercantilism – was the product and object of a rationality of rule which took as its main problematique the strengthening of the state itself – *raison d'état* – in the context of social, political and religious upheaval unleashed by the Reformation, Counter-Reformation, and the decline of feudalism. But it was in the development of this rationality of governing that the seeds for its own decline were sown. The governmentalising state, which developed from the mid-eighteenth century, and which was the product and object of a liberal rationality of government, grew initially out of an internal critique of the techniques of *raison d'état*, most notably of police as a technology of government and its ability to ensure state strength through the meticulous regulation of the daily lives of its subjects. It was through the development and deployment of the statistical analyses that were intended to facilitate and rationalise this exhaustive administrative apparatus of the police, that it was realised that the relationship between population and resources can no longer be managed through such a system or, more accurately, it was 'discovered' that this relationship could not be managed *effectively* by such means. This shift was evident, Foucault claims, in the development, in the latter half of the eighteenth century, of political economy – a mode of economic and political reflection based upon a fundamentally new understanding of 'population'.

For mercantilists, the population was the sum of individual subjects in a territory and the source of the state's strength, to the extent that it contributes to the balance of trade and can fill the ranks of the army; and a collection of subjects whose lives can be controlled in every particular by regulations to ensure their productivity (Foucault, STP: 70). For the political economists of the mid-to-late eighteenth century, population was not the simple sum of subjects who inhabit a territory, but was, in fact, a quasi-natural being dependent upon a series of variables. Some of these variables are natural, such as the climate; but even where those variables upon which population depends are not strictly 'natural' – the tax system, distribution of profits, cultural and religious traditions, and so on – this dependence can be rationally analysed in such a way that the population appears to be 'naturally' dependent on these modifiable factors (Foucault, STP: 366). Statistical analyses 'revealed' the inner dynamics or regularities of the population which were amenable to programming, and thus enabling various forms of governmental interventions (Lui-Bright, 1997: 585). But the particular type of intervention enabled by this reconceptualisation of population as a kind of natural being is important for the development of the governmentalising state as a practice of government, away from the administrative (or police) state. The relation between the sovereign and the population – as opposed to that between the sovereign and a subject, or a collection of subjects – cannot, on this understanding of population, simply be one of obedience or the refusal to obey. The variables upon which population depends are such that they escape the direct action of the sovereign in the form of command-obedience:

> If one says to a population "do this", there is not only no guarantee that it will do it, but also there is quite simply no guarantee that it can do it. If we restrict ourselves to the sovereign-subject relationship, the limit of the law is the subject's disobedience; it is the "no" with which the subject opposes the sovereign. But when it is a question of the relationship between government and population, then the limit of the sovereign's or government's decision is

by no means necessarily the refusal of the people to whom the decision is addressed.

(Foucault, STP: 71)

But to say that the population cannot be changed by *decree* is not to say that it is completely inaccessible and impenetrable to government. On the contrary, the naturalness identified in the fact of population *is* accessible to government, on the condition that its interventions are enlightened, analytical, calculated and calculating (Foucault, STP: 71); in other words, provided that such interventions are based upon knowledge of and respect for the nature of these variables themselves. What does 'naturalness' mean in this context? What does it mean to respect the 'nature' of variables such as the tax system, or prices? It is the naturalness, Foucault writes:

> of those mechanisms that ensure that, when prices rise, if one allows this to happen, then they will stop rising by themselves.... It is a naturalness that is opposed precisely to the artificiality of politics, of *raison d'état* and police.... It is not the naturalness of processes of nature itself, as the nature of the world, but processes of a naturalness specific to relations between men, to what happens spontaneously when they cohabit, come together, exchange, work, and produce.

(STP: 349)

It is, in other words, *society* as a naturalness specific to man's life in common that is brought to light with political economy: society as a field of objects, and as a possible domain of analysis, knowledge and intervention (Foucault, STP: 349).

This characterisation of population as a society, as a kind of quasi-natural being dependent on processes, presents governmental practice with a series of problems to be rationalised, signifying the birth of what Foucault calls 'biopolitics' (Foucault, SMBD: 243–245). The phenomena characteristic of a group of living beings constituted as a population – health, sanitation, longevity, birth rates, and so on – make matters of life and death, birth and propagation, health and illness, and the processes that sustain or retard the optimisation of the life of the population matters of governmental concern (Dean, 1999: 119). Because these matters are themselves dependent upon the social, cultural, environmental, economic, and geographic conditions under which such populations exist, these milieus must also be of concern to government, and it is, in fact, through reasoned intervention in these milieus that the desired effects can be produced in the population itself. In other words, rather than seeking to intervene directly upon individual subjects through police regulation of every aspect of their daily lives, governmental interventions should now act at a certain degree of separation from the individual members of the population, working upon the milieus, or habitats, within which they live, circulate, and interact. Unlike meticulous and exhaustive police regulation, then, government will be effective when it governs at a relative distance, respecting the inner rationality of the processes of population and of those processes upon which population depends. This conceptualisation of population and, thus, a new relationship between population and government, is evidence of a recognition, characteristic of liberalism as a rationality of government, of the inherent limitations of effective government itself.

Unlike notions of police science, liberal government presumes that there is a non-political dimension of existence and that this dimension is "governed by processes that are autonomous from the operation of sovereign authority" (Dean, 1999: 69). The population encompasses a variety of self-regulating domains each of which is subject to its own laws and developmental tendencies and which function, in large part, by perceptions that the participants form in the course of their interactions with each other (Hindess, 2000: 123–124). In other words, individuals and groups engage in a whole series of interactions with each other which are neither constituted nor willed by the state. These interactions, these spheres, constitute a 'society'. But, because the individual members of society are understood to be heterogeneous forms of governed subject – they are economic subjects of interest and, simultaneously, political and legal subjects of rights (Dean, 1999: 147) – the task of the government of the state is to secure the forms of individual liberty required for the effective working of these domains. In other words, liberalism as a rationality of government seeks "to balance the biopolitical imperative of the optimisation of life of the population against the rights of the juridical-political subject and against the norms of an economic government" (Dean, 1999: 62). Liberalism can be understood, then, as a critique of *raison d'état*; as a doctrine of limitation and wise restraint; a rationality of governing which constantly reflects upon the bounds of its own power to know and to act, so as to produce the desired effects of economic, social and political interaction of subjects and the population. Nikolas Rose summarised the "recurrent dilemma" of liberal government as "the fear of not governing enough versus the fear of governing too much" (1993: 292). He continues:

> Liberalism inaugurates a kind of perpetual dissatisfaction with government, a perpetual questioning of whether the desired effects are being produced, of the mistakes of thought or policy that hamper the efficacy of government, the imperative not necessarily to govern more but to govern better.
>
> (Rose, 1993: 292)

Such government is to be effected by establishing mechanisms of security, rather than by exhaustive police regulation. To oppose the two might seem odd as we are used to thinking of the police and security as on the same side of the coin. But the French word that Foucault uses, *sécurité*, is more accurately understood as a 'future-oriented management of risk'. The French word *sureté* is closer to the understanding of security (in political terms) that we might equate, at least in part, with the police today, or with 'national security' (Valverde, 2007: 172). Mechanisms of security are about *managing* processes, rather than controlling them. Their objective, Foucault explains, "is not so much to prevent things as to ensure that the necessary and natural regulations work, or even to create regulations that enable natural regulations to work" (Foucault, STP: 353). The natural phenomena immanent to population that it has become the task of government to manage need to be framed in such a way that they do not 'veer off course'. Government must not try to obsessively control these phenomena – not only does it lack the knowledge and ability to do so, but to try to do so may in fact undermine their proper functioning. It must, rather, create the conditions under which individuals can exercise the various liberties necessary to ensure the proper functioning of these processes. The role of police, under this new system of governmentality, evolves into the more readily recognisable institution that exists today: an instrument by which the occurrence of disorder is prevented. Particular populations, or particular phenomena, where they pose a risk to the security – the proper unfolding – of these processes, can still be subject to detailed regulation. For example, while the system of sovereign criminal law treats a theft as an act to be punished, assemblages of security deal with the phenomenon of theft – turned into an aggregate – as a series of probable events, and set out to govern the general problem of future theft as it affects 'the population' (Valverde, 2007: 172). Criminal law, and the police, will still, of course, have to deal with the individual thief, and the criminal justice system will have to function in such a way as to punish and re-educate/rehabilitate the thief. But government engagement with the problem of theft does not end here. Drawing on bodies of knowledge that deal with criminality, poverty, demography, and so on, which were all developing during this period, government must also seek to understand 'the criminal', 'criminality', the socio-economic conditions which might produce such 'criminality' and 'criminals', so as to act on these conditions in such a way as to reduce the probability of future theft. But because, as we saw earlier, the inhabitants of society are economic subjects, political subjects and legal subjects, the appropriate balance must be struck between these spheres in the creation of these mechanisms/regulations of security. To govern properly, then, to achieve security, "it is necessary to respect the liberty of the governed so that the natural processes of the economy and population might function effectively" (Dean, 1999: 146).

Biopolitics and mechanisms of security also lie behind the development, in the latter half of the nineteenth century, of what came to be known as 'the social question' and the rise of the idea of state welfare. Whereas political economy was primarily concerned with the sanctity and security of the economic processes of population, other bodies of knowledge, or disciplines, which had been forming and developing at the same time – pedagogy, demography, medicine, biology and so on – began to open up new areas of problematisation for biopolitical/liberal government. In states such as the United Kingdom and France, the nineteenth century was a century of commissions of inquiry, censuses, and surveys into poverty, illness, morality, crime, alcoholism, suicide, and many other phenomena. Much as with the development of statistical analyses which gave rise to political economy and a reconceptualisation of the notion of population, these commissions and surveys give to the social a kind of reality with its own regularities, laws and characteristics also amenable to the intervention of government (Dean, 1999: 150). The undesirable social consequences of industrialisation, wage labour and urban existence become the responsibility of government to tame and govern. It is during this period, for example, that we see the emergence of social work, and of schemes for social insurance, and the establishment of public schools and hospitals. This process should not, Rose argues, be understood as part of a single logic or coherent programme of 'state intervention'. Rather, phenomena or problems such as disease, criminality, pauperism, and the breakdown of marital relations, for example, were recoded as 'social' problems with consequences for national well-being calling for authoritative attention. More often than not, however, the impetus for addressing such problems came from the "proselytising of independent reformers", rather than from government ministers (Rose, 1993: 290). At any rate, from the mid-eighteenth through the nineteenth centuries, the role of government comes to be the administration, or management, of the collective life process of 'the population'.

From the early treatises on the art of government in the sixteenth century through to the early twentieth century, the fundamental question of government has evolved from whether one was governing in proper conformity to moral, divine or natural laws, through whether one was governing with sufficient intensity, depth, and attention to detail so as to bring the state to its maximum strength, to, finally, whether one governs between the maximum and minimum fixed by the nature of things (Foucault, BB: 18–19). The practices and techniques of governing change as the problematique of government changes, changing the character of 'the state' as a concrete manifestation of government. It follows, for Foucault, that the emergence of specific phenomena as 'problems' necessitating intervention also relates, fundamentally, to these changes in the rationality and practice of government. These changes in how the practice and rationality of government relates to 'population' are key to understanding the role of migration in relation to the state, and its emergence as a phenomenon in need of management.

Population and Migration

For the administrative state, population is understood as one of the factors, or elements, of a sovereign's strength. Its growth must be encouraged, on the one hand, but on the other, the individuals of this population must also be regulated in their daily lives and activities so as to ensure their productivity and utility for the state. Migration, therefore, occupies a particular place in the administrative state. In general, emigration was to be avoided, since states with which one is in competition would stand to benefit from such emigration, particularly if those emigrating were skilled labourers or capable of bearing arms. For example, an edict issued in 1669 by Louis XIV of France forbade his subjects to leave French territory without permission (Torpey, 2000: 21). In England, statutes prohibited exit from the kingdom without a licence, with the exception of peers, notable merchants, and soldiers (Torpey, 2000: 21). The out-migration of colonial settlement is a notable exception. Although not a topic discussed by Foucault, the mercantilist period – the period of the administrative state – was also a period of colonial settlement beyond Europe, especially in the New World. Spain, France, the Netherlands, and England all sought to establish and grow colonies in the Americas, by sending groups of merchants, traders, and farmers to the resource-rich lands across the Atlantic (Zolberg, 2006: 222). The principal aim of these colonies was to produce goods that would help the parent state maintain a favourable balance of trade. Colonial production and commerce was subject to strict controls by the parent state, and the economic interests of the parent state were to trump the interests of the colonies, and colonists, themselves. Emigration to a state's own colonies was, therefore, a potentially desirable form of migration, so long as such emigration was not so excessive as to diminish the productive capacities of the parent state. In fact, England, in particular, sought to recruit foreign migrants – including those fleeing their country due to religious persecution – to help populate its new colonies (Lachenicht, 2017: 267). Emigration to rival European states, however, was to be avoided. Immigration, according to mercantilist doctrine, was desirable, as it served to increase the productive – or potentially productive – population, which, as we saw above, was an important source of the state's strength.

The flight of the Huguenots from France following the revocation of the Edict of Nantes is a telling example. While the Edict formally expelled the Protestant *clergy* from France, lay people were prohibited from leaving, largely because they tended to be wealthy and skilled labourers. Nevertheless, between 1681 and 1720, approximately one quarter of the French Protestant population did flee and among them were the most wealthy and skilled members of the Huguenot community (Koslowski, 2000: 58). While this migration was problematic for the French state, the displacement of these people was not considered to be a problem for the states in which they sought admittance. These Huguenots *refugiés* not only filled the ranks of the Dutch and English armies, but were generally welcomed as potentially attractive immigrants. Frederick William, the Great Elector of Prussia, issued the Edict of Potsdam within four days of the revocation of the Edict of Nantes, inviting the Huguenots to settle in Brandenburg. In 1709, the British Parliament passed an act naturalising the expelled French Protestants (Soguk, 1999: 90). Parliament proposed naturalisation rather than simply welcoming them as foreign nationals because they believed that naturalisation would be a stronger inducement for similar wealthy, skilled co-religionists to transport themselves and their estates to the kingdom. This does not mean that there was no opposition, at the level of the existing population, to these new arrivals. Local populations often looked upon the religious practices of their supposed co-religionists with confusion and suspicion. But the practices and rationality of governing characteristic of the administrative state do suggest that, at the level of governmental practice, the arrival of such displaced persons did not pose a problem, in and of itself, to the state. It is emigration, rather than immigration, that poses a problem for the administrative state.

For the governmentalising state, population is no longer conceived of simply as a collection of subjects or an element of the strength of the state, but a dynamic totality, a living body, subject to natural and artificial processes, which it is the responsibility of government to preserve, enhance, and protect. As a dynamic totality, the population is also a potential source of disequilibrium and instability (Dean, 1999: 128). Biopolitics, as a mechanism for the management of population, has both positive and negative aspects. Positive aspects include fostering the conditions of life to increase the health and longevity of the population, through interventions in the form of public health and sanitation programmes, for example. But these same conditions can also be fostered by identifying threats to the population, such as unhygienic living conditions, food shortages, disease, and dangerous social elements, and acting upon them to manage the risks that they pose (Foucault, SMBD: 243–245). Government must create mechanisms of security, and forms of intervention in social milieus in such a way as to foster life and productivity, but without over-stepping the mark and governing 'too much' – impeding the liberties of subjects or over-regulating 'natural' processes. For such a state, such a rationality of government, the relationship of migration to population is problematised along a number of axes, including membership, economic concerns, and concerns with public health.

The most obvious of these, and the one which has received the most attention in International Relations and in studies of forced migration, is the spread of immigration and nationality legislation throughout, and beyond, Europe. If the primary concern of government is to foster the conditions of life of its population, this necessarily involves a determination of who is, and who is not, a part of this population – who is and is not a member for whom government is responsible – and ideas of nation and race play an important role in this process (Foucault, SMBD: 276). Throughout the nineteenth century there was a proliferation of nationality legislation in Europe: France in 1804, Prussia in 1842, the Netherlands in 1848, Italy, Russia and Austria in the 1860s, Switzerland in 1874 and Britain in 1870 (Soguk, 1999: 97). Torpey has called the nineteenth century a "golden age of the codification of citizenship laws" (2000: 71), motivated by the need to establish who did and did not have a right to the benefits of membership. However, the prime motivator of this need, according to Torpey, was not nationalism per se, but the decline of serfdom and "the attendant rise in mobility among the popular classes" which began shortly after the Congress of Vienna in 1815 (Torpey, 2000: 72). This is a distinct shift from the period of the administrative state, and earlier, where membership was based on residence in a particular place. In a context where relatively few people moved around, Torpey argues, this *jus soli* approach may have been well suited. Membership rooted in descent, however, was arguably more well suited to a period of drastically increased mobility, allowing states to "hold onto" members of the population who may have been living elsewhere (Torpey, 2000: 72). While the rise of national citizenship was undoubtedly important to the regulation of 'foreigners', the overview undertaken in the preceding pages of the development of the state indicates that there is much more behind the problematisation of migration in this period than the emergence of nationalism and national citizenship.

While the 'line' between national and foreigner was sharpened throughout the nineteenth century with various forms of identification documents and migration-related regulations, this was also a period of much greater freedom of movement (Torpey, 2000: 93). The nineteenth century, then, appears to be a century of contradiction: increased freedom of movement *and* increased regulation of movement and membership. However, these contradictions are immanent to liberal governmentality: practices of liberal governmentality both give birth to and thrive on such contradictions, without being able to resolve/reconcile them, and this is what makes mechanisms of security so central to liberal governmentality.

Mechanisms of security, through which liberal governmentality operates, do not function strictly through binaries or bans, or through seeking to prevent the occurrence of certain phenomena or processes. They seek, rather, to manage them (Bigo, 2002 and 2008). It follows, then, that in the realm of the regulation of movement, mechanisms of security would operate primarily through the identification of risks inherent in movement, and through instituting regulations which seek to mitigate such risks, while, at the same time, preserving the movement necessary for trade and commerce. To put it another way, what is required for the liberal government of populations is "a capacity to distinguish between what can be governed through the promotion of liberty" – including through the promotion of movement – "and what must be governed in other ways" – including through the restriction of movement (Hindess, 2004: 28). On this understanding, liberal complicity in 'illiberal' practices – such as restricting freedom of movement – appear not as aberrations but as a central feature of liberal political reason (Hindess, 2004: 28). Thus, while nationalism may help to account for the rise in citizenship legislation based on national identity, in itself it tells us little about specific proposals for the government of 'risky' populations, or the management of their movement. Many migration-related regulations and forms of documentation facilitating or circumscribing movement during this period had little to do with nationality, strictly speaking. Even the passport had little to do with national identity until the mid-nineteenth century. Prior to this point, in many European states, passports could be issued by one's country of origin or by a host country (Czajka, 2014: 159). Concerns about health and the protection of labour markets play an important role in the problematisation of, and, thus, in attempts to manage, the risks posed by migration.

Around the mid-nineteenth century, legislation appeared in many European states which signalled a move away from the "population is good" mentality of mercantilism and the administrative state. Emigration was decriminalised in the North German Confederation, for example, in 1867 (Torpey, 2000: 95). The end of the Napoleonic Wars saw increased unemployment and depression in Britain, and by 1819 Parliament was relaxing its views on emigration, and was, in fact, making grants to encourage it. In 1819, for example, £50,000 was provided to assist settlement at the Cape (South Africa), building upon a similar provision in 1816 to provide £50,000 to assist the emigration of unemployed labourers (Ward, 1976: 221). In 1824, Britain had a surplus of labour and an unemployment problem, and laws prohibiting the emigration of workmen and artisans were repealed (Ward, 1976: 221), essentially facilitating the export of joblessness. The trade-off for slackening restrictions on departures for the sake of the regulation of the domestic labour market was that access to the territory should, then, be restricted precisely to avoid the problem of accumulating excess labourers or poor in need of relief. At the same time as labour markets were becoming 'national-ised', systems of poor relief were similarly being removed from the responsibility of individual parishes and transferred to the administration of the state. The Poor Law Amendment Act of 1834 saw the national government assume greater responsibility for Britain's poor (Torpey, 2000: 69).

If rates of emigration and immigration needed now to be monitored and managed, rather than prohibited and permitted, so as to ensure the strength of the economy and prevent over-burdening systems of poor relief and newly established social services, then responsibility for public health was also an important concern in this new period of migration regulation, itself linked with the desire for inter-national trade. Governmental approaches to problems of public health and disease shifted in the nineteenth century from a strategy of quarantine – i.e. preventing movement – to a strategy of surveillance – monitoring movement. This was, Salter claims, part of a general shift in government strategies corresponding to the growth of the modern bureaucratic welfare state, and was also part of a recognition that international travel was necessary – particularly as regards trade and commerce – and, in many ways, unstoppable (Salter, 2003: 60).

The US Public Health Service, originally created to provide medical care to sick and disabled seamen, saw its functions gradually expand through the nine-teenth century and, in the latter decades of the 1800s, it became responsible for the monitoring of infectious diseases. In this capacity it became more involved in immigration screening, helping to exclude potential immigrants with con-tagious illnesses. Cholera outbreaks were a particular concern, and medical examinations and exclusion became an integral part of US immigration law. Ships and individuals were required to carry 'certificates of health' in order to be admissible. However, since the states from which many immigrants were arriv-ing to the US were keen to be rid of unproductive or unhealthy populations, these certificates proved relatively easy to come by when issued by authorities in their state of origin, and, as such, were distrusted by US authorities, leading to more restrictive practices (Salter, 2003: 60), for which newly established public health systems could be co-opted. Many of these health-related migration regu-lations were, of course, racially coded, and so I am not claiming that nationalism or racism had nothing to do with these controls. I wish simply to highlight that nationalism or racism are insufficient explanations on their own. While certain laws did place blanket restrictions on entire nationalities – such as the Chinese Exclusion Act of 1882 in the US – many did not, and functioned, rather, to intro-duce breaks within these populations – to 'sift' the more 'dangerous' or risky members of such populations from the less dangerous, allowing freer circulation among the latter than the former. Indeed, that race comes to play a role in migra-tion legislation at all was itself only possible at this point in time because of developments in biology and related concerns for the health of populations (Rose and Novas, 205: 440–443; Foucault, SMBD: 254–258; Crampton, 2007).

As we have seen thus far in this chapter, the political reflections on the art of government and *raison d'état*, the establishment of an exhaustive administrative apparatus to collect information on the population to serve the military and economic growth of the state, the development of statistics and the rise of political economy which problematise the population-wealth nexus, all alter the way the government understands the body of subjects under its control, and the way it governs them. Migration, then, has been problematised in different ways as the rationality of government changed. Whereas population for the administrative state was a 'numbers game' – more population meant more wealth – the governmentalising state developed as population was reconceived, and so the relationship of government to population, and thus to migration, also changed. Population as a living being, with its own processes, and dependent upon other processes, requires careful and reasoned management. Migration is thus, not a phenomenon that either simply increases or decreases the number of subjects and thus the stock of potential wealth, but a phenomenon which can alter the nature of the population itself and, by extension, can then impact on a range of economic and social processes for which government has become responsible. Migration, as a phenomenon, has, thus, been problematised in different ways, and these problematisations are dependent on the 'nature' or 'character' of 'the state' as both an object and reflection of underlying practices of government. This, however, only tells part of the story of the potential for the emergence of 'the refugee (as) problem'. We have seen how the state developed into the kind of entity that could be disrupted by an influx of displaced persons, but it still remains to show why this should become a problem in need of coordinated international attention in the early twentieth century, and not before.

Governing the International

This section addresses how the developments in the rationality and practice of governing, at the level of the state, also reveal shifting understandings of inter-state relations, and, thus, how migration can come to be understood as a process, or phenomenon, in need of *international* cooperation in order to be effectively managed. While Foucault certainly seemed to have seen the state and inter-state system as mutually constitutive (Leira, 2011: 114), his own reflections on 'the international' or the 'inter-state' level are, unfortunately, minimal.

Governmentality beyond the State

Raison d'état, the governmental rationality underpinning the administrative state of the mid-sixteenth to the mid-eighteenth centuries, was concerned, first and foremost, with the practice of rule inside the state and how states project themselves outwards. This rule, however, had a number of 'external' or 'externally related' features, according to Foucault. With *raison d'état*, states understand themselves as situated alongside each other in a space of competition for the first time. This space of competition differs from the dynastic rivalry of princes, Foucault claims, in that it is no longer a question simply of the wealth or status of the sovereign, but of the strength of the state. Force becomes central, and states must attempt to maintain an equilibrium, or balance, between their respective forces. The political technology of police, which we examined earlier, is necessary to ensure the growth of the state's forces from within, whereas a military-diplomatic apparatus is needed to take care of relations of force between states. The objective of this military-diplomatic apparatus is the 'balancing', or equilibrium, of forces. The goal of this 'balancing' is, to the extent that it has a clear goal (Leira, 2011: 123), universal peace, but, in a break from previous thought, this peace will not come from a universal empire but from "plurality maintained as plurality" (Foucault, STP: 297–300). This shift in thought is possible, Foucault claims, because the rationality of *raison d'état* implies three important new ideas: a new relationship between political practice and knowledge; a new relationship between politics and history; and a new relationship between the individual and the state. The first and third ideas are central to the development of the administrative state, which we examined above.

The state is something that exists per se – it is a kind of object, and order of things – and political knowledge deals with the nature of the state to be governed. Government is only possible when the strength of the state is known, because it is only by this knowledge that the strength of the state can be sustained. Concrete, precise, measured knowledge of the forces and resources of the state is, thus, necessary for effective government (Foucault, EWP: 408). The individual is an important part of the state, conceived in this way, but only insofar as his continued existence is *productive* for the state. Government need not worry about individuals as individuals, except in their ability to introduce even minimal changes in the strength of the state (Foucault, EWP: 409). It is the second idea, the new relationship between politics and history, Foucault claims, that lies at the root of the new imperative towards a balance of forces and the development of a permanent military-diplomatic apparatus in Europe. The forces of the state, which can be known through the collection of concrete and precise knowledge, have to be increased because each state is in *permanent* competition with other states. Belief in the coming of the *respublica Christiana*, the last empire before the return of Christ, was eroding, and being replaced with the idea of politics as concerned with the struggle and competition between a multiplicity of states in an unlimited history (Foucault, EWP: 409). The 'inter-state' level is thus conceptualised as a collective of similar units, in permanent competition with each other, in a history understood for the first time as open-ended.

However, the broad brushstrokes with which Foucault paints this picture of 'Europe' during the period of the administrative state stand in marked contrast to the finer-grained portrait characteristic of his reflections on the development of rule 'inside' the state. Not only does Foucault fail to explain how this 'equilibrium of forces' is to be maintained in practice, but his remarks about this second new idea of *raison d'état* in particular have been revealed as problematic. Foucault appears to over-estimate the changes in thinking about history and politics in this period (Leira, 2011: 126–127), glossing over the extent to which the dominant understanding of history was still cyclical, rather than linear and open-ended, and reads systemic thinking into the theorists of *raison d'état* which was, on more detailed accounts, largely absent. Examples of system-level thought during this period are in fact scarce and brief. In his examination of the period, Osiander highlights that while the notion of equilibrium is evident in the sources of the seventeenth century, it is applied with regard to individual actors (states/kingdoms) rather than being understood as "a structural feature of the international system as a whole" (Osiander, 1994: 80). While this may seem only of semantic importance it indicates a lack of consciousness or reflectivity about anything we might call an international or inter-state 'system' at this time. Similarly, Bartelson, in his *Genealogy of Sovereignty*, argues that if by 'system' we mean "a totality which is something more than the sum of its constituent parts, yet something presumably different from" – as Foucault claims – "a universal *respublica Christiana*" or a universal moral community (of which Grotius and Pufendorf both wrote), then there was no such object of knowledge called an international system evident in political reflection at this time (Bartelson, 1995: 137). This is not to say, however, that the problem of how to interact with relatively similar polities did not arise under *raison d'état*, but these interactions were of a limited kind, and focused on a limited purpose: to maintain an equilibrium of forces so as to introduce a degree of predictability to prevent war (Bartelson, 1995: 181).

Liberal governmentality – the political rationality of the governmentalising state – by contrast, is a rationality of governing concerned not with the strength of the state for its own sake, but with managing the health, well-being, and prosperity of the population. Developing initially out of the birth of political economy, but later drawing on domains of knowledge made possible by the problematisations of biopolitics, the various phenomena characteristic of population, and the various natural and artificial processes upon which it depends, and in relation to which it develops, come to be understood as less place-bound than the population itself. That is to say, while each state is responsible for the well-being and security of its own population, the phenomena and processes which affect each state's population, and thus the risks that need management, are not themselves contained or strictly containable within the boundaries of the state. This expansion of understanding begins first with the economy and increasingly global trade, and it is in relation to this economic thought that an understanding of, or reflection on, a 'system' within which states are situated emerges. In contrast to mercantilist thinking, in which competition between states is a zero-sum game – whatever one state gains must necessarily be a loss for another state – for political economy, competition, under conditions of market freedom, is a mode of mutual enrichment. Foucault sees in the treatises of the political economists the formation of a new idea of Europe:

It is a Europe of collective enrichment; Europe as a collective subject that, whatever the competition between states, or rather through the competition between states, has to advance in the form of unlimited economic progress.

(Foucault, BB: 54)

This idea of progress, of a European progress, is a fundamental theme in liberalism and overturns the classical *raison d'état* concern with an equilibrium of forces, although these concerns do not disappear completely (Foucault, BB: 54). But this progress requires continuous 'inputs':

> [I]f freedom of the market must ensure the reciprocal, correlative, and more or less simultaneous enrichment of all the countries of Europe, for this to function, and for freedom of the market to thus unfold according to a game that is not a zero-sum game, then it is necessary to summon around Europe, and for Europe, an increasingly extended market and even, if it comes to it, everything in the world that can be put on the market.
>
> (Foucault: BB: 54–55)

This unlimited character of European economic development views the whole world as 'summonable' around Europe, to exchange on a European market. This is significant, Foucault claims, not because this is the first time that Europe thinks about the world – it is not – but because it is the first time that Europe appears *in its own eyes* as having to have the world for its unlimited market (Foucault, BB: 55). If, as Bartelson, Osiander, and Leira claim, contra to Foucault's own claims about *raison d'état*, the self-reflectivity of states in the sixteenth century was not accompanied by self-reflectivity about being part of a system (Leira, 2011: 131), then this systemic self-reflectivity does seem to appear in the economic thought of the late eighteenth century.

Liberal governmentality appears, on this account, to be a governmental rationality that has the entire planet for its horizon (Foucault, BB: 56). It is in this context that late eighteenth-century projects/treatises for peace and international organisation emerged. Foucault's claim that a new form of political calculation on an international scale emerged in the late eighteenth century "absolutely does not mean that every other form of reflection, calculation, analysis, and governmental practice disappears", far from it (Foucault, BB: 58). What Foucault was attempting to show is that a particular form of reflection, analysis, and calculation appeared at this time which was integrated into political practices (Foucault, BB: 58–59). When combined with the biopolitical imperatives of liberal governmentality, and the inability to contain the phenomena which affect the health and prosperity of individual populations, interaction between states must necessarily expand beyond the diplomatico-military concerns with war, peace, and the size of armies. We can see this in the emergence of new forms of international governmental activity/practice, beyond the traditional concerns of war and peace, as the nineteenth century progressed.

Governance and Humanitarianism

Coordination between states was by no means a new phenomenon in the nineteenth century. The formation of military alliances, for example, had long been a feature of international politics. The nineteenth century, however, was a period of considerable expansion in inter-state cooperation and coordination, beyond the concerns of war and peace, in ways that reflected the shifting nature and concerns of the state, developing into international practices of governance. It was also a period that saw the birth of humanitarianism, which itself reflected many of the same concerns as liberal governmentality and came to serve an important role in the management of populations.

Inter-state cooperation in the nineteenth century began in familiar terms, with the Congress of Vienna of 1815, the purpose of which was to re-establish order in Europe in the wake of the Napoleonic Wars and establish a system for monitoring, or balancing, the military power of the key European states. However, overt military concerns were not the sole focus of the work of the Congress. It also established the world's first intergovernmental organisation: the Central Commission for the Navigation of the Rhine. The purpose of this Commission was, essentially, to maximise the potential of the river – which crossed a number of jurisdictions – for commerce. Free navigation of the river was the ultimate goal, ensuring that traffic on the river would be treated fairly, equally and as favourably as possible (Jacobsen, 1979: 33). A similar Commission was also established for the navigation of the Danube, at the Congress of Paris in 1856 (Jacobsen, 1979: 33). Conferences and Congresses became a more frequent occurrence as the nineteenth century progressed, attempting to coordinate pressing international problems such as sanitation, health, trade and commerce, and communications. In the area of health and sanitation, for example, eleven International Sanitary Conferences were held between 1851 and 1903.[1] Topics of discussion at these Conferences included the causes of cholera – whether it was caused by microbes, or by miasmas (it is worth remembering that at this point the germ theory of disease was not yet accepted) – and the merits of different methods of controlling the spread of diseases: hygiene, sanitation, and quarantine. Britain was a staunch opponent of absolute quarantine as "inimical to free commerce, a source of hardship and oppression to travellers, traders and residents alike" (Salter, 2003: 59), its opposition showing the important connections between health, trade, and regulating the circulation of goods and people. As Salter argues:

> Whereas national policies were prompted by the concern for the nation's health against foreign diseases, international conferences on the cholera epidemic recommended ways that travel could be facilitated through monitoring and the dissemination of information about disease and its prevention. Thus, between 1860 and the late 1930s, except during times of war, the desire to increase trade and travel trumped the desire for security.
>
> (Salter, 2003: 60–61)

These International Sanitary Conferences were the direct precursors of the League of Nations Health Organisation, whose three essential functions were: the centralisation and standardisation of information on health, hygiene, sanitation, and disease; education in proper methods for quarantine and treatment; and the coordination of States Members in preventing the spread of diseases (Salter, 2003: 61). The role of expert knowledge was central not only to the Health Organisation, but also the international conferences which preceded it, and this reliance on expertise beyond government was another notable feature of nineteenth-century inter-state cooperation and coordination.

In addition to sending delegates to intergovernmental conferences and congresses, governments also sent delegates to observe and participate in non-governmental conferences and congresses, organised around a number of different themes and disciplines. International meetings were held on topics as diverse as archaeology, criminology, demography, education, medicine and hygiene, raw materials, and the protection of nature (Herren, 2001: 123). These conferences became important forums for technical collaboration and information-sharing on topics, issues and problems that "went beyond the capacity of foreign ministries, and which needed the analysis of 'experts' rather than diplomats" (Herren, 2001: 123). This increasing cooperation, between state ministries and with learned societies and unions, was also, Herren argues, conducive to the development of administrative units at international and state levels for specific issue areas or problems. For example, officials from domestic postal ministries took part in the Congresses of the Universal Postal Union, an intergovernmental organisation established to govern international postage rules (Herren, 2001: 128), and, likewise, telegraph offices sent delegates to international meetings on the telegraph system (invented in the mid-1830s). In 1865, the International Telegraph Union (now the International Telecommunications Union) was established as a means of ensuring that the equipment, operating and administration procedures in different countries using the telegraph were compatible (Jacobsen, 1979: 34). By the time the League of Nations was established in the wake of the First World War as a formal international governance organisation there was, thus, a developing tradition of inter-state cooperation and coordination on a wide range of issues and problems beyond immediate military concerns. Equally important, however, to our examination of how it became possible for 'the refugee (as) problem' to emerge in the early decades of the twentieth century, is the development of humanitarianism in the nineteenth and early twentieth centuries.

Alms giving, charity, and philanthropy are by no means strictly modern phenomena, but during the nineteenth century they begin to proliferate outside of the realm of private individuals and take on a more public, organisational and governmental character. In his history of humanitarianism Barnett charts how the nineteenth and early twentieth centuries were characterised by a "growing zeal" for creating standing bodies, organisations, and institutions which were "self-consciously organised around the principles of rationality" (Barnett, 2011: 21), and whose activities were characterised by a "growing confidence in scientific knowledge and its application to human affairs" (Barnett, 2011: 52). Moreover, humanitarianism came to be associated with compassion across boundaries and not only with 'the needy' close to home. In the domestic sphere, the discourse of 'progress' and 'improvement' was central. Mere charity was thought to bring out the worst in people: simply providing food or immediate relief was thought to encourage dependence, ill-discipline and irresponsibility. And so, humanitarian organisations sought not just to provide immediate relief, but to foster moral and civic virtues in the poor, to enable those capable of 'improvement' to improve themselves. Not coincidentally, the efforts of humanitarians and the interests of capitalist enterprise dovetailed. Rapidly increasing industrialisation and urbanisation were giving birth to a variety of social ills, such as alcoholism and prostitution, as a result of the growth of urban slums, shortages of work, and a growing and mobile labour force. Alcoholism, in particular, posed a challenge for industrialists as "a significant hindrance to a stable and compliant labour force", and so many industrialists supported temperance movements and organisations that encouraged sobriety to enable individuals to become self-disciplined and responsible workers (Barnett, 2011: 24). In line with liberal economic thought, many humanitarians turned not to the state to effect such social change, but to the market, utilising the knowledge of experts and new developments in social sciences.

But humanitarianism was not only concerned with 'domestic' issues. Humanitarian organisations were also established to save soldiers and civilians during war, to abolish the international slave trade, and to address the adverse consequences of slavery. The world's first official international humanitarian organisation, the International Committee of the Red Cross – the organisation whose pleas to the League of Nations on behalf of Russian refugees prompted the first coordinated international actions for/on refugees – was founded in 1863 by Henry Dunant, inspired by witnessing the gruesome aftermath of the Battle of Solferino during the Second Italian War of Independence in 1859. In the fight against slavery, abolitionists in Britain sought not only to abolish slavery itself, but also to 'save' the freed slaves from the evil consequences of freedom unaccompanied by self-discipline, education, or religious belief (Barnett, 2011: 60). Barnett argues that these humanitarian (but also often deeply paternalistic) discourses fed into colonial practices of governing in a way which drew on the growing responsibility of the state to its citizens. During the *laissez-faire* era of the early nineteenth century, individuals had largely to fend for themselves, and various charitable and reform-minded organisations stepped in where the state refused or failed to tread (Barnett, 2011: 24). As this *laissez-faire* approach receded in the latter years of the nineteenth century and the early years of the twentieth, the state accepted more responsibilities for the welfare of its population. The aftermath of the First World War would not only see the state take a more direct role in humanitarian practice, but also the rapid expansion of humanitarianism as both a doctrine and practice by which individuals and groups felt and acted upon a sense of responsibility not only to those 'in need' close to home, but also to distant strangers, including those displaced across borders and without means of providing for themselves. The First World War saw the creation of a number of humanitarian organisations, many of which would play a key role in assisting refugees. Two notable examples are the Save the Children Fund, founded in England in 1919, to alleviate starvation among children in

Germany and Austria-Hungary, and Near East Relief, an American organisation founded in 1915 in response to the Armenian Genocide, and focused primarily on providing assistance to women and children. Near East Relief established and ran orphanages throughout the Middle East following the end of the war, and provided teaching in trades and agriculture to enable orphans to become self-supporting (Hope-Simpson, 1939: 176–179). These two organisations, along with the ICRC, were three of the largest organisations involved in providing and coordinating relief and assistance to refugees in the years following the First World War, and drew upon, and themselves contributed to, a rapidly developing sense of responsibility towards even distant 'others'.

Managing Movement

It is against the background of governmentality, this grid of intelligibility for the emergence of the various practices of governing examined above, and not simply of nationalism, that efforts to govern population movement internationally should be understood. This background provides the immediate context for the emergence of 'the refugee (as) problem'. In this final section I focus on this immediate context: efforts to govern international movement in the form of the international passport regime.

As we have already seen, regulations on movement, either in the form of laws prohibiting or permitting movement, or in the development of various forms of documentation facilitating or curtailing movement, had emerged in relation to a number of different concerns, rooted in the responsibility of government for the health, well-being, and economic prosperity of the population. As we have also seen, these regulations were not manifestations of simplistic binaries – such as that of the always unwanted foreigner versus the always welcome citizen – but became, as the governmentalising state developed, a technology for managing risk. It was in the wake of the First World War that an international cooperative effort on the regulation of movement occurred for the first time. Until the First World War, state regulations on movement were ad hoc, in that they developed, changed, receded, and re-emerged at different times in different states, and in relation to different concerns – ranging from cholera outbreaks to economic downturns and conflict. Regulations lacked uniformity almost across the board, and by the early years of the twentieth century, many states had ceased to require passports for international travel at all. The outbreak of world war, however, saw the universal imposition of strict controls on the movement of one's own nationals – in order to track combatants and deserters – and of foreign nationals – in order to defend the state against spies and military threats (Salter, 2003: 78). Interestingly, however, many people seemed to think that the imposition of such movement controls was temporary and that, after world politics settled down again, they would cease to be necessary (Salter, 2003: 77). Very soon after the conclusion of the Paris Peace Conference, the League of Nations facilitated international discussions aimed at the abolition of passport controls. While these efforts were ultimately unsuccessful and the 'temporary' passport controls of the war years became permanent, there are a couple of features of both the effort and the codification of a movement regime that are relevant for our purposes.

The new international movement regime was codified, in October 1920, at the Conference on Passports, Customs Formalities and Through Tickets, under the auspices of the League of Nations Provisional Committee on Communications and Transit. The preamble of the resolution adopted by the conference reveals the dual concerns of its efforts:

> The International Conference ... charged with the study of the methods necessary to facilitate international passenger traffic by rail, at present more especially hindered by passport and Customs formalities.... Convinced that the many difficulties affecting personal relations between the people of various countries constitute a serious obstacle to the resumption of normal intercourse and to the economic recovery of the world; Being of the opinion, further, that the legitimate concern of every Government for the safeguarding of its security and rights prohibits, for the time being, the total abolition of restrictions and that complete return to pre-war conditions which the Conference hopes, nevertheless, to see gradually re-established in the near future; Proposes....
>
> (League of Nations, 1920: Preamble)

The driving force behind the conference appears to have been the desire to facilitate the economic reconstruction of Europe, for which travel was understood to be central. However, the statement above also recognises that, even if the ultimate goal was the abolition of wartime movement controls, in the immediate term the national security interests of states need to be taken into account. The conference appears then, as a balancing act between two imperatives: a liberal-economic imperative of reconstruction facilitated by freedom of movement, and a security imperative requiring restrictions on such movement. The broader economic context of these state deliberations on passport controls is evident not only in the statement quoted above, but also in the make-up of the body of delegates conducting the negotiations. Rather than consisting solely of councillors or ministers of states' foreign or interior ministries, delegates were also drawn from European railway companies, from customs bureaus, communications ministries, and departments of finance (League of Nations, 1920: 55–58), indicating that the regulation of cross-border movement was understood at the time not to simply be a question of national security and a need to keep out foreigners, but as more akin with the Foucauldian understanding of mechanisms of security characteristic of liberal governmentality outlined above. Mechanisms of security seek to manage, rather than control, processes, so as to keep a handle on risks posed to those same processes. To completely eliminate all passport controls so soon after a world war, in which states maintained real concerns about spies and Communist agitators, would have been to fail to manage risks to the physical safety of the population and, in the case of the fear of Communism, the fragile economic position of many states. However, to attempt to completely ban all cross-border movement would have been to fail to manage the risks to the natural functioning of economic and social processes, as trade, travel and communications were considered central to economic development. It could be argued, then, that the conference was an expression of what Rose referred to as the recurring dilemma of liberal governmentality: "the fear of not governing enough versus the fear of governing too much" (Rose, 1993: 292).

The codification of the regime itself is also important. The Conference made a series of recommendations to governments in relation to passports, visas, customs barriers and through-tickets, but it is the recommendations on passports that are of most relevance here. The conference established a uniform type of 'ordinary' (as differentiated from 'diplomatic') passport, which would be identical for all countries, and which would supersede all other types of passport previously issued by individual states (League of Nations, 1920: Art.1). The conference also mandated the periodic sharing of information with the League of Nations by governments concerning passports (and customs formalities), with such information, where suitable, to be shared "for the benefit of the public" (League of Nations, 1920: Art.17). Introducing a uniform passport system to replace the largely ad hoc and diverse systems of individual states can be understood as an effort to ensure that cross-border movement, even though subject to regulation, would nevertheless be as efficient as possible and minimise disruption, as far as possible. The introduction and imposition of uniformity in the documentation regulating international travel reflects that cross-border movement has become an issue of international concern, and not merely a state's 'own business'; the policies pursued by individual states are understood as impacting on the potential prosperity of all. These new international travel regulations create, for the first time, an internationally mandated and recognised 'regularisation' of cross-border movement, enabling the conceptualisation of 'irregular', and thus potentially threatening, destabilising, risky, cross-border movement. It was precisely this kind of movement that became of concern to the League of Nations in 1921, in the form of almost one million Russians stranded in the countries surrounding the former Russian empire.

It is, thus, within this context that the concerns voiced so loudly by states in discussion of the Russian refugee question when the matter was put before the League of Nations by the Red Cross can be understood. In Chapter 1 we saw that the concerns most frequently raised by states were concerns about the social undesirability of the Russian refugees, about existing unemployment and the potential of the refugees to make unemployment problems worse, and about the expense of providing food and shelter to the refugees. As a mass of unknown and unclaimed individuals they were potentially risky and so their movement needed to be managed. However, precisely because they were unclaimed by their state – they had, in fact, been denationalised – their movement could not be managed in the same way as the movement of the citizens of other states could be managed: they were not entitled to passports and what identification documents they did have were no longer recognised. A new mechanism, therefore, needed to be devised to manage the risk of their presence and potential onward movement. One way of managing the potential risk posed to the domestic population by their presence and potential onward movement, was the tactic that many states initially employed of trying to 'quarantine' the refugees: states had reported to the League of Nations, ahead of its first conference on the issue, that they had felt it necessary to keep the Russian refugees in concentration camps, for military and political reasons. Once state representatives met to discuss what collectively could be done about the Russian refugees, they decided to develop a travel document to enable them to move in a regular manner, to enable them to conform to the new 'rules of the game', but, just like with movement of others, they would also require visas to facilitate that movement. Importantly, as has been shown by the examination undertaken in this chapter of the development of the state and international system, these concerns, and the mechanisms developed to try to address them, could not have emerged at just any point in the long history of human displacement. That they became concerns at all, and, further, that they became concerns for the attention of the international community, depended upon both the state and the international community existing in such a way as to have these concerns, and to be in a position to try to address them. And so, while then-Deputy High Commissioner for Refugees W. D. Smyser is right that people have been displaced from their homes "probably since the dawn of the human community" (Smyser, 1985: 154), it was only with the emergence of the political rationality of population management underpinning the development of the modern state and state system that this displacement could be conceptualised as a distinct 'refugee problem'.

Conclusion

This chapter set out to answer the question of why, despite the fact that population displacement is arguably an age-old phenomenon, it only emerges as a distinct *problem* in the early decades of the twentieth century. Rather than simply a result of increased numbers of displaced persons, or the spread of the *nation*-state throughout Europe in the wake of the First World War, this chapter argued that the problematisation of population displacement was also a result of the changing character of the state and international system and their concomitant political rationalities. Using Foucault's lectures on the state and governmentality at the Collège de France as a lens through which to explore the development of the state and state system, we saw how changes in the problematique of government led to changing problematisations of population movement.

When something called 'the state' first entered into reflected governmental practice in the mid-sixteenth century, the primary concern of government, as a rationality and practice, was to ensure the continual growth of the strength of the state. Population was conceptualised as the sum of subjects inhabiting a territory and, as such, serves as an important source of state strength, understood as a source of wealth. According to such a rationality of government, growth of the population, and ensuring that each individual member is as productive as possible, will ensure the growth of the wealth and thus the strength of the state.

Emigration thus needs to be prohibited, and immigration encouraged. In the mid-eighteenth century the rationality of governing shifted, and population was conceptualised in a different way. No longer simply the sum of subjects in the state and thus the source of the state's strength, the population was now understood as a quasi-natural being, with its own processes, and dependent upon a number of natural and artificial variables for its health, well-being, and productivity. The responsibility of government was no longer to obsessively regulate the daily lives of each member of the population to ensure their productivity, since this kind of obsessive regulation could produce the opposite effects to those intended. Government must, rather, recognise when it must not intervene, when it must refrain from action, when and how it must let the 'natural' processes of population and the variables upon which it depends, take their own course. Government must, in other words, govern according to the immanent rationality of these economic, biological, and social processes. This concern with ensuring the security of these processes – enabling them to function according to their own rationality – involves identifying potential threats to them, and acting so as to *manage* those threats/risks. Migration comes to be problematised differently, as a result not only of the rise of nationalist and race-thinking, but also as a result of concerns about health and economic progress. It is now immigration that poses a risk to the population, rather than emigration. But, the binary of prohibition-permission is substituted for monitoring and management, an approach that sifts populations, rather than banning or quarantining them, to identify risky/dangerous subgroups or individuals to be subject to increased regulation, while preserving the circulation of people and goods necessary for the proper functioning of economic and social processes.

This shifting rationality of government was evident also in changes beyond the state. *Raison d'état*, the rationality of government of the administrative state, is primarily concerned with the rule of the inside, and does not reflect on an 'outside' except in terms of the balance, or equilibrium of forces enabling greater prediction in state relations. The horizon of liberal governmentality, the rationality of government of the governmentalising state, however, does not stop at the boundaries of the state, because the processes and variables upon which the health, well-being, and prosperity of its population depend are not themselves so bounded. Effective management of these processes will thus require coordination with other actors – states and organisations. The international system thus also developed into the kind of entity for which population displacement – as unmanaged and thus risky migration – became a problem, and the kind of entity capable – or thought to be capable – of addressing such a problem through developing a system to manage it. The international passport system that was institutionalised after the First World War was the first such attempt that the international community made to manage migration, and it was precisely this system that the Russian refugees, whose assistance was the 'birth' of the modern refugee regime, could not conform to. While the previous chapter explored how understanding of a distinct 'refugee problem' develops in the first half of the twentieth century, the next chapter turns its focus to how this 'problem' is managed.

Note

1 Proceedings of the various Conferences can be accessed at: http://ocp.hul.harvard.edu/contagion/sanitaryconferences.html.

References

Barnett, M., *Empire of Humanity: A History of Humanitarianism* (Ithaca: Cornell University Press, 2011)

Bartelson, J., *A Genealogy of Sovereignty* (Cambridge: Cambridge University Press, 1995)

Bigo, D., "Security and Immigration: Toward a Critique of the Governmentality of Unease" in *Alternatives: Global, Local, Political* 27(1) (2002): 63–92

Bigo, D. "Security: A Field Left Fallow" in Dillon, M., and Neal, A. (Eds), *Foucault on Politics, Security and War* (Basingstoke: Palgrave Macmillan, 2008): 93–114

Crampton, J. W., "Maps, Race and Foucault: Eugenics and Territorialization Following World War One" in Crampton J. W., and Elden, S. (Eds), *Space, Knowledge and Power: Foucault and Geography* (Aldershot: Ashgate, 2007): 223–244

Czajka, A., "Migration in the Age of the Nation-State: Migrants, Refugees, and the National Order of Things" in *Alternatives: Global, Local, Political* 39(3) (2014): 151–163

Dean, M., *Governmentality: Power and Rule in Modern Society* (London: SAGE, 1999)

Dean, M., *Critical and Effective Histories: Foucault's Methods and Historical Sociology* (New York: Routledge, 2003)

Elden, S., "Governmentality, Calculation, Territory" in *Environment and Planning D: Society and Space* 25 (2007): 562–580

Foucault, M., "Political Technology of Individuals" in Faubion, J. (Ed.), *The Essential Works of Foucault 1954–1985, Volume 3: Power* (London: Penguin, 2000): 403–417

Foucault, M., "The Subject and Power" in Faubion, J. (Ed.), *The Essential Works of Foucault 1954–1985, Volume 3: Power* (London: Penguin, 2000): 326–348

Foucault, M., *Society Must Be Defended: Lectures at the Collège de France, 1975–1976* (London: Penguin, 2004)

Foucault, M., "What Our Present Is" [1981] in Lotringer, S. (Ed.), *The Politics of Truth* (Los Angeles: Semiotext(e), 2007): 129–144

Foucault, M., *Security, Territory, Population: Lectures at the Collège de France, 1977–1978* (Basingstoke: Palgrave Macmillan, 2009)

Foucault, M., *The Birth of Biopolitics: Lectures at the Collège de France, 1978–1979* (Basingstoke: Palgrave Macmillan, 2010)

Gordon, C., "Governmental Rationality: An Introduction" in Burchell, G., Gordon, C., and Miller, P. (Eds), *The Foucault Effect: Studies in Governmentality* (Chicago: University of Chicago Press, 1991): 1–51

Haddad, E., *The Refugee in International Society: Between Sovereigns* (Cambridge: Cambridge University Press, 2008)

Herren, M., "Governmental Internationalism and the Beginning of a New World Order in the Late Nineteenth Century" in Geyer, M. H., and Paulmann, J. (Eds), *The Mechanics of Internationalism: Culture, Society, and Politics from the 1840s to the First World War* (Oxford: Oxford University Press, 2001): 121–144

Hindess, B., "Divide and Govern" in Ericson, R. V., and Stehr, N. (Eds), *Governing Modern Societies* (Toronto: University of Toronto Press, 2000): 118–140

Hindess, B., "Liberalism: What's in a Name?" in Larner, W., and Walters, W. (Eds), *Global Governmentality: Governing International Spaces* (London: Routledge, 2004): 23–39

Hope-Simpson, Sir J., *The Refugee Problem: Report of a Survey* (Oxford: Oxford University Press, 1939)

Jacobsen, H. K., *Networks of Interdependence: International Organizations and the Global Political System* (New York: Alfred A. Knopf Inc., 1979)

Johnson, A., "Foucault: Critical Theory of the Police in a Neoliberal Age" in *Theoria* 141(61) (2014): 5–29

Koslowski, R., *Migrants and Citizens: Demographic Change in the European State System* (Ithaca: Cornell University Press, 2000)

Lachenicht, S., "Refugees and Refugee Protection in the Early Modern Period" in *Journal of Refugee Studies* 30(3) (2017): 261–281

Larner, W., and Walters, W., "Global Governmentality: Governing International Spaces" in Larner, W., and Walters, W. (Eds), *Global Governmentality: Governing International Spaces* (London: Routledge, 2004): 1–20

League of Nations, "Conference on Passports, Customs Formalities and Through Tickets" in *League of Nations Official Journal* 1(8) (1920): 52–64

League of Nations, "The Question of the Russian Refugees – Covering Letter and Memorandum by the Secretary General, and Annexes" in *League of Nations Official Journal* 2(3–4) (1921): 225–230

Legg, S., "Foucault's Population Geographies: Classifications, Biopolitics and Governmental Spaces" in *Population, Space and Place* 11 (2005): 137–156

Leira, H., "Taking Foucault Beyond Foucault: Inter-State Governmentality in Early Modern Europe" in Kiersey, N. J., and Stokes, D. (Eds), *Foucault and International Relations* (London: Routledge, 2011): 113–133

Lemke, T., " 'The Birth of Biopolitics': Michel Foucault's Lecture at the Collège de France on Neoliberal Governmentality" in *Economy and Society* 30(2) (2001): 190–207

Lemke, T., "An Indigestible Meal? Foucault, Governmentality and State Theory" in *Distinktion: Journal of Social Theory* 8(2) (2007): 43–64

Lui-Bright, R., "International/National: Sovereignty, Governmentality and International Relations" in Crowder *et al.* (Eds), *Australian Political Studies 1997: Proceedings of the 1997 APSA Conference Vol. 2*: 581–597

Marrus, M., *The Unwanted: European Refugees in the Twentieth Century* (Oxford: Oxford University Press, 1985)

Osiander, A., *The States System of Europe, 1640–1990: Peacemaking and the Conditions of International Stability* (Oxford: Oxford University Press, 1994)

Rose, N., "Government, Authority and Expertise in Advanced Liberalism" in *Economy and Society* 22(3) (1993): 283–299

Rose, N., and Novas, C. "Biological Citizenship" in Ong, A., and Collier, S. J. (Eds), *Global Assemblages: Technology, Politics, and Ethics as Anthropological Problems* (Oxford: Blackwell, 2005): 439–463

Salter, M., *Rights of Passage: The Passport in International Relations* (Boulder: Lynne Rienner Publishers, 2003)

Sawyer, S. W., "Foucault and the State" in *The Tocqueville Review* 36(1) (2015): 135–164

Smyser, W. D., "Refugees: A Never-Ending Story" in *Foreign Affairs* 64(1) (1985): 154–168

Soguk, N., *States and Strangers: Refugees and Displacements of Statecraft* (Minneapolis: University of Minnesota Press, 1999)

Torpey, J., *The Invention of the Passport: Surveillance, Citizenship and the State* (Cambridge: Cambridge University Press, 2000)

Valverde, M., "Genealogies of European States: Foucauldian Reflections" in *Economy and Society* 36(1) (2007): 159–178

Ward, J. M., *Colonial Self-Government: The British Experience, 1759–1856* (Basingstoke: The Macmillan Press, 1976)

Zolberg, A., "Managing a World on the Move" in *Population and Development Review* 32(1) (2006): 222–253

3 Power, Knowledge, and the Subject

Managing the Refugee (as) Problem

The previous two chapters unpacked the relationship between 'the refugee problem' and the refugee regime, first by exploring the formative years of the development of the refugee regime to reveal that it was created, primarily, to address the problems that the existence and presence of refugees posed to states rather than addressing the problems that refugees themselves face, and second, by investigating the historical conditions of possibility for the emergence of this problem. By employing Foucault's analysis of the development of the state as an object and practice of government, the previous chapter demonstrated how 'the refugee (as) problem' was able to emerge once population was conceptualised as a quasi-natural being, dependent upon a number of natural and artificial processes, the management of which became the responsibility of government. Population movement shifted from a phenomenon to be either prohibited or permitted in order for the state to realise the potential inherent in the size of its population, to one that must, in the interests of the proper unfolding of the natural and artificial processes upon which population depends, instead be managed. Migration thus appeared as a general phenomenon in need of management, with a nascent regime of cross-border movement regulations systematised after the First World War. The appearance of almost one million individuals suddenly unable to conform to these new procedures of migration management posed a more specific problem within this broader problematisation of cross-border movement that then needed to be managed. The international refugee regime examined in Chapter 1 was the apparatus established for such management. This chapter turns its attention to *how* 'the refugee (as) problem' is managed.

In establishing a refugee regime to help states manage the presence and movement of these newly problematised figures, a new legal subjectivity was created – the Refugee – which gives access to a limited set of rights and protections in states other than one's own. With the creation of the refugee regime, another dimension of 'the refugee (as) problem' was, thus, opened up, still guided by the underlying conceptualisation of refugees as problematic figures of burden: the problem of managing *access* to this legal subjectivity and the rights and protections that accompany it. Just as the confluence of the breakdown of feudalism and the upheavals of the Reformation and Counter-Reformation provided the impetus for the emergence of a general problematic of government, the development of which led to the problematisation of migration and the need for it to be managed, the confluence of the breakdown of colonialism and the advent of the travel and communications revolution in the latter half of the twentieth century provided the impetus for the rapid expansion of this access-management dimension of 'the refugee (as) problem'.

Building upon the insights of the previous chapter that a problem can only be managed by being known, and the more 'accurately' it can be known the more 'effectively' it can be managed, this chapter examines the role that knowledge production plays in the effective management of 'the refugee (as) problem'. Turning to Foucault's work on the relationship between knowledge, truth, power, and subjectivity, this chapter argues that in order for the international refugee regime to effectively manage 'the refugee (as) problem' in line with its principles of burden-limiting/shifting and self-interest it needs to 'know' both the individuals and the phenomenon in need of management, and that the knowledge and management of one both necessitates and facilitates knowledge and management of the other. As such, the chapter will examine two practices, or processes, of knowledge production in relation to 'the refugee (as) problem': the refugee status determination process, and the development of Refugee Studies as a discipline. The chapter argues that these two practices of knowledge production serve as both the legitimation for, and a key component of, managing access to Refugee[1] status as a way to manage 'the refugee (as) problem'. The production of academic knowledge provides a grid of specification against which different categories of migrant – or different subjectivities – can be produced; and the status determination process then works to assign individuals to one of these subject positions. This joint operation enables states and UNHCR to more 'accurately' sift populations on the move so as to more effectively manage them. This practice differentially restricts or enables the legitimate exercise of choice and agency on the part of such migrants in seeking solutions to their displacement, or to the problems for which displacement is itself a partial solution, and keeps them locked within the statist framing of the problem of migration management. The consequences for those subject to the operation of these processes of knowledge production is of central concern to this chapter, as it is in the recognition of these consequences that the need for reconceptualising 'the refugee problem' arises – a task undertaken in Chapters 4 and 5.

The chapter is structured as follows. First, an overview is given of key developments in the production of academic knowledge about refugees and forced migration, including how these developments in knowledge production have provided the 'scientific' rationale for specific policies designed to manage access to Refugee status. Second, Foucault's understanding of the relationship between power, knowledge, truth and the subject is summarised. The refugee status determination process is examined in the third section and these Foucauldian reflections applied to the process of truth- and identity-production operative within it. The final section addresses the consequences of these practices of knowledge production: the production of subjectivity and the differential agency and choice that accompany it.

Understanding (Forced) Migration

While academic work on refugees was not unheard of in the inter-war period or years immediately following the establishment of UNCHR, such work tended to be restricted to historical surveys of the work of refugee organisations (e.g. Holborn, 1956), or in-depth examinations of particular refugee groups (e.g. Hope-Simpson, 1939) (for a good summary of early work on refugees, see: Black, 2001; Skran and Daughtry, 2007). With decolonisation came a recognition that the "non-Western world was in such a state that it would regularly produce refugee crises", and refugee movements ceased to be considered atypical (Lippert, 1999: 314). Since then there has been a dramatic growth in the production of knowledge about refugees. Such knowledge has been produced in a range of disciplines, including law, anthropology, and sociology, but has also coalesced into an inter-disciplinary 'discipline' of its own: Refugee Studies. Barry M. Stein was the first to develop a university course on refugees and displacement, in 1975, and he was one of the first to conceive of Refugee Studies as a new area of investigation for social science. In a special issue of *International Migration Review*, he and his co-editor, Silvano Tomasi, called for the establishment of a discipline to produce the knowledge necessary to address refugee movement:

> [W]e are not just calling for more research on refugees. Rather, we seek to provoke new thinking and promote a comprehensive, historical, interdisciplinary and comparative perspective which focuses on the consistencies and patterns in the refugee experience. Ideally, such work should build the foundation of a new field of Refugee Studies, clarify concepts, formulate the questions to be addressed more precisely and define the parameters and priorities of such studies. The ultimate objective must be the development of a new body of knowledge, the cataloguing and evaluation of existing programs, and, perhaps most importantly, the establishment of an institutional memory for policy makers and operational personnel.
>
> (Stein and Tomasi, 1981: 6–7)

The academic community was quick to respond to their call. The Refugee Studies Programme at Oxford University began in 1982, followed in 1985 by the creation of an Inter-University Consortium for Refugee Research involving government officials, scholars, and aid workers. In 1988, also at Oxford, a new academic, peer-reviewed journal, the *Journal of Refugee Studies*, was established as "an intellectual opening through which patterns in crises, movements, behaviours, and policies could be inspected, explanations given, and new concepts refined" (Lippert, 1999: 316). On the other side of the Atlantic, at York University in Canada, the Refugee Documentation Project was established in 1982, which became the Centre for Refugee Studies in 1988. They too publish an academic journal, *Refuge*, dedicated to the study of refugees. In addition to *Refuge* and the *Journal of Refugee Studies*, there are now dozens of journals dedicated to the study of refugees, forced migration and displacement, and UNHCR and other organisations working in the field of forced migration also fund and produce their own research. Refugee Studies has produced a vast body of knowledge about refugees, but there are two developments in particular that are central to the management of 'the refugee (as) problem': the development of the 'myth of difference' in the 1980s, and the conceptualisation of the 'migration-asylum-nexus' in the 1990s.

The rapid expansion, through the 1980s, of Refugee Studies coincided with developments in travel and communications which enabled easier, quicker, and cheaper access to the states of the global North by refugees from the global South, a recession sparked by the 1973 OPEC oil crisis which led to a resurgence of protectionism towards domestic labour markets in the face of rising unemployment, and the restriction of refugee resettlement programmes – which had focused mainly on refugees from Communism who possessed 'ideological value' for Western states – across the global North. As these resettlement programmes were reduced, refugees were effectively 'transformed' into 'asylum seekers', "who now had to arrive independently and prove their claims" (Koser, 2001: 88), and the early years of the 1980s saw increasing restrictions on asylum seekers, and the asylum process, in industrialised countries in order to manage these unplanned arrivals. This confluence of events and academic developments was not merely a coincidence. Refugee Studies did not develop in a vacuum or in quarantine from the world of policy, and nor did policy-makers view Refugee Studies scholars as ivory-tower academics, unconnected to the 'real world' and producing knowledge of purely academic interest. Far from it.

The rapid expansion of Refugee Studies scholarship in the early 1980s 'revealed' what were supposedly fundamental differences between Refugees as defined in the Convention, and the individuals and groups displaced by events occurring in the global South. These 'new' refugees fled situations of generalised violence and civil war, rather than persecution for their political opinions, religion or ethnicity (Chimni, 1998: 356). Such wars or situations of violence were the result of failures of post-colonial governance – conflicts over resources, or weak governments unable to get a hold of gang violence. These differences, it was argued, rendered the early Cold War practice of resettlement – which had been the favoured practice for the ideologically valuable refugees from Communism – inappropriate and ineffective, elevating repatriation to the top of the hierarchy of 'solutions' to displacement. Repatriation was even attributed by some Refugee Studies scholars to refugees in the global South as their own preferred solution (Chimni, 1998: 364). The increased numbers of people from the global South claiming protection as Refugees in the global North were constructed, on the basis of these assumptions, to be in many cases spurious – their asylum claims were merely a cover for economic migration. For B. S. Chimni, these differences are a 'myth', based less upon "extensive studies of the complex issues involved, [than] the outcome of a marriage between convenient theory, untested assumptions, and the interests of states" (Chimni, 1998: 364–365). Claudena Skran, one of the few Refugee Studies scholars known for historical research, similarly argues that such differences between the 'new' refugees and 'traditional' (read, European) Refugees are significantly overblown (Skran, 1995: 5). Regardless of the intrinsic academic merit of these assertions of difference, for governments already concerned about immigration in the wake of a recession and which were now facing an increase in the number of refugees seeking admittance, such knowledge provided the 'scientific' rationale and legitimacy for the creation of restrictive asylum policies (Chimni, 2009: 14) which, it has been argued, were designed to enable authorities to decline access to Refugee status (Koser, 2001: 181). Such policies took two main forms: restricting access to territory and reforming asylum processes. The first option is typified by the UK where, from the mid-1980s, the government imposed stringent visa requirements on foreign nationals seeking to enter the UK, and imposed sanctions against carriers transporting individuals to the UK who lacked the proper paperwork (Zolberg, 1989: 280). These policies were intended to restrict access to British territory as only those on British territory are entitled to lodge a claim for Refugee status. The second approach was typified by West Germany. Also in the mid-1980s, the West German government began to reform its asylum procedures, reducing the work and support schemes that those claiming Refugee status were entitled to, introducing poor living conditions, and speeding up the whole process of status determination (Zolberg, 1989: 280).

These policies received renewed academic legitimation and tools in the 1990s and into the 2000s in the form of the 'migration-asylum-nexus'. One of the effects of the attempts by Northern states to restrict refugee resettlement and access to legal migration routes and asylum processes, has been an increase in 'illegal' border crossings and human smuggling (not in itself a new method employed by refugees to escape persecution) by asylum seekers and other migrants (Johnson, 2014: 51). This led to the elaboration of the 'migration-asylum-nexus', which recognises the inherently blurred nature of the lines between refugees (Convention and otherwise) and 'economic migrants'. As summarised by Castles in 2007, the migration-asylum-nexus is a concept intended to articulate that the artificial lines drawn between 'economic' migration and 'forced' migration do not correspond to the reality of migration processes, and that it is often not possible to attain the neat separation between the two that the refugee regime appears to require. Not only do refugees and economic migrants often make use of the same routes and mechanisms to facilitate mobility, but the causes and motivations of both are often 'mixed':

> Countries with weak economies, increasing inequality and widespread impoverishment tend also to have tyrannical rulers, weak state apparatuses, and high levels of violence and human rights violations. Thus the conditions that cause economic migration are closely linked with those that cause forced migration, leading to the migratory movement of people with 'mixed motivations'.
>
> (Castles, 2007: 26)

The purpose of the elaboration of the 'migration-asylum-nexus' was primarily to criticise the definition of a Refugee in the 1951 Convention as too narrow, a definition based upon a distinction between 'forced' and 'voluntary' migration – corresponding to 'political' and 'economic' reasons for flight – that is impossible to draw with any real accuracy in practice (Scheel and Ratfisch, 2014: 931). However, since all knowledge is "dual use" (Chimni, 2009: 14), the concept was deployed in the realm of policy in a fashion arguably at odds with the initial motivation behind its development. Recognition of 'mixed flows', both for UNHCR and state actors, necessitated the development of ever more 'accurate' refugee status determination procedures, so as to enable the accurate and efficient 'sorting out' of populations on the move problematised anew by the mixed nature of migratory flows (Scheel and Ratfisch, 2014: 934). These more accurate processes – which could take advantage of technological developments in biometrics such as fingerprinting, retina scanning, and others (Muller, 2004: 52–53) – are intended to enable authorities to separate the 'genuine refugee' from the 'economic migrant' or 'bogus asylum seeker', and facilitate the swift repatriation of the latter to his/her country of origin.

The utilisation of the 'migration-asylum-nexus' and the 'myth of difference' thus come to function hand in hand in the contemporary management of 'the refugee (as) problem'. As knowledge about refugees and forced migration has increased, so too have the categories of 'migrant'. The proliferation of categories, labels, or subjectivities (different scholars use different terms) – 'refugee', 'asylum seeker', 'environmental refugee', 'irregular migrant', 'economic migrant', and so on, that have emerged from the academic study of refugees and forced migration (Zetter, 2007) – are, as Hayden points out, efforts on the part of scholars, politicians, and aid workers, to distinguish motivations for moving and thus construct categories of people in relation to space and rights (Hayden, 2006: 471). The result of these developments in academic knowledge of refugees has not been the revision of the definition in the 1951 Convention so as to provide its protections to the wider range of individuals in need of it – which one might expect if the purpose of the regime was to address the issues that forced migrants face. The response, in fact, has remained faithful to the foundation of 'the refugee (as) problem' – that the refugee is a burden for which the state, if at all possible, will try not to take responsibility. The restriction of access to the already limited protection and assistance provided by the refugee regime is now to be effected through the deployment of the legal status guarding these same protections – Refugee – in order to manage other potential figures of burden: people who flee desperate situations and seek a new life abroad. Refugee status has itself become a tool to be used to manage 'the refugee (as) problem'. These academic developments have provided 'scientific' rationale and legitimation to governments seeking to justify these policies. This is not to claim, of course, that Refugee Studies scholars have been working at the behest of governments. Rather that, regardless of the intentions or motivations of such scholars, the knowledge they have produced has been put to work by other actors – state authorities, UNHCR, and others –

in order to manage 'the refugee (as) problem' by regulating access to Refugee status. There is, in other words, an integral relationship between knowledge production about a 'problem' and the management of that problem; a relationship central to, and elaborated in detail in, Foucault's work, to which we now turn before exploring the refugee status determination process in more detail.

Power/Knowledge, Truth, and the Subject

In an essay entitled 'The Subject and Power' Foucault states that the consistent goal of his diverse works on mental illness, medicine, sexuality, prisons, and the history of the social and human sciences had been "to create a history of the different modes by which, in our culture, human beings are made subjects" (Foucault, EWP: 326). He identifies and examines three "modes of objectification" by which this transformation is facilitated. The first is the "modes of inquiry that try to give themselves the status of sciences" and he is referring here, primarily, to his investigation in *The Order of Things* of the development of the 'human sciences' of economics, philology, and biology which are dependent upon and reinforce the existence of Man as a speaking, labouring, and living being. In *The Order of Things* Foucault argues that 'Man' is

> not simply a thing that has been waiting for all eternity for scientific knowledge to take it as an object and for philosophical speculation to take it as a source of value; rather, it is a particular concern which arose as a consequence of precise transformations affecting the practice of empirical knowledge at a particular point in time.
>
> (Maniglier, 2013: 104)

The human sciences claim to give us 'truth' about Man, and thus take Man as an object to be known and about whom knowledge can be produced. We could arguably conceive of Refugee Studies, or Forced Migration Studies, as another example of this type of "mode of objectification". The second of the modes of objectification by which human beings are made subjects are "dividing practices" whereby "the subject is either divided inside himself or divided from others" (Foucault, EWP: 326). Examples of this include the divisions between the mad and the sane, the sick and the healthy, and criminals and "good boys" that were the focus of *Madness and Civilisation*, *The Birth of the Clinic*, and *Discipline and Punish*, respectively. In each of these cases the processes of social objectification and categorisation give human beings both a social and a personal identity, transforming them into certain kinds of subjects, and in so doing render them objects of knowledge. The third and final mode of objectification that Foucault highlights, and which was the focus of his work at the time of 'The Subject and Power', is that concerning the way a human being turns him- or herself into a subject. In the second and third volumes of his *History of Sexuality* he examines how individuals have learned to recognise themselves as subjects of "sexuality" (Foucault, EWP: 327). Such 'subjectification' takes place through a variety of operations by individuals on their own bodies, souls, thoughts and conduct, entailing a process of self-understanding, mediated by an external authority figure such as a confessor or psychoanalyst (Rabinow, 1984: 11).

Foucault's earlier studies of these modes of objectification – his works on madness, medicine, and the human sciences – are often referred to as his 'archaeological' works, which focused on the discursive formation of bodies of knowledge. His later works – on criminal punishment and sexuality – are 'genealogical', and in them the archaeological examination of discourse is supplemented by an examination of the influence of power relations on the development of discursive knowledge. In examining the discursive formation of bodies of knowledge, Foucault begins from the position that at any given period there are substantial constraints, beyond those of grammar and logic, on how people are able to think and speak, and that these 'discursive practices' can be recovered through the study of the material traces left behind by a particular historical period and culture – the 'archive'. The focus of archaeology is not, as Rousse explains, the specific bodies of knowledge (*connaissance*) of disciplines such as psychology, medicine, or economics, but this deeper epistemic context and conditions (*savoir*) within which such bodies of knowledge became intelligible and authoritative (Rousse, 2005: 96). Foucault argued that particular investigations were structured by

> which concepts and statements were intelligible together, how those statements were organised thematically, which of those statements counted as 'serious', who was authorised to speak seriously, and what questions and procedures were relevant to assess the credibility of those statements.
>
> (Rousse, 2005: 96)

Foucault's individual archaeologies revealed that the 'knowledge' of any given discipline in the human and social sciences was not the "sum of what was thought to be true, but the whole set of practices, singularities, and deviations of which one could speak" in that particular discourse (Foucault, AK: 201).

Foucault's earliest study of mental illness had led him to the conclusion that there was no discourse-independent object 'madness', the truth of which psychiatry and psychology could claim to have any privileged access to (Gutting, 1989: 55–61). The objects of discourse for investigation in the human and social sciences are not already existing and awaiting the advent of scientific investigation to discover them in their true form – as the traditional view of scientific progress suggests (Foucault, AK: 49). Rather, they are the result of the interplay of sets of rules governing what Foucault calls "surfaces of emergence", "authorities of delimitation" and "grids of specification". Those rules governing "surfaces of emergence" derive from the social norms which separate objects characterised in a certain way from a social context and transfer them to the domain of the discursive formation (what Foucault would later designate as a "dividing practice"). For example, the family, the immediate social group, and the religious community all had thresholds of acceptable behaviour beyond which the term 'madness' would have been applied, confinement of the 'mad person' been demanded, and responsibility for explanation and treatment placed on the medical profession (Sheridan, 2005: 96). Those to whom society gives the authority of deciding what objects belong to a discursive formation are "authorities of delimitation". In the nineteenth century, medicine – as an institution possessing its own rules, a group of individuals constituting the medical profession, a body of knowledge and practice, and a public authority recognised by law and practice – became the major authority in society that delimited, designated, named and established madness as an object of examination (Foucault, AK: 46). "Grids of specification" are systems according to which different kinds of objects are divided, contrasted, related, regrouped, and classified as objects of discourse. A person may merit classification as 'mad' not only in relation to social customs and by authoritative judgement, but also by virtue of where (s)he stands in relation to the behaviour of others – where one stands in relation to a 'norm' (Gutting, 1989: 234). What we 'know', then – about mental illness and 'the insane', or about recidivism and 'the delinquent', or about migration and 'the refugee' – is a function of practices, sites from which statements emerge, and concepts and their modes of integration, rather than a collection of things judged to be 'true'. Or, to put it another way, these things are judged to be true because they are a function of these practices, sites, and concepts. Foucault's 'archaeologies', of madness, medicine, and the human sciences, revealed that there were important shifts in what counted as serious discussions of madness, disease, wealth, and so on, but he came to the realisation that the rules of discourse alone could not explain the occurrence of these shifts, or why they took the form that they did. Foucault's 'genealogical' works supplement this archaeological analysis of discourse with a complementary analysis of the relation of discursive knowledge to the power structures of society (Gutting, 1989: 260).

Foucault understands power as a relation, rather than an institution, a structure, or a strength we are endowed with (Foucault, HS: 93). Unlike more traditional (political) theories of power, which assume that power resides in the hands of the sovereign, and is wielded over individuals in and through the sovereign's commands, rendering such subjects free from power wherever they are out of reach of the sovereign (Allen, 2002: 132–133), Foucault argues not only that power relations exist throughout social relations of all kinds, but that power is a productive as well as repressive force; power forms knowledge and produces discourse (Foucault, EWP: 120). On this understanding, it would be misguided to imagine that knowledge can only exist where power relations are suspended, and that knowledge can only develop outside of its injunctions, demands and interests (Foucault, EWP: 131). Foucault does not mean by this that those 'in power' dictate to those producing knowledge (although public – and perhaps to a similar extent, private – funding of research does add an interesting dimension to consider). Rather, power relations and discourses (or knowledge) mutually constitute one another by rendering the social world into a form that is both knowable and governable, each dependent on the other (Simons, 1995: 27). As Hall explains, knowledge linked to power not only assumes the authority of 'the truth' but has the power to *make itself true*: all knowledge, once applied in the world, has real effects and, in that sense at least, becomes true. Further, knowledge, once used to regulate the conduct of others, entails restraint, regulation, and the disciplining of practices (Hall, 1997: 49). Thus, Foucault states, "there is no power relation without the correlative constitution of a field of knowledge, nor any knowledge that does not presuppose and constitute at the same time, power relations" (Foucault, DP: 27). This led Foucault to speak not of the 'Truth' of knowledge in an absolute sense – a truth which remained so for all time regardless of context – but of discourse sustaining a 'regime of truth' (Foucault, EWP: 132). This relationship between power, knowledge, truth, and their 'effect' – the subject – is perhaps best illustrated by Foucault's examination of disciplinary power and disciplinary techniques.

Power/Knowledge, Truth, and the Subject in Discipline and Punish

Discipline and Punish begins with illustrations of two different modalities of power: the 1757 execution of the regicide Damiens, representing the manifestation of sovereign power on the body of the condemned man; and a timetable for the House of Young Prisoners in Paris, from the 1830s, which represented a novel form of power – disciplinary power. These illustrations represent, for Foucault, a profound shift in the relationship of the body to power. Throughout the eighteenth century the body was no longer simply the site upon which the power of the sovereign was manifested, but became a site of a meticulous observation of detail, a site of 'discipline' through which docile and 'useful' bodies might be created (Foucault, DP: 138–139). A new 'economy' of power was established, in the sense that procedures were established that "allowed the effects of power to circulate throughout the entire social body" in ways much more efficient, less wasteful and less risky than the techniques previously employed – such as the gruesome public execution of Damiens (Foucault, EWP: 120). In various sites, such as schools and factories, whole bodies of methods, knowledge, descriptions, plans and data were developed, at first in response to particular needs, but which converge, overlap, and gradually produce the blueprint of a general method of domination which made individuals into specific subjects (Foucault, DP: 141). This new technique of power – disciplinary power – creates a subject who is self-monitoring, developmental, and productive, and it operates according to a number of techniques or mechanisms, most notably through normalising judgement and the examination.

At the heart of disciplinary systems functions a small penal mechanism different in its focus from those of judicial and sovereign power. Disciplinary power is concerned less with violations of law than with 'non-observance' of practices. Disciplinary sites – workshops, schools, the army – were subject to a series of micro-penalties: of time, where lateness, absence and interruption becomes punishable; of activity, whereby negligence and inattention become punishable; of behaviour, by which impoliteness and disobedience become punishable; of the body, by which irregular gestures and lack of cleanliness are punishable; and so on (Foucault, DP: 178). In other words, the whole domain of non-conforming becomes punishable. However, unlike the punishment of the law characteristic of sovereign power – such as that displayed in the execution of Damiens – disciplinary punishment is corrective rather than retaliatory: the goal of disciplinary punishment is to reform. To this end, punishment is but one element of a double system – gratification-punishment – and it is this system that operates in the process of training and correction: observance of expectations of behaviour are rewarded, and non-observance is punished, leading subjects to adjust their behaviour accordingly. This mechanism makes possible the definition of behaviour and performance on the basis of two opposed values of good and bad: "instead of the simple division of the prohibition as practised in penal justice, we have a distribution between a positive and a negative pole" (Foucault, DP: 180). All behaviour falls somewhere within this field. What is differentiated under this system is, however, not acts, but individuals themselves – their nature, potential, level, or value. In short, disciplinary power

> refers individual actions to a whole that is at once a field of comparison, a space of differentiation and the principle of a rule to be followed. It differentiates individuals from one another ... it introduces, through this value-giving measure, the constraint of conformity that must be achieved. Lastly, it traces the limit that will define difference in relation to all other differences, the external frontier of the abnormal. In short, it normalises.
>
> (Foucault, DP: 183)

This 'norm' – of behaviour, ability, activity, achievement – is a measure which the 'disciplines'[2] themselves create. As Ransom explains, one way of training individuals to do something is to establish standards to act as performance goals. Each individual will display a certain aptitude in learning or executing such tasks, and this allows a ranking to be traced around a norm of performance (Ransom, 1997: 47–48). From the accumulation of distinctions and valuations in reference to this 'norm', a particular conception of the 'truth' about human beings emerges: "the 'natural' body is capable of repeating exercises for specific periods of time; the mind, 'on average', is capable of absorbing only so much instruction", and so on (Ransom, 1997: 48). These 'natural' traits are natural only in relation to the tasks set by the disciplines, and so while these truths are not 'false' they do lack foundational ontological status (Ransom, 1997: 50). They are, nevertheless, used as standards against which the behaviour and abilities of individuals are measured, and the normalising judgements they produce can, and do, facilitate and justify exclusions from the human community, such as of the mad, the sick, and the sexually 'abnormal'.

The principles and practices of observation and normalising judgement are joined in another key technique of disciplinary power: the examination. A prime example of the power-knowledge nexus, the examination combines the deployment of force and the establishment of truth. It places the individual within a field of surveillance and situates them in a network of writing. The procedures of examination as they developed in hospitals, armies, and schools were accompanied by a system of registration and documentary accumulation to enable the efficient transmission of information along the hierarchy of observation. Related to this placing of the individual into a field of documentation, which enables knowledge about individuals and groups to be efficiently collected and transmitted, the examination makes each individual 'a case', but a case which "at one and the same time, constitutes an object for a branch of knowledge and a hold for a branch of power" (Foucault, DP: 191). As Foucault explains, the case is "the individual as he may be described, judged, measured, compared with others, in his very individuality; and it is also the individual who has to be trained or corrected, classified, normalised, excluded" (Foucault, DP: 191). The examination, thus, fixes, in both a ritual and 'scientific' way, the individual to his/her own particularity. But this particularity is not some internal essence that makes one person different from another, but particularity in comparison to others and effectuated by relation to a 'norm' (Foucault, DP: 192).

Foucault's examination of disciplinary power, of (academic) disciplines, and of modern political rationality that was the subject of the previous chapter, reveals that power, knowledge, truth and the subject are linked in circular relation with each other, by rendering the social world into a form that is knowable and thus governable. Methods of government render phenomena – such as the people under its jurisdiction, or a person moving across borders – subjects – such as population, or an irregular migrant – amenable to (scientific) study. Simultaneously, scientific methodologies provide knowledge of these subjects that render them amenable to government (Simons, 1995: 27). The unregulated, and increased, movement of (potentially risky or needy) individuals presents a problem to the state that must be managed. Knowledge produced about (forced) migration and about individuals 'on the move' enables their more efficient management and provides the rationale for the implementation of specific policies for such management.

Foucault is concerned with revealing the ways in which power and knowledge manufacture subjects, normalise behaviour, and thus tie individuals to 'their' 'identity'- as a 'homosexual', a 'delinquent', an 'insane person'. He is not primarily concerned with the 'truth' of the claims made by the disciplines he examines, but with the way in which relations of power with which they are intimately related

> categorise[s] the individual, mark[s] him by his own individuality, attach[es] him to his own identity, impose[s] a law of truth on him that he must recognise and others have to recognise in him. It is a form of power that makes individuals subjects.
>
> (Foucault, EWP: 331)

Such subjectification is produced and effectuated in relation to a 'norm', and these norms become the criteria by which such subjects are excluded, to a greater or lesser extent depending on the subject, from 'normal' society; and the forms of knowledge upon which these practices rest become the justification for such continued exclusion. 'Better' understanding of the phenomenon of forced migration enables the creation of a continuum of migration categories, or migrant 'types', plotted in relation to the 'norm' of the territorially bound citizen. Different migrants can then be located on the continuum according to the factors governing their movement, and affording to each position varying degrees of choice and legitimate agency. The 'legitimacy' of the factors governing their movement in turn provides the criteria for excluding such individuals from the protections of the refugee regime and inclusion in a new community. The refugee status determination process is the primary tool through which such subjectification is produced. As demonstrated in the following section, the refugee status determination process, via an economy of truth, 'sifts' the body of people on the move irregularly, producing subjects which can then be managed appropriately/ effectively. The process itself, and the knowledge upon which it relies, become the justification for the exclusion or inclusion of these subjects.

Refugee Status Determination and the Political Economy of Truth

In 2015 the United Nations estimated that around 244 million people were classed as 'international migrants' – individuals who live in a country other than the country in which they were born (United Nations, 2015). Of these 244 million, around 20 million have been identified as falling within the remit of the international refugee regime, and entitled to the protections and rights of the 1951 Refugee Convention. Access to those protections is dependent upon being recognised as a Refugee, the definition of which is laid down in Article 1:

> The term 'refugee' shall apply to any person who:
> (2) …owing to a well-founded fear of being persecuted for reasons of race, religion, nationality, membership of a particular social group or political opinion, is outside the country of his nationality and is unable or, owing to such fear, is unwilling to avail himself of the protection of that country; …
>
> (United Nations, 1951: Art.1A(2))

In order to gain this recognition, an individual must be judged by the appropriate authorities to: have crossed an international border, have a fear that they will face persecution if returned to their country of origin, that such a fear of persecution is based on their religion, race, nationality, political opinion, or membership of a particular social group, and that such a fear of persecution is 'well-founded' – the subjective frame of mind of the asylum seeker must be supported by an 'objective' situation (UNHCR, 2011: 11). The Convention itself is silent on the process by which an individual would be recognised as a Refugee, and so the status determination process is left up to individual states, although this can be carried out by UNHCR with the permission of the relevant government (Storey, 2013: 116). Although each state can institute its own process, the basic practices are similar across the states of the global North, and will usually involve an interview with the asylum seeker to determine the specifics of his/her case, a review of the evidence by an appropriate authority, and a process for appealing a negative outcome. UNHCR has issued its own guidance on refugee status determination (UNHCR, 2011), and this guidance is intended to assist state authorities in assessing claims for refugee status.

In the United Kingdom, the Home Office is responsible for all aspects of immigration and asylum policy and control. There are currently two bodies within the Home Office with direct responsibilities on asylum screening: UK Visas and Immigration (UKVI) and the UK Border Force. The Asylum Casework Directorate within UKVI makes formal decisions on asylum claims, by conducting interviews and investigations into their veracity. The UK Border Force is responsible for initial asylum screening at the UK borders and, formally, makes no decisions on asylum, sending reports of the initial screening interview to the Asylum Casework Directorate, who then decide whether and how to proceed with a claim (Jubany, 2017: 57).[3] Applications for protection under the 1951 Convention can be made at the border upon arrival, or 'in-country', at the Asylum Intake Unit in Croydon, London. Upon lodging a claim for asylum, the applicant is taken to a screening interview to establish his/her identity and collect fingerprints and other biometric data, basic personal details, information on the individual's travel route to the UK, and the reasons for claiming asylum. At this point the applicant's details, including biometric data, are checked against a centralised European identity database, EURODAC (European Dactyloscopy), to see if (s)he has made an asylum claim in another EU state or if there are any criminal proceedings against the applicant in another state. In either of these circumstances it is likely that the applicant will be detained while deportation to the appropriate country is arranged. If the decision is made to proceed with the asylum claim, a formal interview is conducted at a later date, lasting several hours and following a question and answer format, with the focus placed on establishing the basic chronology of the story and testing its 'credibility' (Gibb and Good, 2013: 293). Following the interview, the caseworker must make a decision about whether or not to grant asylum. Under UK immigration rules there are a number of possible outcomes. The applicant could be granted: Refugee status; Humanitarian Protection if judged as not eligible for Refugee status but still in need of international protection; limited leave to remain if judged as not eligible for international protection but there are reasons for allowing the applicant to remain on a temporary basis; or asylum and any other form of protection could be refused (United Kingdom Home Office, 2016: 13–14).

The key phrase of the 1951 Convention definition, and thus the aspect of an asylum claim upon which its success or failure will most often depend, is the applicant's "well-founded fear of being persecuted". The determination of whether or not to grant Refugee status will therefore primarily require an evaluation of the applicant's statements, making the *credibility* of both the applicant and his/her story the main focus of the determination process. UNHCR guidance states that the basic requirement for an asylum seeker's account to have credibility is that it should be "coherent and plausible" and "not run counter to generally known facts" (UNHCR, 2011: 39). The claimant must tell his/her story, and must impart his/her experiences and fears to the caseworker, who must then judge the validity of these claims against what is known about a particular country or situation, in order to establish the credibility of the applicant and his/her case. The credibility assessment focuses on both the 'internal' credibility of the applicant and his/her story – focusing on consistency and appropriate levels of detail – and the 'external' credibility of the story – how well the account holds up against knowledge of an "objective situation" (UNHCR, 2011: 11). The main source of information used in the determination process to assess external credibility is 'Country of Origin Information' (COI), contained in reports produced by the Home Office Country of Origin Information Service (COIS) (Gibb and Good, 2013: 298). These reports contain no analysis or explanation and can most accurately be described as collections of quotes from risk analysis firms, media sources, NGOs, and so on, with almost all sources included being English-language sources. It is not, however, sufficient that an asylum seeker's account be externally credible – i.e. that it accords with what is known about an objective situation. The account must also be internally credible – i.e. it must be judged that this account genuinely is an account of the applicant's experience. There is no single COI-equivalent body of knowledge to assist the caseworker in assessing internal credibility, but a passage from the 2012 Asylum Policy Instructions provides a helpful indication of the kinds of factors that might indicate the credibility of the applicant:

> It is reasonable to expect, subject to mitigating circumstances, that an applicant relating an experience that occurred to them will be more expressive and include sensory details such as what they saw, heard, felt or thought about an event, than someone who has not had this experience … it is a reasonable expectation for an applicant to recount an event to the level of detail that can be reasonably expected of an individual who has experienced the claimed event.
>
> (United Kingdom Home Office, 2012: 14)

A negative credibility finding can have a serious detrimental effect on the possibility of the success of an asylum claim. A caseworker evaluation of whether an asylum seeker is in need of international protection often requires decision-makers to decide whether they *believe* the applicant's evidence about these past and present events and how much weight to attach to that evidence. The status determination process is one in which the story of the applicant is 'tested' against objective evidence, to reveal its truth or falsity, and revealing, by extension, the true identity of the applicant: genuine refugee, or bogus asylum seeker? Individual in need of international protection, or an economic migrant in disguise? The proper course of action can then be employed in order to manage that particular individual: allow the refugee to remain in the UK, with access to the rights and protections of the Convention, thereby regularising their presence; permit the individual to remain in the UK but without the full protections and rights accompanying Refugee status; or detain the individual pending deportation to their country of origin, nullifying the risk posed by their irregular and unauthorised presence.

However, this picture, of the use of objective knowledge to reveal truth, belies the extent to which the status determination process is one of the *production* of knowledge and the *production* of truth, to facilitate the management of people 'on the move'. Refugee status determination does not function to 'reveal' the truth about an applicant's identity but to manufacture such an identity, and it does so via an economy of truth: certain types and sources of knowledge are privileged in advance of the asylum encounter, and this hierarchy of knowledge and truth is reproduced by the status determination process itself. This 'truth' can then be employed in the service of the management of populations by assigning a specific subjectivity to the individual, thereby letting the state know what is to be done with that particular individual. The process is, in other words, "a particular knowledge-power constellation" (Chimni, 2009: 15), a "dividing practice" which, in rendering individuals as objects of knowledge, makes them into certain types of subject.

Asylum and the Political Economy of Truth

Even though the status determination process often turns on the decision the case-worker must make about whether they believe the applicant's evidence, or that the applicant's evidence could be believed, the determination process is not presented – by UNHCR or Home Office guidance, at least – as a competition between two 'subjective' positions, that of the applicant and that of the caseworker. The case-worker's position, as portrayed in the guidance, is rescued from being 'merely' subjective by the use of supposedly 'objective' information, namely Country of Origin Information. A study by the Immigration Advisory Service in 2010 found that 97 percent of all UK asylum caseworkers used COI in all or the majority of their cases, but only 36 percent of these caseworkers *analysed* the information contained therein (Tsangarides, 2010: 18). These numbers appear to be reflective of a certain level of trust in the accuracy and objectivity of the information, a level of trust that has been observed by others (Hardy, 2003: 474). Earlier iterations of the Asylum Policy Instructions produced by the Home Office listed COI as the only reference under a heading of 'Objective Evidence' (United Kingdom Home Office, 2012: 10), and these sources of information were often preceded in the guidance by the word 'objective' (for example, United Kingdom Home Office, 2012: 14, 15). The most recent guidance no longer contains these overt messages of objectivity, but it is still clear that COI is taken to be authoritative. This is reflected in the importance noted in the guidance of the correlation of the asylum seeker's account of his/her reasons for fleeing his/her country of origin with this country information:

> The claimant's testimony and other evidence should be consistent with information (COI) about events in the country of persecution and with any other available information or expert evidence ... the greater the correlation between aspects of the account and external evidence, the greater the weight caseworkers should attribute to those aspects.
>
> (United Kingdom Home Office, 2015a: 15)

Where COI supports the claimant's account of a past or present event, and the account is 'internally consistent ... sufficient in detail and/or plausibility, the material fact should be accepted' (United Kingdom Home Office, 2015a: 16).

If information contained in the COI report contradicts an asylum seeker's case as presented to the caseworker, the COI is often considered authoritative and the applicant's credibility is undermined. This process of determining 'external' credibility functions according to, and entrenches, a hierarchy of knowledge according to the provenance of such knowledge: the subjective knowledge of the asylum seeker occupies the lowest rank and can be discounted, or is at the very least considered to be suspect, when it fails to match the higher-ranked, 'objective', knowledge produced by the government. Other bodies of supposedly 'objective' knowledge are also used to establish the credibility of the asylum seeker. The UK Home Office began using 'language analysis' in 2001 in order to establish the 'true' national origin of the claimant. Here, even the possession of identity documents testifying to a claimant's nationality can be distrusted or disbelieved if an 'expert' language analyst decides that an applicant does not come from where (s)he claims. As Campbell demonstrates, language analysis is used by the Home Office in such a way that the applicant's own origin is made to conform to the belief that language and national borders coincide – an applicant's claim to originate from, for example, Eritrea, can be rendered suspect by a determination of a 'language analyst' that the applicant speaks a language also found in Ethiopia (Campbell, 2012: 676). As Jubany recounts from her observation of the work and training of UK Border Force officers, trainers make a clear distinction between what asylum seekers 'say' and 'the facts', underlining the need to be wary of the applicants' intentions. Asylum seekers are presented to new recruits as "simply presenting a 'version' of reality, while the immigration officer has the exclusive task of establishing what that reality is" (Jubany, 2017: 128–129).

The 'internal' credibility of the asylum seeker's story is equally important to the status determination process, and it is here that Foucault's concept of the 'norm' is most clearly at work. A recent UNHCR report into European asylum procedures, including the process in place in the UK, discovered that authorities in charge of status determination often use the demeanour of an applicant as a measure by which to assess that applicant's credibility (UNHCR, 2013: 189). Jubany similarly noted that applicants for protection have to meet officers' "essentialised views on the features and behaviours" about different populations:

> Explicit behaviours, performances or even appearances are expected from men and women by the officers as per the sex-gender identities formed by

the ethno-androcentric views of the west. These beliefs, obviously shaped by officers' own experiences, conform to what are seen as 'normal' expectations from any man or woman. This tends to imply that women are expected to behave in a nourishing, submissive and sensitive way, whilst men have to behave in a stronger, persistent and rational way.

(Jubany, 2017: 168–169)

Failure to conform to these norms renders an applicant – and his/her claim – suspect in the eyes of the border agents.

The paradigmatic example of the function of the 'norm' in refugee status determination is the case of asylum seekers claiming Refugee status on the basis of sexual orientation.[4] Even though UNHCR and UK guidance both state that the appearance or demeanour of an applicant – such as "effeminate demeanour in gay men or a masculine appearance in lesbians (or the absence of such features)" – should not influence the assessment of credibility (United Kingdom Home Office, 2011: 10), no guidance is given as to what factors should influence credibility in the place of stereotypes, or latent views about 'normal' or expected behaviour of certain groups. A report into the experiences of LGBTQ individuals claiming asylum in the UK confirmed that LGBTQ asylum seekers frequently face difficulty being believed by caseworkers due to reliance on 'norms' of homosexual or heterosexual behaviour (Cowen *et al.*, 2011). The UK Asylum Policy Instructions on assessing claims based on sexual identity states that:

Evidence of existing or former heterosexual relationships or parenthood (both of which may need to be explored at interview) must not be automatically taken as evidence of a lack of credibility.

(United Kingdom Home Office, 2015b: 17)

At first glance these appear to be highly reasonable guidelines, and yet the fact that heterosexual relationships do need to be explained at interview, and that a lack of previous homosexual relationships *could* mean that an applicant does not have the sexual identity (s)he claims to have betrays the latent role of homosexual and heterosexual 'norms' in the status determination process. Studies of status determination in Europe, Australia, Canada and the USA have revealed that, in the case of claims for Refugee status on the basis of sexual orientation, national authorities tend to rely on generalised assumptions of 'traditional', 'normal', or 'expected' homosexual behaviour. Berg and Millbank's study of refugee status determination between 1994 and 2007 in North America, Australia and the UK revealed numerous instances of decision-makers drawing conclusions about the claimants' sexuality based on the idea of sexual identity development following a linear process of self-knowledge: moving from denial or confusion, to 'coming out' as a self-actualised lesbian or gay man. Such assumptions evident in the asylum determinations included the idea that it is 'typical' for homosexuals to become aware of their sexual orientation in adolescence, and of negative decisions being upheld on appeal on the basis of a lack of such self-awareness (Berg and Millbank, 2009: 206–208; Millbank, 2009). Even in cases when the cultural relativity of sexual identity was acknowledged in the status determination process, this was often done in such a way as to deprive the applicant of the power to categorise his/her own experiences. For example, applicants claiming to be homosexual whose only same-sex experiences were early in life, and related to cultural norms of sexual segregation prior to marriage, were readily characterised as having a "youthful transient phase" or engaging in "sexual play" regardless of the applicant's proclaimed self-identity (Berg and Millbank, 2009: 208). In addition to this 'norm' of a linear progression of sexual self-awareness, decision-makers also expected that members of sexual minorities would, as a matter of course, form a sense of group identity and either join or demonstrate knowledge of lesbian or gay groups in their home countries and countries of asylum. Where this could not be demonstrated, negative credibility findings were often the result (Berg and Millbank, 2009: 210).

Psychiatric examinations have been used in the past in order to establish whether or not an applicant is a homosexual or bisexual person in various European countries, most notably in Austria, Bulgaria, the Czech Republic, Germany, Poland and Romania (Jansen and Spijkerboer, 2011: 49). They have also been used in the UK asylum determination process, and McGhee explores the Foucauldian implications of such a practice in his examination of the case of Romanian asylum seeker Ioan Vraciu. Vraciu arrived in the UK via Calais and claimed asylum on the basis of his political activity in Romania. His initial claim was denied and at his appeal he revealed, for the first time, that he feared return to Romania on account of his homosexuality. His only homosexual partner had been arrested and imprisoned in Romania, Vraciu refused to give his name to UK authorities, and he could not produce any witnesses to corroborate his claim as he had not 'come out' to anyone (McGhee, 2000: 31). These circumstances were taken as too damaging to his credibility to overturn the original decision, and Vraciu then re-appealed. At his second appeal hearing the representative for the Home Office requested that he undergo a medical examination in order to establish the veracity of his claim to be a homosexual. This suggested production of homosexual identity "from the signs of sexual acts and ... hallmarks of ... (mis)use of the body" was a way to bring to light the sign of an 'authentic' or 'inauthentic' homosexual identity through medical practices of truth (McGhee, 2000: 39). The requested medical examination was avoided by the suggestion of Vraciu's lawyer that he undergo a psychiatric evaluation instead. His lawyer believed that declaring one's homosexuality should be sufficient, but since it proved not in fact to be sufficient to convince the tribunal, the only other option was to obtain a psychiatrist's report as a means of 'authenticating' his identity. In doing so, Vraciu's lawyer discovered the "key to the game of truth at work within 'the law'; that is, there is an order of discourse, an economy and hierarchy of discursive value before the law when it comes to knowledge of sexual identity" (McGhee, 2000: 42). In the absence of the actual report, one can assume that in order to 'diagnose' Vraciu's homosexuality the psychiatrist made use of prior knowledge of 'characteristic homosexuality' – a "range of factors, a typology of details, which are considered to denote a homosexual propensity" (McGhee, 2000: 44–45). What is important here is that Vraciu's mode of giving evidence had not significantly altered, but, crucially, *who* he had told these details to, had. As Foucault explains in *The History of Sexuality*:

> If one had to confess, this was not merely because the person to whom one confessed had the power to forgive ... but because the work of producing the truth was obliged to pass through this relationship if it was to be scientifically validated. The truth did not reside solely in the subject who, by confessing, would reveal it wholly formed.
>
> (Foucault, HS: 66)

In Vraciu's case, then, the psychiatrist became the authorised hearer, and then the authorised speaker (the "authority of delimitation"), who was to exchange Vraciu's confessed secrets for a psychiatric interpretation of their 'truth'. This brings to light not only the fundamental issue of who has the authority to 'know' sexuality and how sexuality itself is to be 'knowable', but also, fundamentally, who has the authority to *speak* this 'truth'. Vraciu's assertion that he was homosexual was not enough:

> What the Vraciu case opens to academic scrutiny is the realisation that the person who is alleging to be a homosexual cannot be the author of his own subjectivity before the law; he remains an object, whose legal subjectivity must be made for him by an authorised knower and speaker of it.
>
> (McGhee, 2000: 43)

We can see from this brief discussion of the operation of the 'norm' in the status determination process that individuals going through status determination are not in charge of the truth of their own experiences, identities, fears and status. Even when they are required to speak, their words must be exchanged for the words of an authorised speaker – an authority of delimitation – in order for what they know to count as 'credible knowledge'.

The arguably subjective nature of such judgements of 'credible homosexuality' related to the norm of the 'real' or 'typical' homosexual, and the inconsistency that can and does arise in status determination as a result, is behind the drive in academic psychiatry, sociology and medicine to provide more 'objective' guidance for decision-makers, and not solely in relation to sexual orientation (Berg and Millbank, 2009). Herlihy, Gleeson and Turner qualify their study on the common assumptions which underpin asylum judgements in the UK with the following:

> What these findings do not tell us is which of these assumptions are consistent with current knowledge on human behaviour, particularly during and following situations of danger, and the process of remembering and presenting an account of possibly traumatic situations in the context of a legal

process. Empirical knowledge is deemed to be the best knowledge available in medical and many other settings.

(Herlihy *et al.*, 2010: 365)

Herlihy *et al.* conclude by stating that further research efforts are needed to identify which of these assumptions can be said to be well founded – i.e. consistent with empirical findings – and which are not, and that cross-disciplinary research is needed where answers are not readily available. There is, they argue, a need for a broader evidence base concerning memory and the asylum process, and the impact of traumatic experiences, depression, and forced migration, in order to help produce a "more robust system (with fewer false positives as well as false negatives), one better able to achieve fair decisions for all" (Herlihy *et al.*, 2007: 4).

This drive to produce asylum guidance more grounded in empirical knowledge of the impact of traumatic experiences on memory recall has begun to bear fruit. The Istanbul Protocol, prepared in line with developments in medicine and psychiatry, sets out accepted standards on the investigation and documentation of torture and ill treatment that its proponents argue should, if followed, result in the production of evidence appropriate for use in asylum claims. The Protocol contains a scale according to which physical scarring and/or injuries can be judged from "not consistent" to "diagnostic of" the trauma described. In the case where no immediate physical scarring or injuries are present, the Protocol's instruction is to consider whether psychological findings are "consistent with" or "expected and typical reactions to" the alleged report of torture (Wallace and Wylie, 2013: 756). The Protocol recommendations have been incorporated into guidelines produced by the International Association of Refugee Law Judges in the attempt to deliver some measure of uniformity to status determination processes. While increased knowledge of the physical and psychological manifestations of torture and ill treatment, the effects of traumatic experiences on the ability to impart a narrative, and of differing cultural experiences of sexual identity would certainly contribute to mitigating the 'lottery' of the system – surely a noble cause in and of itself – this drive for knowledge is revelatory of an unfortunate, but not necessarily intended, consequence.

What drives these (social) scientific investigations into cultural experiences of sexual identity and behaviour, the impact of trauma on memory and communication, and the physical and psychological manifestations of torture, is not to better know the *individual* but to better know the *phenomena* under investigation; to better construct the continuum of behaviour, activity, ability, reaction, and so on, along which to place and categorise individuals; to paint a clearer picture of the grids of specification, and the 'norm' according to which individuals can be separated and classified. Rather than the operation of the gratification-punishment nexus serving to lead individuals to alter their behaviour in pursuit of the 'norm', as in the case of disciplinary institutions such as schools and prisons, and in refugee status determination and the bodies of knowledge upon which it relies, the central importance of Foucault's conception of the norm is in the referral of "individual actions to a whole that is at once a field of comparison and a space of differentiation" (Foucault, 1995: 183). For example, the Istanbul Protocol questions for expert medical reports require the physical and psychological attributes of the asylum applicant to be judged in relation to a whole field of norms, which we can see by focusing on just one of the questions:

> (iii.) Given the fluctuating course of trauma-related mental disorders over time, what is the time frame in relation to torture events? Where is the individual in the course of recovery?
>
> (Wallace and Wylie, 2013: 756)

The norms evident here include mental 'health' against which mental 'disorder' is measured and characterised; the 'normal' trajectory of any given mental disorder against which the development of a particular individual's diagnosed disorder is measured; and the 'normal/average/optimum' time frame of recovery post-torture event against which the individual in question is located. A similar variety of 'norms' could also be isolated in the psychiatric discourse on the impact of traumatic events to memory recall, and a continuum laid out along which a particular individual's abilities could be placed. The singular homosexuality which has so permeated popular culture and the status determination process becomes fractured into a proliferation of culturally specific homosexualities, allowing for more 'accurate' knowledge of a particular individual's homosexuality in relation to his/her culture's 'typical' experience. Such 'refined' knowledge could indeed result in a 'fairer' status determination system, and rein in the subjective elements of the decision-making process by making asylum judgements more 'accurate'. It is not my intention to claim that this is an ignoble enterprise, but it does not challenge – it reinforces – the fundamental economy of truth at work in determining refugee status: the refugee still cannot escape the hierarchy of truth within which his/her discourse is discounted or rendered suspicious, and stands in need of translation and verification by others. This may result in more accurately producing Refugees – individuals who conform to the narrow definition of a Refugee in the 1951 Convention – but this does little for those still in need of international protection of their rights but who cannot conform to this definition. A negative asylum judgement, it is worth noting, is not, strictly speaking, a judgement that an individual does not *need* protection of some kind, but a judgement that (s)he does not meet the criteria of the 1951 Convention definition, and is, thus, not entitled to its protections.

As McGhee's study of the Vraciu case so ably demonstrated, refugees are not in charge of the 'truth' of their own experiences and identities. At every stage of the determination process their subjective knowledge must be validated by the 'objective' knowledge produced by others – its very objectivity deriving at least in part from its not being produced by the applicant. The 'truth' of Vraciu's homosexuality could only, in the opinion of the Home Office and the tribunal, be produced by medical or psychiatric examination. Similarly, allegations of torture are often subject to validation by physical or psychiatric evidence by a suitably qualified and recognised medical professional. In this quest for knowledge and truth, "asylum has become the realm of scientists, doctors and other professionals, which leaves the applicant without an audible and understandable voice" (Puumala, 2017: 66). The refugee's story of past persecution or fear of future persecution must accord with the 'objective' knowledge on his/her country of origin, and perceived or actual discrepancies must be explained to the satisfaction of the decision-maker. The refugee's story and behaviour must fit at every stage the expectations of decision-makers, and the 'norms' or 'grids of specification' according to which they make their decisions, and where it cannot or does not, his/her credibility is damaged and his/her request for asylum may be denied. There is, thus, a regime of truth at work here, which masks relations of power. Few would deny that refugees are caught up in power relations, but for the scholarship examined above, the way to mitigate the potential negative effects of this is through more 'accurate', 'refined' knowledge. My point here, drawing on Foucault, is that knowledge itself cannot be extricated from relations of power: if something is constituted as an area of investigation, this is because relations of power have established it as a possible object, and power can only be exercised over something that techniques of knowledge and procedures of discourse are capable of investing in (Simons, 1995: 27). Power, in producing certain kinds of subjects, necessitates certain ways of knowing them so that they may be better governed. Thus, in this (refugee) regime of truth, academic knowledge serves to enable decision-makers to more accurately assign the individual to his/her 'real' identity – 'genuine refugee' or 'failed asylum seeker', a.k.a. 'economic/irregular migrant' – so that (s)he may be more effectively managed. Not only is such knowledge no less subjectivising in its accuracy, as we shall see below, but it also conforms to the underlying rationality of 'the refugee (as) problem'.

National asylum systems, such as that in place in the UK, can afford to take heed of developments in psychiatry, medicine, and others, in order to produce more 'accurate' outcomes because the myth of difference and the migration-asylum-nexus have provided the 'scientific' rationale for restricting access through these 'improved' procedures, rendering these more 'accurate' judgements less risky for the state. The most recent UK Asylum Policy Instructions contain a measure of 'credibility' which is arguably the clearest sign thus far that the status determination process functions to assist the state in shifting the burden of the refugee on to others. A number of 'behaviours' are listed which "must always be treated as damaging to the claimant's credibility", including "failure to take advantage of a reasonable opportunity to make an asylum or human rights claim while in a safe country" (United Kingdom Home Office, 2015a: 39). While many other behaviours listed are qualified by a "reasonable explanation defence", no such qualification is permitted in relation to failure to claim asylum in a country through which an applicant transited on his/her way to the UK. Failure to claim asylum in a country to which deportation is permitted under the EU's Dublin II Regulation must always be taken into account in assessing the general credibility of the applicant, and caseworkers are permitted, but not required, to take into account failure to claim asylum in other countries as well (United Kingdom Home Office, 2015a: 40). These factors have nothing to do with the specifics of an individual's claim for Refugee status – his/her actual experiences or fears – but exist purely in order to enable the shifting of that individual on to another state.

Subjectivity and Agency

As Simons points out, "a vast range of social practices seek to justify themselves by reference to a true discourse, yet should be subject to a politically motivated critique, along with the will to truth on which they rest" (1995: 44). The production of discourse and knowledge of the refugee and 'the refugee problem' is not apolitical or disinterested. Discourse, as Foucault shows us, is not just a description of a thing already existing; the intersection between knowledge and power produces subjects. The historically contingent modern form of this intimate relationship produced the refugee, made her a 'problem', and seeks to 'manage' her, but the technologies employed to do so only entrench her subjectification further.

Refugee status determination is a key technology in the management of 'the refugee (as) problem' through policing access to the status of Refugee and, as such, can be understood as a Foucauldian 'dividing practice' – one of the modes of objectification by which individuals are made into subjects. Dividing practices work through social processes whereby "the subject is either divided inside himself or divided from others" (Foucault, EWP: 326), giving the individual both a social and a personal identity. The 'Refugee' is divided from the 'citizen' and the refugee status determination process divides the 'asylum seeker' from the 'Refugee'. But the status determination process can also – and very often does – deny Refugee status to asylum seekers, and when this happens the asylum seeker becomes something else: a person with 'humanitarian protective status', a person with 'limited leave to remain', or a 'failed asylum seeker' (which, in the eyes of the society in which (s)he has sought admittance could also render him/her an 'illegal immigrant', an 'economic migrant', or a 'criminal'). The status determination process is, therefore, a process which literally fabricates subjects (Scheel and Ratfisch, 2014: 928). These are 'artificial' subjectivities to the extent that those assigned to them often do not imagine their own identities and presence "in terms of the categories and statuses that are produced" (Puumala, 2017: 86; see also Chimni, 2009: 12; Hayden, 2006: 472–473), and yet these 'artificial' categories and statuses not only have a significant impact on an individual's ability to continue living his/her life in a manner of their own choosing, but are also themselves judgements on the legitimacy of his/her previous exercising of agency by deciding to migrate at all.

As soon as the status determination process begins, the individual becomes a 'case' and is situated within a field of documentation. Fingerprints, photographs and personal information are collected and passed from authority to authority as a written record of an individual's 'identity'. Asylum seekers in the UK are then issued with biometric identity cards containing their personal details and fingerprints. While the claim is investigated, the asylum seeker must live at a specified address and report to police stations or other authorities on a regular basis. The biometric identity card must be presented in a number of situations and everyday transactions, including the reporting procedure, claiming support, and accessing healthcare (Ajana, 2013: 589–590). The identity of 'asylum seeker' allows access to certain benefits and entails rejection from others. When the status determination process, as it often does, denies Refugee status to an applicant, she can become a 'failed asylum seeker'. In this event she now faces deportation either to her country of origin or to a 'safe third country', but her biometric data remains in the EURODAC database for ten years. In addition to remaining tied to a biometric field of documentation and being followed by the identity of 'failed asylum seeker' should she try to move around Europe, or cross European borders again in the future for any reason, the very idea of a 'failed asylum seeker' means that the reasons for migration and/or the manner in which such migration occurred are judged to have been 'illegitimate'. This rendering of individuals as certain kinds of subjects on the basis of the legitimacy/regularity of their movement across borders or their reasons for doing so, gets to the very heart of the assumptions of legitimate agency and choice built into the subjectivity of the refugee, in both the formal legal sense, and the broader non-legal subjectivity of the humanitarian victim.

The academic 'discovery' of the complex nature of migratory processes has given life to a concern on the part of states and UNHCR with 'irregular secondary movements' on the part of refugees. Irregular secondary movements are movements "that occur from initial areas of safety to newer destinations for the purpose of claiming asylum, irrespective of whether persons have been officially recognised as refugees previously, and in the absence of authorisation or (usually) sufficient documentation for travel" (Zimmermann, 2009: 74–75). Such movements are, certainly in the eyes of states in the global North, assumed to be voluntary and thus not deemed warranted or acceptable under the refugee regime. Indeed, UNHCR recognises such movements as a "growing concern" (UNHCR, 2000: 6). Susan Zimmermann discusses the concept of irregular secondary movements in the context of a group of Somali refugees who found their way to Europe after initially fleeing to countries bordering Somalia. In these areas that have "for the most part provided a means of escape from the dangers at home, but little more besides", risk and uncertainty often prevail (Zimmermann, 2009: 76). However, due to the focus on the need for safety in the definition of a Refugee, movements from these areas to newer ones have tended to appear less 'genuine'. For the Somali refugees interviewed in Zimmermann's study, being a refugee "meant more than having to leave a home because of safety fears due to wider effects of insecurity, and beyond escaping from those threats, being a refugee meant escaping to other more viable conditions" (2009: 83). It meant needing to achieve something in exile that had been lost in the process of gaining safety.

While Foucault is often criticised for an essentialist notion of the subject – he is either committed to its death, or is accused of having such a restrictive notion of subjectivity that one can *only* be a criminal, or mental patient or homosexual

– his notion of subjectivity is not, in reality, so restrictive: we can be many sub-jects at once, but some may be more constraining than others (see Allen, 2000, for an in-depth examination of these critiques). In the case of the refugee regime, it is a matter of fact that individual refugees are more than simply refugees, but for the functioning of the refugee regime and international system, the only iden-tity that matters, the only subjectivity that matters, is the one assigned to the individual by the status determination process. Rather than recognising the fact that those who flee their homes may seek more than the charity begrudgingly provided by the international community, any such desires that they may enter-tain are almost instantly and universally dismissed as illegitimate. The Somali refugees interviewed in Zimmermann's study revealed a combination of 'push' and 'pull' factors involved in their decisions to leave the immediate (and often deficient) physical safety of nearby countries and travel to Europe to claim asylum. These included being unable to return to Somalia (a 'legitimate' reason), conditions for refugees in nearby areas (only 'legitimate' if such conditions amount to persecution), and what was held to exist for them in Europe (an 'ille-gitimate' reason rendering their migration 'irregular' by default) (Zimmermann, 2009: 84). Nearby countries offered short-term solutions, and greatly restricted what could be achieved in terms of settlement once outside Somalia: "all per-ceived that Europe would be safe and would offer work, education, homes and stability that they needed" (Zimmermann, 2009: 88). In deciding to head to Europe, all sought to achieve a long-term solution to the situations that they found themselves to be in, and to have a 'life' rather than just be alive and living with difficulty (Zimmermann, 2009: 84). Similar circumstances, motivations, and experiences have been found in a recently concluded study of migrant jour-neys across the Mediterranean. Syrian, Afghan, Iranian, Eritrean, Sudanese, Somali, and Iraqi refugees were interviewed in Greece, Malta, Italy, and Germany, and many of those interviewed spoke of how the difficulties that they faced in the first countries to which they fled had driven them to move on, often irregularly, and come to Europe (Squire *et al.*, 2017: 44, 54, 61, 62, 91). However, rather than accepting these interests as rightly belonging to refugees, both states and UNHCR have increasingly used them to justify attempts to prevent or deter asylum seeking (Scheel and Ratfisch, 2014). The implication of this is that the refugee should simply accept the lower standards of protection and life prospects available elsewhere – such as a camp near the border of their country of origin – where physical safety can, perhaps, be achieved but where insecurities of different forms are still present and cannot be countered while remaining there. To do anything else makes one an 'irregular migrant', a 'bogus asylum seeker', an economic migrant in disguise, with the restrictions and bar-riers accompanying such a status, because a 'genuine' refugee seeks safety from persecution, not 'economic gain'. As Watson argues:

> The normative ideal for refugees is the 'real' or 'good' refugee that flees to the nearest state, stays in a refugee camp awaiting resettlement or repatria-tion, all the while fully cooperating with the local authorities in whatever

decisions are made regarding their welfare. They are to be passive and speechless. The 'bogus' or 'bad' refugee circumvents the 'queue' by traversing multiple states to make an asylum claim in a Western liberal state, is uncooperative with authorities and attempts to be an active participant in matters regarding his or her welfare.

(Watson, 2009: 41)

The two underlying conceptualisations of 'the refugee' – the burden and passive victim in need of charity – thus work hand in hand, and are assisted by the refugee status determination process and by developments in knowledge about refugees and forced migration. If the refugee is merely a humanitarian victim then what they need is physical security, and this can be provided just as easily in, for example, Kenya, as in the UK. The burden of providing (a home) for the refugee can then be justifiably shifted onto Kenya. Kenya then employs enforced encampment to relieve itself of the burden of the refugee, because the refugee's 'needs' can just as easily be met in a UNHCR-run camp as they can by allowing the refugee to integrate into Kenyan society. In other words, the construction of 'the refugee' as a passive victim of circumstance in need of humanitarian assistance provides a justification for the logic of burden-shifting of the refugee regime, which is effectuated in part by the operation of the refugee status determination process. It also provides an underlying grid of specification against which to judge any particular refugee, to discover the extent to which their behaviour conforms, or fails to conform, to this 'ideal'; to this picture of the 'genuine' refugee.

Conclusion

The foundational assumption of this book is that how one addresses a problem is dependent, in large part, on what one understands that problem to be. In Chapter 1 we saw that the development of the international refugee regime during the inter-war and immediate post-war period could be understood as the result of a battle between two different – although related – understandings of 'the refugee problem' in need of a solution. Charitable organisations appeared to be focused upon alleviating the concrete problems that individuals faced in becoming displaced, whereas states appeared to be focused on alleviating the problems that these displaced individuals posed to states themselves. It was argued that, ultimately, the state's understanding of 'the problem' took precedence, with the international refugee regime instituted to help states manage 'the refugee (as) problem'; to manage the presence of these figures of burden. This regime was built upon two key principles: burden-limiting/shifting and self-interest. Rather than permitting these figures of burden and pity full membership of the states in which they found themselves, states created a regime of limited rights and freedoms based upon the creation of a limited new legal status which marginally included them but still allowed for their exclusion. Chapter 2 then examined why, despite forced migration being an arguably age-old phenomenon, it emerged as a problem in need of the coordination and attention of the international community only in the early years of the twentieth century. This was not an explanation of the causes of 'the refugee (as) problem' but of the development of its conditions of possibility. By employing Foucault's analyses of the development of the state as an object and practice of government, we saw how 'the refugee (as) problem' is able to emerge once population is conceptualised as a quasi-natural being, dependent upon a number of natural and artificial processes, the management of which becomes the responsibility of government. Population movement shifts from a phenomenon to be either prohibited or permitted, in order for the state to realise the potential inherent in the size of its population, to one that must, in the interests of the proper unfolding of the natural and artificial processes upon which population depends, instead be managed. Migration thus appears as a general phenomenon in need of management, with a nascent regime of cross-border movement regulations systematised after the First World War. The appearance of almost one million individuals suddenly unable to conform to these new procedures of migration management posed a more specific problem within this broader problematisation of cross-border movement that then needed to be managed. The international refugee regime examined in Chapter 1 was the apparatus established for such management.

This chapter examined how practices and processes of knowledge production are central to the management of 'the refugee (as) problem', by guarding access to Refugee status. Knowledge produced in the academic sphere about refugees and forced migration provides the 'scientific' rationale for governmental policies restricting access to Refugee status, and this restriction is then effectuated through the refugee status determination process – a process which itself manufactures different 'migrant subjects' who are differentially included or excluded, based largely on judgements of the inherent (il)legitimacy of the motivations behind their cross-border movement.

The conceptualisation of 'the refugee (as) problem' thus leads to certain ways of trying to manage this problem, which do not appear to have at the centre of concern the problems or wishes of refugees themselves. For 'the refugee (as) problem', what is needed is to find places to put refugees, with that place dependent not upon the refugee's own choice, but upon the needs, concerns, and exigencies of states. For 'the refugee (as) problem', the refugee is both a figure of burden, to be shifted onto other actors – other states or charitable organisations such as those running refugee camps in the global South – and a passive victim of circumstance who should simply accept the charity offered by the international system and take no active part in finding solutions to their own problems – certainly not when such action takes the form of border-crossing without permission. Recognition of the agency of refugees – of their decisions to cross borders as an immediate 'solution' to the problems and dangers that they face – manifests in the attempt to use such agency against them in order to manage cross-border movement more generally. The events of the summer of 2015, in which European television screens were full of images of the bloated, lifeless bodies of refugees who had drowned trying to cross the Mediterranean, are only the latest manifestation of the awful potential consequences of constructing the refugee as 'the problem'; an understanding of the problem that, as was demonstrated in Chapter 1, is as old as the refugee regime itself. But if the way one addresses a problem depends on what one understands that problem to be, could we think of different ways to address 'the refugee problem'; ways that place the concerns of refugees at the centre? It is to this task that the remaining two chapters of this book turn, by utilising the work of Hannah Arendt.

Notes

1 From this point on in the book, where I use the term 'Refugee' I refer to the legal status or to those in possession of formal legal status in accordance with Article 1 of the Refugee Convention.
2 The dual meaning of the term 'discipline' is central to Foucault's examination of disciplinary power.
3 Despite *formally* playing no role in making asylum decisions, the reports of initial screening interviews conducted by UK Border Officers and sent to the National Asylum Allocation Unit are often simply 'rubber-stamped' by caseworkers in the NAAU and, thus, play a significant role in deciding how a claim will be dealt with: whether it will be dismissed, whether it will be dealt with in a 'Fast Track' process, or whether it will be examined on its merits. These reports are thus not, as the Home Office claims, simply reports on the 'facts' of the case, but also contain a subjective 'appraisal' of the case presented and the individual seeking asylum (Jubany, 2017: 57).
4 While sexual orientation is not a category defined in the Convention, UNHCR has nevertheless recognised that LGBTQ individuals can face persecution on a number of the Convention grounds, including "membership of a particular social group" (UNHCR, 2012: 11–13).

References

Ajana, B., "Asylum, Identity Management and Biometric Control" in *Journal of Refugee Studies* 26(4) (2013): 576–595
Allen, A., "The Anti-Subjective Hypothesis: Michel Foucault and the Death of the Subject" in *The Philosophical Forum* 31(2) (2000): 113–130
Allen, A., "Power, Subjectivity and Agency: Between Arendt and Foucault" in *International Journal of Philosophical Studies* 10(2) (2002): 131–149
Berg, L., and Millbank, J., "Constructing the Personal Narratives of Lesbian, Gay and Bisexual Asylum Claimants" in *Journal of Refugee Studies* 22(3) (2009): 195–223
Black, R., "Fifty Years of Refugee Studies: From Theory to Policy" in *International Migration Review* 35(1) (2001): 57–78
Campbell, J., "Language Analysis in the United Kingdom's Refugee Status Determination System: Seeing through Policy Claims about 'Expert Knowledge'" in *Ethnic and Racial Studies* 36(4) (2012): 670–690
Castles, S., "The Migration-Asylum Nexus and Regional Approaches" in Kneebone, S., and Rawlings-Sanaei, F. (Eds), *New Regionalism and Asylum Seekers: Challenges Ahead* (New York: Berghahn Books, 2007): 25–42
Chimni, B. S., "The Geopolitics of Refugee Studies: A View from the South" in *Journal of Refugee Studies* 11(4) (1998): 350–374

Chimni, B. S., "The Birth of a 'Discipline': From Refugee to Forced Migration Studies" in *Journal of Refugee Studies* 22(1) (2009): 11–29

Cowen, T., *et al.*, *Sanctuary, Safety and Solidarity: Lesbian, Gay, Bisexual, Transgender Asylum Seekers and Refugees in Scotland* (2011), available at: www.equality-network. org/wp-content/uploads/2013/05/Sanctuary-Safety-and-Solidarity.pdf (last accessed 10 May 2017)

Foucault, M., *Discipline and Punish: The Birth of the Prison* (New York: Vintage Books, 1995)

Foucault, M., *The History of Sexuality, Volume 1: The Will to Knowledge* (London: Penguin, 1998)

Foucault, M., "The Subject and Power" in Faubion, J. (Ed.), *The Essential Works of Foucault 1954–1985, Volume 3: Power* (London: Penguin, 2000): 326–348

Foucault, M., "Truth and Power" in Faubion, J. (Ed.), *The Essential Works of Foucault 1954–1985, Volume 3: Power* (London: Penguin, 2000): 111–133

Foucault, M., *The Archaeology of Knowledge* (London: Routledge, 2004)

Gibb, R., and Good, A., "Do the Facts Speak for Themselves? Country of Origin Information in French and British Refugee Status Determination Procedures" in *International Journal of Refugee Law* 25(2) (2013): 291–322

Gutting, G., *Michel Foucault's Archaeology of Scientific Reason* (Cambridge: Cambridge University Press, 1989)

Gutting, G., "Michel Foucault: A User's Manual" in Gutting, G. (Ed.), *The Cambridge Companion to Foucault* (Cambridge: Cambridge University Press, 2005): 1–28

Hall, S., *Representation: Cultural Representation and Signifying Practices* (London: SAGE, 1997)

Hardy, C., "Refugee Determination: Power and Resistance in Systems of Foucauldian Power" in *Administration & Society* 35(4) (2003): 462–488

Hayden, B., "What's in a Name? The Nature of the Individual in Refugee Studies" in *Journal of Refugee Studies* 19(4) (2006): 471–487

Herlihy, J., Gleeson, K., and Turner, S., "What Assumptions about Human Behaviour Underlie Asylum Judgements?" in *International Journal of Refugee Law* 22(3) (2010): 351–366

Herlihy, J., and Turner, S., "Asylum Claims and Memory of Trauma: Sharing Our Knowledge" in *British Journal of Psychiatry* 191 (2007): 3–4

Holborn, L., *The International Refugee Organization – A Specialized Agency of the United Nations: Its History and Work* (London: Oxford University Press, 1956)

Hope-Simpson, Sir J., *The Refugee Problem: A Report of a Survey* (Oxford: Oxford University Press, 1939)

Jansen, S., and Spijkerboer, T., *Fleeing Homophobia: Asylum Claims Related to Sexual Orientation and Gender Identity in Europe* (Amsterdam: Vrije Universiteit Amsterdam, 2011), available at: www.refworld.org/docid/4ebba7852.html (last accessed 10 May 2017)

Johnson, H., *Borders, Asylum, and Global Non-Citizenship: The Other Side of the Fence* (Cambridge: Cambridge University Press, 2014)

Jubany, O., *Screening Asylum in a Culture of Disbelief: Truths, Denials and Skeptical Borders* (Basingstoke: Palgrave Macmillan, 2017)

Kagan, M., "Is Truth in the Eye of the Beholder? Objective Credibility Assessment in Refugee Status Determination" in *Georgetown Immigration Law Journal* 17(3) (2003): 367–416

Koser, K., "New Approaches to Asylum?" in *International Migration* 39(6) (2001): 85–102

Lippert, R., "Governing Refugees: The Relevance of Governmentality to Understanding the International Refugee Regime" in *Alternatives: Global, Local, Political* 24(3) (1999): 295–328

Maniglier, P., "The Order of Things" in Falzon, C. *et al.* (Eds), *A Companion to Foucault* (Chichester: Blackwell Publishing, 2013): 104–121

McGhee, D., "Accessing Homosexuality: Truth, Evidence and the Legal Practices for Determining Refugee Status – The Case of Ioan Vraciu" in *Body and Society* 6(1) (2000): 29–50

Millbank, J., "From Discretion to Disbelief: Recent Trends in Refugee Determinations on the Basis of Sexual Orientation in Australia and the United Kingdom" in *The International Journal of Human Rights* 13(2–3) (2009): 391–414

Muller, B., "Globalization, Security, Paradox: Towards a Refugee Biopolitics" in *Refuge* 22(1) (2004): 49–57

Puumala, E., *Asylum Seekers, Sovereignty, and the Senses of the International: A Politico-Corporeal Struggle* (London: Routledge, 2017)

Rabinow, P., "Introduction" in Rabinow, P. (Ed.), *The Foucault Reader* (New York: Pantheon Books, 1984): 3–29

Ransom, J., *Foucault's Discipline: The Politics of Subjectivity* (Durham, NC: Duke University Press, 1997)

Rousse, J., "Power/Knowledge" in Gutting, G. (Ed.), *The Cambridge Companion to Foucault* (Cambridge: Cambridge University Press, 2005): 95–122

Scheel, S., and Ratfisch, P., "Refugee Protection Meets Migration Management: UNHCR as a Global Police of Populations" in *Journal of Ethnic and Migration Studies* 40(6) (2014): 924–941

Sheridan, A., *Michel Foucault: The Will to Truth* (London: Taylor and Francis, 2005)

Simons, P., *Foucault and the Political* (London: Routledge, 1995)

Skran, C., *Refugees in Inter-War Europe: The Emergence of a Regime* (Oxford: Oxford University Press, 1995)

Skran, C., and Daughtry, C. N., "The Study of Refugees before Refugee Studies" in *Refugee Survey Quarterly* 26(3) (2007): 15–35

Squire, V., *et al.*, *Crossing the Mediterranean Sea by Boat: Mapping and Documenting Migratory Journeys and Experiences*, (2017) Final Project Report, available at: www. warwick.ac.uk/crossingthemed (last accessed 15 May 2017)

Stein, B. N., and Tomasi, S. N., "Foreword" in *International Migration Review* 15(1/2) (1981): 5–7

Storey, H., "Consistency in Refugee Decision-Making: A Judicial Perspective" in *Refugee Survey Quarterly* 32(2) (2013): 112–125

Tsangarides, N. (Ed.), *The Refugee Roulette: The Role of Country Information in Refugee Status Determination* (Immigration Advisory Service: Research, Information and Policy Unit, 2010), available at: www.refworld.org/pdfid/4b62a6182.pdf (last accessed 12 May 2017)

United Nations, *Convention relating to the Status of Refugees* (United Nations Treaty Series Vol. 189, No. 2545) (1951): 138–220

United Nations Department of Economic and Social Affairs, "International Migrant Stock 2015" (2015), available at: www.un.org/en/development/desa/population/migration/data/estimates2/estimates15.shtml (last accessed 12 May 2017)

UNHCR, *Handbook on Procedures and Criteria for Determining Refugee Status under the 1951 Convention and the 1967 Protocol Relating to the Status of Refugees* (Geneva: UNHCR, 2011)

UNHCR, *Guidelines on International Protection No. 9: Claims to Refugee Status Based on Sexual Orientation and/or Gender Identity within the context of Article 1A(2) of the 1951 Convention and/or its 1967 Protocol Relating to the Status of Refugees* (2012), available at: www.refworld.org/docid/50348afc2.html (last accessed 12 May 2017)

UNHCR, *Beyond Proof: Credibility Assessment in EU Asylum Systems* (Brussels: UNHCR, 2013)

United Kingdom Home Office, "Sexual Orientation Issues in the Asylum Claim" (2011), available at: www.refworld.org/docid/4eb8f0982.html (last accessed 14 May 2017)

United Kingdom Home Office, "Considering Asylum Claims and Assessing Credibility" (2012), available at: www.refworld.org/docid/5449ffa84.html (last accessed 14 May 2017)

United Kingdom Home Office, "Assessing Credibility and Refugee Status", *Asylum Policy Instruction* (2015a), available at: www.gov.uk/government/uploads/system/uploads/attachment_data/file/397778/ASSESSING_CREDIBILITY_AND_REFUGEE_STATUS_V9_0.pdf (last accessed 14 May 2017)

United Kingdom Home Office, "Sexual Identity Issues in the Asylum Claim", *Asylum Policy Instruction* (2015b), available at: www.gov.uk/government/uploads/system/attachment_data/file/404372/EXT_Asylum_Instruction_Sexual_Identity_Issues_in_the_Asylum_claim_v5_20150211.pdf (last accessed 14 May 2017)

United Kingdom Home Office, "Information about Your Asylum Application" (2016), available at: www.gov.uk/government/publications/information-leaflet-for-asylum-applications (last accessed 14 May 2017)

Wallace, R., and Wylie, K., "The Reception of Expert Medical Evidence in Refugee Status Determination" in *International Journal of Refugee Law* 25(4) (2013): 749–767

Watson, S. D. *The Securitization of Humanitarian Migration: Digging Moats and Sinking Boats* (New York: Routledge, 2009)

Zetter, R., "More Labels, Fewer Refugees: Remaking the Refugee Label in an Era of Globalization" in *Journal of Refugee Studies* 20(2) (2007): 172–192

Zimmermann, S., "Irregular Secondary Movements to Europe: Seeking Asylum Beyond Refuge" in *Journal of Refugee Studies* 4(1) (2009): 74–96

Zolberg, A., et al., *Escape from Violence: Conflict and the Refugee Crisis in the Developing World* (Oxford: Oxford University Press, 1989)

4 Hannah Arendt and the Refugee Problem

Worldlessness and Superfluity

[T]he world is not humane just because it is made by human beings, and it does not become human just because the human voice sounds in it, but only when it becomes the object of discourse.... We humanize what is going on in the world only by speaking of it, and in the course of speaking we learn to be human.

(Arendt, MDT: 24)

Introduction

One of the twentieth century's most influential political theorists, Hannah Arendt was also a refugee. Forced to flee Germany in 1933 after her arrest for research-ing 'everyday' anti-Semitism in German civil society, she lived the life of a stateless person for 18 years. Taking refuge first in France, she worked with a number of Jewish organisations, preparing Jewish youths for a new life in Pales-tine, and assisting fellow Jewish refugees in Paris. When France fell to the advancing German armies in 1940, Arendt was imprisoned in Gurs, a camp in the south-west of France. After managing to escape she was reunited with her husband, Heinrich Blücher, and they made their way to Lisbon to await a boat to America. Arendt and Blücher travelled to the US in 1941, but she remained stateless until her naturalisation as an American citizen in 1951. In her 1951 book *The Origins of Totalitarianism* she set out how the existence of refugees is inextricably tied into the internal structures and logic of the nation-state and the expansion of the nation-state system, and these insights have influenced more critically minded refugee studies scholars ever since. Much of the work that spe-cifically builds upon Arendt's insights on the refuge problem is characterised by a focus on the paradox of human rights that her analysis revealed. These works rightly highlight the problems inherent in an unreflective legalistic approach to refugee protection (e.g. Benhabib, 2004; Gündoğdu, 2015; Hayden, 2008 and 2009; Isaac, 1996; Oudejans, 2014; Owens, 2010; Parekh, 2004). To assume that the expansion and entrenchment of a global human rights framework in the years since Arendt wrote *Origins* has rendered her analysis obsolete is to fall into the same trap as the "well-meaning idealists" (Arendt, OT: 279) of the inter-war years of which Arendt was so scathing: simply enumerating new declarations of rights leaves the structural roots of the refugee problem unchanged. Ultimately, the human rights regime has not succeeded in displacing sovereignty from its position atop the hierarchy of ordering principles in international life. While these analyses successfully highlight how and why Arendt's analysis of human rights and migration are still relevant despite the passing of over six decades, there are other facets of Arendt's broader body of work, not explicitly related to her reflections on right and refugees, that can fruitfully be brought to bear upon our understanding of, and approaches to, the refugee problem.

This chapter begins the shift in focus/understanding of the refugee problem and the search for solutions from the problem that refugees pose to states – the refugee *as* problem – to the problems faced by refugees in becoming displaced. To this end I will revisit Arendt's well-known analysis of the structural causes of displacement within the context of her philosophical and political reflections on the 'world' and 'world alienation' to bring to light what makes this structural problem such a personal problem for those produced by it, positing that this is best understood, in Arendtian terms, as 'worldlessness' and 'superfluity'. The chapter will then utilise these reflections to reveal why the three durable solutions to displacement, focused as they are on formal remedies to structural rather than existential problems, are insufficient to address the problems that *being* a refugee presents for those ejected from the state-citizen-territory trinity. This reading of Arendt's work through the idea of 'world' forms a theoretical base from which to begin, in the next chapter, to conceptualise 'solutions' to this reframed understanding of the refugee problem – solutions which place the experience of refugees at the centre of concern rather than the exigencies of the sovereign state and state system.

Arendt on Refugees

Arendt's most sustained reflections on refugees and the refugee problem appear in the ninth chapter of *The Origins of Totalitarianism*, 'The Decline of the Nation State and the End of the Rights of Man'. Arendt's analysis of the refugee problem begins with the aftermath of the First World War, and the attempts to create functional, ethnically homogeneous successor states out of the collapse of the Russian, Ottoman and Austro-Hungarian empires. The Peace Treaties and Minority Treaties which brought the war to a close divided the territories and attempted to manage the ethnic composition of the new states. In those successor states where ethnic homogeneity proved too difficult to produce through population transfer, the population was divided into groups with separate statuses and differential positions in relation to the rights of citizenship and the right to govern. Some groups were designated as 'state people' and were entrusted with government. Others were "silently assumed" to be equal partners in government, even though they were not – such as the Slovaks in Czechoslovakia, or the Croats and Slovenes in Yugoslavia. Out of the remnants were isolated a third group of nationalities designated as 'minorities', who were to be governed by special regulations, would not share in government, and whose rights were to be guaranteed not by the state in which they resided but by the League of Nations

(Arendt, OT: 270). While minorities had certainly existed before, this was the first time that millions of people were formally recognised as existing outside of normal legal protection, and in need of an additional guarantee of their rights from an outside body – the League of Nations – rather than being able to rely on the state for such protection (Arendt, OT: 275). By openly stating that persons of different nationality needed a law of exception until or unless they were completely assimilated, the Minority Treaties stated what until then had only been implied in the nation-state system: that only nationals could be citizens and enjoy the full protection of legal institutions. The minorities themselves, and those denied minority status, came to understand their own struggles not as struggles for equal rights within the state, but as national struggles for states of their own (Arendt, OT: 273–274). This tacit admission of the conquering of the state by the nation would be confirmed not just by these successor states intent on repressing, oppressing, and eventually expelling their minorities, but also by the established nation-states of Western Europe with the appearance of the stateless (refugees).[1] It was the appearance of this group that would shatter the illusion that this was only a problem in the "belt of mixed populations", and reveal that the rights of man, which supposedly grounded such established states, were in reality simply an illusion, which had lasted only as long as the comity of European nations had lasted.

In theory, a number of mechanisms existed to deal with the legal anomaly of the stateless – asylum, repatriation, and naturalisation – all of which proved impotent as states attempted to hide their exclusionist tendencies by claiming that the sheer number of stateless persons rendered them powerless to solve the problem. Repatriation measures failed when there was no country to which these people could be returned as their countries of origin simply refused to claim them. Naturalisation similarly proved a failure when states responded to the influx of stateless persons by cancelling earlier naturalisations, which only compounded the problem. Since legal deportation of stateless persons was not an option because no other state would lay claim to them, the whole matter was swiftly transferred to the police and a system of reciprocal illegal deportations was triggered all over mainland Europe (Arendt, OT: 280–287). The paradoxical result of this was that it was in the one sphere in which state sovereignty is, theoretically, absolute – the control of entry of foreign nationals – that states violated each other's sovereignty as an expression, and attempt to regain control, of their own. The exhortations of societies for the protection of human rights fell on deaf ears and they were unable to understand what to Arendt seemed obvious: that protection abroad, in practice, is based upon one's status as a citizen of a foreign friendly nation and not, as natural rights or human rights theories claim, on account of one's status as a rights-bearing individual (Oudejans, 2014: 10). The fact that states either would not or could not protect the rights of those who had lost nationally guaranteed rights revealed a paradox at the heart of the system of rights upon which the modern state was supposed to be founded; and the stateless became the living, breathing embodiment of this paradox.

Arendt locates the source of this paradox of rights in the 'Declaration of the Rights of Man and of the Citizen' of the French Revolution. Until the upheaval of the revolution, rights and privileges had been derived from one's position in society and had been guaranteed by social, spiritual and religious forces, rather than by government and constitution (Arendt, OT: 291). The revolution turned this system on its head, and the rights of man were proclaimed as the foundation of all law, with Man himself (not one's station, or God, or the customs of history) as their source. The context of such declarations is vital for Arendt: "Man appeared as the only sovereign in matters of law *as the people was proclaimed the only sovereign in matters of government*" (Arendt, OT: 291; emphasis added). The sovereignty of the people, established by the revolution, was proclaimed in the name of Man, and thus, Arendt argues, "it seemed only natural that the 'inalienable' rights of man would find their guarantee and became an inalienable part of the right of the people to sovereign self-government" (Arendt, OT: 291). What is significant here is that the human being of the declarations of rights – Man – was an abstract being who seemed to exist nowhere, for all people appeared to live in some kind of social order. The whole question of human rights, therefore, was blended from the beginning with the question of national emancipation.

This identification of the rights of man with the rights of peoples in the European nation-state system remained relatively unproblematic while all people were considered to belong to a state. However, as Gündoğdu highlights, the precarious balance established by the French Revolution between 'nation' and 'state' – between the state as the supreme legal institution charged with the protection of inhabitants in a territory, and the nation as the community composed of those who belong by right of origin and fact of birth – became imperilled with the rise of nationalism which turned the nation into a new absolute (Gündoğdu, 2011: 11–12). The state gradually lost its representative function and became an instrument of the nation, transforming the 'citizen' into the 'national'. With the conquering of the state by the nation it became ever more obvious that not all people in Europe did *belong* to a state, despite their *physical presence* within one state or another, and the millions forced to wander the European continent became the walking embodiments of the reality that "the moment human beings lacked their own government and had to fall back upon their minimum rights [their supposedly inalienable human rights], no authority was left to protect them and no institution was willing to guarantee them" (Arendt, OT: 292).

The peculiar situation of the stateless was not that their rights had been violated, but that they were completely right*less*. In losing their homes – "the entire social texture into which they were born and in which they established for themselves a distinct place in the world" (Arendt, OT: 293) and government protection (equivalent to the loss of legal status in *all* countries) – what the stateless lost was not the right to freedom of movement, or of equality before the law. The soldier, Arendt explains, can be denied his right to life, and the criminal his right to freedom, but in neither case has a loss of *human* rights taken place. The calamity of the rightless is that they are no longer part of any community whatsoever: their plight is not that they are not equal before the law, but that no law exists for them. She continues:

> Neither physical safety – being fed by some private welfare agency – nor freedom of opinion changes in the least their fundamental situation of rightlessness. The prolongation of their lives is due to charity and not to right, for no law exists which could force the nations to feed them; their freedom of movement, if they have it at all, gives them no right to residence which even the jailed criminal enjoys as a matter of course; and their freedom of opinion is a fool's freedom, for nothing they think matters anyhow.
>
> (Arendt, OT: 295–296)

It was for this reason that Arendt considered efforts at 'solving the problem' by enumerating new declarations of rights to be hopelessly inadequate. What the various declarations of rights failed to grasp was that "it was not the loss of specific rights but the loss of a community willing and able to guarantee any rights whatsoever that had been the calamity of ever-increasing numbers of people" (Arendt, OT: 297). It was this fundamental deprivation of rights that had remained unaddressed, and this was a problem not of geographic space but of political organisation. The fundamental deprivation of human rights is manifested "first and above all in the deprivation of a place in the world which makes opinions significant and actions effective" (Arendt, OT: 296). In other words, the stateless lost their 'right to have rights'.

Arendt does not explicitly add much flesh to the bones of this now famous conception of a 'right to have rights'. A veritable cottage industry of scholarship has emerged which sets itself the task of explicating exactly what she meant by the language she chose – a *right* to *have rights* – and on what she grounds this right given her scepticism of naturalistic fallacies (e.g. Cohen, 1996; Gündoğdu, 2011; Ingram, 2008; Kesby, 2012; Michelman, 1996; Näsström, 2014; Rancière, 2004; Schaap, 2011). In many of these works the right to have rights is understood as, and abbreviated to, the right to citizenship within the nation-state. While recognising the importance of citizenship to Arendt, I contend that examining her broader body of work reveals that this approach to the right to have rights, and of addressing the problems of rightlessness faced by refugees, is to ignore the profound problems that Arendt also had with citizenship and politics in modernity for all, not just the stateless. It was these broader problems that animated her call to re-imagine the very *nature of the communities* to which such a right to have rights would correspond, and this is the context within which we need to understand her reflections on refugees, and the problems that refugees face. And so, rather than focusing on the terminology of the right to have rights I propose focusing instead on Arendt's description of this condition: the loss of a place in the world which makes opinions significant and actions effective. What does she mean by this? What does it mean for opinions to be significant and actions effective? And why would losing the significance of opinions and effectiveness of actions be to lose one's place in the *world*? It is only by answering these questions that we can see what *kind* of 'place' it is that is lost and begin to ask how such a place might be reclaimed. I contend that the place in the world that refugees lose, and which characterises their predicament, should not automatically be understood either as a purely physical place, or reduced to citizenship in the nation-state. What becomes clear from an analysis of Arendt's reflections on politics is that while there is certainly a legal aspect to this place in the world – citizenship is certainly important for Arendt – this 'place' also needs to be understood in terms of the lived experience of being-in-the-world-with-others, and that this cannot be automatically regained simply through being provided with a physical space in which to live, or by acquiring citizenship in a state, as citizenship has become merely a degraded formality under modern political conditions. The next section will, therefore, explain Arendt's unique conceptualisation of the 'world', and her thoughts on action and opinion.

The World, Action, and Opinion

The world occupies a special place in Arendt's thought, rooted in her experience and analysis of the rise of totalitarianism, but she has a quite particular understanding of what 'the world' is. While many may use the words 'world' and 'earth' synonymously, Arendt felt that there was an important distinction between them. The earth is that "limited space for the movement of men and the general condition of organic life", while the world is the condition under which, and realm within which, specifically *human* life can be at home on earth (Arendt, HC: 52, 134). The earth and the world are, thus, different dimensions of the earth that we inhabit, rather than geographically distinct spaces, and so humans have both an earthly and a worldly existence. Whereas mankind shares the earth with all living things and his *earthly* existence is guaranteed as a matter of course by the continued existence of the earth,[2] the continued existence of the world, and man's ability to be at home in it, is not a matter of course, and this is because the world is the result of human activity, rather than natural process. Individuals are born into the world as strangers and, Arendt claims, we need to engage in various activities in order to create a home for ourselves in it. The *vita activa* is the name Arendt gives to human life in so far as it is engaged in these activities, and it consists, primarily, of labour, work and action.[3] Labour is the activity which corresponds to the biological process of the human body, and is conditioned by life itself; that is, the natural biological process of physical life requires that we engage in the cyclical process of production and consumption in order to sustain it. Work is the activity that corresponds to the "unnaturalness of human existence" and provides an artificial world of things, distinctly different from all natural surroundings, among which, and in relation to which, human life proceeds. Action is "the only activity which goes on directly between men without the intermediary of things or matter" and is conditioned by plurality: "the fact that men, not Man, live on the earth and inhabit the world" (Arendt, HC: 7). The world, for Arendt, is thus both material and immaterial; quasi-objective and inter-subjective. The material world, the world as human artifice, is created by human beings in their capacity as *homo faber* – man the creator – and consists mostly, but not exclusively, of objects for use: buildings, bridges, tools, works of art, and laws and constitutions. This man-made world gives a stability and solidity to human life and provides a degree of protection against nature (Arendt, HC: 136). It possesses a permanency that the individual life does not, and yet, through being inhabited and used, it decays and thus requires maintenance to remain fit to house human life. The human artifice, while consisting of things, is only *quasi*-objective because these objects derive their meaning and utility from the relation they hold to human beings.

The material world, which is the product of work, is overlain by the immaterial, phenomenal, inter-subjective world, as both a *public space* and a *common* world, which is the ephemeral 'product' of action and speech (Arendt, HC: 182–183). The world as 'space of appearance' is the locus wherein, through speech and action, men appear to each other *qua* men – as the distinct individuals that they are, with their unique perspectives on the world shared in common. While all species on earth are distinguished from each other, only humans can *express* this distinction and communicate *themselves*: "in acting and speaking, men show who they are, reveal actively their unique personal identities and thus *make their appearance in the human world*" (Arendt, HC: 179; emphasis added). This appearance, however, is only possible when one is with others, as one cannot appear to nobody. The space of appearance, "the space where I appear to others as others appear to me", is therefore public by definition. And yet, it does not always exist; it does not exist outside, or independently, of the individuals who constitute it, but nor can it be reduced to such individuals (Arendt, MDT: 4). It is, rather, an inter-subjective 'in-between': a realm which arises through the actions of men and women and which, through their continued action and speech when oriented towards it, relates and separates them as a table unites and separates those who sit around it (Arendt, HC: 52). This *common* world is what we enter at birth and leave behind in death, and as such it transcends our lifespan into the past and future alike (Arendt, HC: 55). But, importantly, the common world can only survive the coming and going of the generations to the extent that it appears *as* public. This is because, as distinct from the reality of biological life, which can be confirmed on one's own through the operation of the senses – and for which, therefore, labour is so vital an activity (Gündoğdu, 2015: 138) – the reality of the *world* is only guaranteed by the presence of others: as the ephemeral 'product' of human action and speech, its reality depends entirely "upon human plurality, upon the constant presence of others who can see and hear and therefore testify to its existence" (Arendt, HC: 95). This presence of others in their plurality is necessary for the reality of the world because, though the common world is the common meeting-ground of all, those who are present have different locations in it, and

> only where things can be seen by many in a variety of aspects without changing their identity, so that those who are gathered around them know they see sameness in utter diversity, can worldly reality truly and reliably appear.
>
> (Arendt, HC: 57)

The material and immaterial worlds are, thus, related to each other in a number of ways. The material world is the stable, non-natural environment which protects human life against nature and within which human life unfolds – it thus shelters both the worldly and non-worldly activities of the *vita activa*; it provides the 'stage' upon which action and speech occur and create the immaterial world of the web of human relationships; and it also gives rise to the specific, objective, worldly interests of individuals, about which action and speech (or opinion) are most often concerned.

The inter-subjective world; the world of narratives, history, memory, and meaning, which occurs within, and which often relates specifically to, the material world of human artifice, is the 'product' of the action and speech of human beings in their plurality. Plurality is the condition of action and speech for the simple fact that if men were endlessly reproducible repetitions of the same model then they would need neither speech nor action to make themselves understood. It is precisely because we "are all the same, that is human, in such a way that nobody is ever the same as anyone else who ever lived, lives, or will live" that plurality is the condition of human action (Arendt, HC: 8). Through acting and speaking "we insert ourselves into the human world, and this insertion is like a second birth, in which we confirm and take upon ourselves the naked fact of our original physical appearance" (Arendt, HC: 177). To act, then, means in its most general sense to take an initiative, to begin, but this beginning is the beginning not only of something but *someone*. Action discloses the identity of the *who* in contradistinction to *what* somebody is, and this disclosure is implicit in everything somebody says or does (Arendt, HC: 179). *What* we are is a combination of our distinctive physical identities – which appear in the world by the mere fact that we are there and without any special effort on our part – and our particular traits, talents, virtues, shortcomings, and roles that we play in society – over which we maintain a considerable degree of control. But *who* we are, our unique identity, is "revealed only in acting and speaking, and it can be hidden only in utter passivity and silence" (Fuss, 1979: 160). This does not mean that action merely expresses a pre-existing identity, nor that the identity of the actor is purely performative. Rather, the identity of the actor is in part constituted through the action itself. As Arendt explains in *The Life of the Mind*, when I act

> I am not merely reacting to whatever qualities may be given me; I am making an act of deliberate choice among the various potentialities of conduct which the world has presented me. Out of such acts arises finally what we call character or personality, the conglomeration of a number of identifiable qualities gathered together into a comprehensibly and reliably identifiable whole, and imprinted, as it were, on an unchangeable substratum of gifts and defects peculiar to our soul and body structure.
>
> (Arendt, LM: 37)

Whilst we decide when and how to act and speak, we are not in control, or possession, either of the 'who' that we reveal in the course of such action and speech, or of their consequences – whether we will achieve the end we seek or do justice to the principle which inspired us to act. What we do and say falls into a pre-existing "web of human relationships", within which they initiate new processes, which are themselves affected by, as they affect, the wills and intentions of other actors and speakers (Fuss, 1979: 163). Together, our words and deeds, and the consequences which they give rise to once they enter the pre-existing web of human relationships, start a new process which "eventually emerges as the unique life story of the newcomer [the actor], affecting uniquely the life stories of all those with whom he comes into contact" (Arendt, HC: 184). The 'who' that is revealed piecemeal throughout our lives in everything that we say and do is thus revealed in the fullness of time only to the 'storyteller' – to those who speak about us and our words and deeds once we have finished acting or once we are gone. We can act and speak with specific intentions and particular goals in mind, but because our deeds and words fall into this pre-existing web of relationships, within which others then re-act, we have no control over the chains of actions that our initiative will set off. As such, we are dependent upon others to act with us in pursuit of our projects. This is what Arendt refers to as the interdependence of action (HC: 189), and is a theme that we will return to in the next chapter. For now, however, it is sufficient to note that, in order for others to join with us in speech and action, our initiative must be seen and heard, and must be recognised as an occasion for response by others.

Each individual, then, apart from being an actor and a speaker, is also a witness, or a spectator, testifying to what takes place from the vantage point of his own irreducibly unique perspective (Fuss, 1979: 165). And this brings us to the importance of opinion, and its worldly (and thus relational) nature. If most action takes the form of speech, then what differentiates speech as action from other kinds of speech – such as the expression of pain, or the relation of desires – is that it tends to take the form of opinion (Herzog, 2014: 193). Arendt follows Socrates in understanding opinion, or *doxa*, as the formulation in speech of what *dokei moi*; that is, "of what appears to me" (Arendt, PP: 14) – how one experiences the world from one's own specific standpoint (Parekh, 2008: 77–78). Rather than subjective fantasy and arbitrariness – as we are, perhaps, used to conceiving of opinions, where the phrase "I'm entitled to my opinion!" is frequently used to shut down conversation or debate – this understanding of opinion as *doxa* takes its starting point in the world as it appears, recognising, as highlighted above, that the world opens up differently to every individual according to his/her position in it. When I form an opinion, Arendt argues, I consider a given issue

> from different viewpoints, by making present to my mind the standpoints of those who are absent; that is, I represent them. This process of representation does not blindly adopt the actual views of those who stand somewhere else, and hence look upon the world from a different perspective; this is a question neither of empathy, as though I tried to be or to feel like somebody else, nor of counting noses and joining a majority but of being and thinking

in my own identity where actually I am not. The more people's standpoints I have present in my mind while I am pondering a given issue, and the better I can imagine how I would feel and think if I were in their place, the stronger will be my capacity for representative thinking and the more valid my final conclusions, my opinion.

(Arendt, BPF: 241)

Opinions, while subjective to the extent that they are developed, held, and related by individuals, are at the same time worldly and relational. Our opinions take their bearings from the world as it appears to us, and develop by seeking out and engaging with the standpoints of others, with our opinions becoming more or less 'valid' the more or less they are 'representative' – not in the sense of how many others *share* a particular opinion, but how many *different* perspectives on the world and given issue we have tried to take account of in coming to our own. This means, by extension, that my ability to form my own opinion on the world depends upon the availability of the opinions of others, and, further, that the opinions of those others are also reliant upon my own. My own opinions – how the world "appears to me" – are not only important to and for myself, but to and for others in comprehending, navigating, acting within and thus co-constituting the world we share in common.

Both action and opinion, then, are fundamentally dependent upon the presence and recognition of diverse others, both in each individual's ability to form opinions and to act in the world, and in order for those opinions and actions to be worldly – to be meaningful to others. With a clearer grasp on how Arendt conceptualises the world, action and opinion, we can return to the plight of the displaced in order to explain why the fundamental loss that they experience is the loss of the significance of opinion and effectiveness of action, and why the significance and effectiveness of opinion and action require a place in the world.

Refugees, Worldlessness, and Superfluity

In what way have refugees lost the effectiveness of action and the significance of opinion? It surely cannot be that they live completely separately from any other people – we need only watch the evening news to see that this is not the case. But while this may not be the case physically, it is, arguably, the case phenomenologically – one can be isolated from others while still being physically among, or visible to, them. We can understand how by turning to another way in which Arendt describes this loss. In 'We Refugees' and *The Origins of Totalitarianism* Arendt writes that one of the first losses that refugees suffer is the loss of their homes – the "entire social texture" into which they were born and "in which they established for themselves a distinct place in the world" (Arendt, OT: 293). This loss of home meant the loss of the "familiarities of daily life", of occupations and "the confidence that they are of some use in this world", and of their language, "the naturalness of reactions, the simplicity of gestures, the unaffected expression of feelings" (Arendt, JW: 264). This initial loss was compounded by the loss of government protection, which turned out to mean the loss of legal status in all countries. But what made these losses unprecedented was not the loss of home itself, but "the impossibility of finding a new one" (Arendt, OT: 294). There was no empty spot on earth where the stateless could go and create new homes for themselves, but this reality was a problem not of geographical but political space. Humanity has "reached the stage where whoever was thrown out of one of these tightly organised closed communities found himself outside of the family of nations altogether" (Arendt, OT: 294).

It was only with such a "completely organised humanity" that the loss of home and political/legal status become identical with expulsion from humanity. As Nicholas Xenos explains, the nation-state is an organised 'community' which requires the loss of home in order to find it in the *homeland* (Xenos, 1993: 425). Referring to Simone Weil's interpretation of French history in *The Need for Roots*, he explains:

> The process of nation-building over a period extending from the thirteenth century through the French Revolution gradually supplanted complex, fragmented, sometimes overlapping local identities in favour of a single, undifferentiated national identity. This is a history of struggle, of conquest and assimilation of Corsicans, Bretons, Burgundians, Basques, Alsatians, and so on. It culminated in the doctrine of the sovereign nation in 1789, a doctrine that paradoxically predicated national identity upon a radical break with the past.
>
> (Xenos, 1993: 426)

The result of this process is that the nation-state, by supplanting all other communities, stands alone as the one unifying identity, object of allegiance, and place of belonging in the modern era. Whether by assimilation or expulsion "the home is exchanged for the homeland, which exists as an imagined necessity rather than as a lived or historical contingency" (Xenos, 1993: 424). The extent to which Arendt considered nationality to have conquered any other form of meaningful identification with others, or ways of belonging to the world, can be seen in her description of the reactions of the stateless to their condition. Stripped of their rights, ejected from their states, and welcomed nowhere, the refugees were reduced to the "abstract nakedness of being nothing but human" (Arendt, OT: 300). They understood that

> this was their greatest danger. Because of it they were regarded as savages and, afraid that they might end up being considered beasts, they insisted on their nationality, the last sign of their former citizenship, as their only remaining and recognised tie with humanity ... people cling to their nationality all the more desperately when they have lost the rights and protection that such nationality once gave them. Only their past with its 'entailed inheritance' seems to attest to the fact that they still belong to the civilised world.
>
> (Arendt, OT: 300)

Action and opinion only become effective and significant (in the sense that they disclose our individuality and contribute to the building of the common world) in a community which is willing to recognise them as such. When Arendt claimed that a refugee can enjoy greater freedom of movement than a jailed criminal and yet still be without human rights (Arendt, OT: 286) she meant that the jailed criminal, while having his civic rights curtailed, is still recognised as a member of the community in which he is imprisoned. His treatment is related, fundamentally, to what he himself has done, and the recognition (albeit in the form of condemnation) of his own individual actions. The refugee, in contrast, is treated not according to anything that she may have said or done, but by what she unavoidably is: a person lacking a home and legal status; a person who is no longer a recognised member of a community, no longer a person whose speech and action are meaningful for the community. This is why Arendt referred to the 'freedom of opinion' retained by refugees – the right to think whatever they please – as "a fool's freedom, for nothing that they think matters anyhow" (Arendt, OT: 296): their opinions are treated as wholly without consequence for anyone else. They are, in other words, superfluous. They are not only treated unjustly; they are not only oppressed; they are "made expendable from a properly human world" (Hayden, 2009: 3). What they say and do fail to be recognised by others as events to which to respond in the co-constitution of the common world, and since this failure to be recognised deprives one of the possibility of creating the world with others, it is to be worldless.

Action and speech are, in themselves, the least tangible and most fragile of all human activities, and yet are also, at the same time, the most distinctively human. In *The Human Condition* Arendt explains that "in order to become worldly things, that is, deeds and facts and events and patterns of thought or ideas, they [our actions and opinions] must first be seen, heard and remembered and then transformed into things" (Arendt, HC: 95). Without others to see and hear and testify to the refugee's existence, her thoughts, words, and actions wither on the wind almost as soon as they are spoken or performed. But being-with-others should not be mistaken for being physically visible to others. One can be physically visible to others and still be isolated from them. Being-with-others is a matter of recognition of our *individuality* – our own unique position and view on the world we share in common – rather than of our common membership in the human species which presents itself to others without any initiative on our part. And this recognition is achieved through equality which, far from being a natural condition, is, rather, an artificial construct based upon legal personhood. Equality, Arendt writes, "is not given us, but is the result of human organization ... We are not born equal; we become equal as members of a group on the strength of our decision to guarantee ourselves mutually equal rights" (Arendt, OT: 301). In no longer belonging to a community in which one is judged by one's actions and opinions, the displaced are thrown back upon their mere givenness; they appear to others only as 'whats' and not as 'whos'.

The worldless existence of the displaced comes into relief most clearly in the refugee camp, which Arendt referred to as "the only practical substitute for a non-existent homeland ... the only 'country' the world has to offer the stateless"

(Arendt, OT: 284). Camps remain (in the eyes of the state) the preferred domicile for refugees on the assumption that their condition is temporary (Gündoğdu, 2015: 140). Those kept within them are not permitted to work outside of the camp, are limited in the jobs they can perform within the camp, and are almost completely reliant on humanitarian organisations for food, water, and other basics to fulfil human needs (Agier, 2011). Many camps are isolated from population centres, and curfews make it illegal for refugees to be outside of the camp after certain hours. The 'logic of temporariness' of refugeehood is reflected in the material construction of the camp: plastic tarpaulins for tents, and rudimentary shacks for 'feeding centres'. The shelters that refugees live in are ill-suited to be transformed into homes, built instead for providing shelter from the elements, and often failing even in this most basic of functions. UNHCR and other aid agencies do seek to provide more than physical protection and the basics of human survival, but the camp is designed as a temporary space – even if in reality it becomes the opposite – and is subject to an administrative logic which leaves little room for the establishment of private, social and public lives for refugees warehoused within them. If the world as human artifice is characterised by its stability and permanence relative to the human lives it protects from nature, then the environment of the refugee camp is a poor substitute: filled with objects for consumption rather than use, not built to last, and cut off from the outside world. While concerted efforts have been made in recent years by agencies running refugee camps to include refugees in governance structures, this is not in itself sufficient to overturn the logic of temporariness and necessity that pervades camp life. To live a life so burdened by necessity means, above all,

> to be deprived of the reality that comes from being seen and heard by others, to be deprived of an objective relationship with them that comes from being related to and separated from them through the intermediary of a common world of things, and to be deprived of the possibility of achieving something more permanent than life itself.
>
> (Arendt, HC: 58)

The human masses sealed off within these "humanitarian spaces without exit" (Dubernet, 2001) are "treated as if they no longer existed, as if what happened to them were no longer of any interest to anybody" (Arendt, OT: 445). This description resonates with Arendt's critique of slavery in *The Human Condition*: "the curse of slavery consisted not only in being deprived of freedom and of visibility, but also in the fear of these obscure people themselves 'that from being obscure they should pass away leaving no trace that they have existed' " (Arendt, HC: 55).

Durable Solutions and a Place in the World: The Shortcomings of the Refugee Regime

The international refugee regime, created to solve 'the refugee (as) problem' is, I suggest, ill-suited to solving the problems of worldlessness and superfluity experienced by the displaced. Refugee status is a poor substitute for the kind of legal personhood necessary to ensure the possibility of a truly worldly existence, and the three durable solutions of resettlement, repatriation, and local assimilation are not only the *gift* of the state but are out of reach of the majority of the global refugee population, and also bound by the same temporary logic as Refugee status itself. This is not to say that the solutions to 'the refugee (as) problem' have no discernible impact also on alleviating the problems that refugees face, but since they are characterised by the structural need to *find places to put people*, until such time as refugees can repatriate, we should bear in mind their shortcomings when it comes to addressing the existential problems of worldlessness and superfluity that refugees experience.

The rights and benefits which attach to Refugee status, enumerated by the Refugee Convention, have not changed significantly since the conventions with which Arendt was familiar from the inter-war years. These rights are, broadly speaking, social and economic rights. Rights concerning moveable and immoveable property, access to courts, education, housing and social welfare, and access to wage-earning employment are all undoubtedly important rights which enable the refugee to rebuild some semblance of a 'normal' life in her country of refuge, but access to these rights is not the same in every state: there are, as Vincent Chétail observes, "as many refugee statuses as there are state parties to the Geneva Convention, insofar as the content of the applicable standards to aliens and nationals is primarily determined by the legislation of each individual state" (Chétail, 2014: 42). Moreover, the Refugee Convention, and thus Refugee status, is marked by its absence of protection for civil and political rights. The Convention even goes so far as to expressly deny such rights to refugees: Article 15 only guarantees rights of "non-political and non-profit-making associations and trade unions" (United Nations, 1951). When the Convention was being drafted the words "non-political" were not present; they were added at the insistence of states during the 1951 Conference of Plenipotentiaries.

In line with the discussion in Chapter 1 of the logic of 'burden-shifting' underpinning the development of the refugee regime, states, with the support of the UN Secretary General, were adamant that Refugee status was not akin to citizenship, and that states were under no obligation to grant citizenship to any refugee. In the Secretary General's memoranda to the Ad hoc Committee which drafted the Refugee Convention, he sought to assure states that

> Decision[s] of the State in granting naturalisation is absolute. It cannot be compelled to grant its nationality, even after a long waiting period, to a refugee settled in its territory, since naturalisation confers on the naturalised citizen a series of privileges, including political rights.
>
> (United Nations, 1950: 24)

Refugee status, then, is a far cry from the kind of legal personhood that can not only act as a bulwark against worldlessness, but can enable and facilitate worldliness. Rather than simply a status as a right-and-duty-bearing subject, legal personhood, for Arendt, endows our actions with a meaning that they would otherwise lack and gives some kind of unity to different aspects of one's life story (Gündoğdu, 2015: 99). In *On Revolution*, Arendt explains that the word 'personhood' derives from the Latin *persona*, which denotes "the mask ancient actors used to wear in a play" (Arendt, OR: 106). *Persona*, for the Romans, also had a metaphorical meaning, which they used to distinguish between citizens and private individuals. Advancing a somewhat unusual etymological interpretation of *persona*, and referring to the mask as a metaphor for legal personhood, Arendt breaks it down into *per-sonare*, which means to "sound through", referring to the "broad opening at the place of the mouth through which the individual, undisguised voice of the actor could sound" (Arendt, RJ: 12). This mask, the *persona*, had two crucial functions: "it had to hide, or rather to replace the actor's own face and countenance, *but in a way that would make it possible for the voice to sound through*" (Arendt, OR: 106; emphasis added). Legal personhood, the equality that we guarantee ourselves as recognised members of political communities, is an artificial mask that not only disguises the countenance of its wearer – the dark background of mere givenness – but which allows the voice – as expression of plurality – to sound through. Vitally important to understand for our later endeavours, however, is that personhood "is not merely a juridical tie between an individual and a state. More importantly, it is an artificial convention that *institutes relationships among different individuals*" (Gündoğdu, 2015: 105; emphasis added). Arendt explains the importance of the mask of legal personhood to the recognition of plurality (between individuals and not just with the state) when she remarks that:

> If a Negro in a white community is considered a Negro and nothing else, he loses along with his right to equality that freedom of action which is specifically human; all his deeds are now explained as 'necessary' consequences of some 'Negro' qualities; he has become some specimen of an animal species, called man. Much the same thing happens to those who have lost all distinctive political qualities and have become human beings and nothing else.
>
> (Arendt, OT: 301–302)

Legal status is, thus, valuable, but it is valuable only to the extent that it enables, or supports, the existential aspects of living in the world with others. It is valuable to the extent that it confers significance on opinions and enables actions to be effective. This implies that legal status can fail to be such a guarantee, or that it can poorly enable such experience. While Refugee status can, on paper, provide access to important socio-economic rights that can help refugees regain a foothold in the world as human artifice, Refugee status cannot provide the kind of mask necessary to ensure one's access to the political realm of action and speech, and, thus, access to the inter-subjective world of action, speech, collective endeavour and remembrance. It is, to remain with the mask metaphor, perhaps best understood as a mask which only partially disguises the countenance of the wearer, but which lacks "the broad opening at the place of the mouth through which the individual, undisguised voice of the actor could sound" (Arendt, RJ: 12).

What, then, of the three so-called 'durable solutions'? Repatriation, resettlement, and local integration are not addressed in themselves within the legal framework of refugee protection since they are the gift of the state. UNHCR is mandated to assist refugees in accessing a durable solution (UNHCR, 1950: 2(d–f)), but cannot itself provide such a solution: repatriation relies on there being material changes of circumstance in the country of origin, whereas local integration and resettlement involve long-term (but not necessarily permanent) immigration, the control of which the state retains. In an ideal world, resettlement and local integration would lead automatically, and quickly, to full citizenship within the state, but this is neither a current legal requirement nor current practice. The difficulties in accessing resettlement and local integration, and the prioritisation in recent years of repatriation – even when it is neither voluntary nor safe – have already been addressed in the first chapter of this book, and they have also been well documented elsewhere.[4] What is less often discussed is the cessation clauses of the 1951 Refugee Convention and how these might impact on the ability of the durable solutions to address the problems of worldlessness and superfluity that refugees face.

Article 1, Section C of the Refugee Convention stipulates that Refugee status will cease to apply to any person who voluntarily re-avails him/herself of the protection of his/her country of nationality, or re-establishes himself there; it will cease to apply to any person who acquires a new nationality and enjoys the protection of the country of that nationality; and it will cease to apply when the circumstances in connection with which he has been recognised as a Refugee have ceased to exist. Given that states are under no obligation to enable refugees to gain citizenship in their country of refuge, it stands to reason that resettlement and local integration are 'durable solutions' only for as long as any individual remains entitled to Refugee status. Once the situation from which the refugee fled is considered to have changed – and while the Convention is silent on who makes this decision, it has in practice been the state of refuge, sometimes in partnership with UNHCR – then Refugee status ceases, the refugee becomes simply another migrant and can, in theory and, increasingly, in practice, be sent back to his/her country of origin. In the absence of any further detail in the 1951 Convention itself, UNHCR has issued guidance for states regarding the implementation of the cessation clause (UNHCR, 2003), stating that cessation should not result in refugees being left with uncertain status or being returned to "volatile" situations (UNHCR, 2003: 3). But while the guidance calls for fair, clear and transparent procedures for determining general cessation (UNHCR, 2003: 3), the recognition that cessation of status and probable return to the country of origin will result in a significant rupture in the lives of refugees – effectively rendering them worldless once again – appears in the guidance simply as an unfortunate but inevitable consequence, rather than a fundamental problem in and of itself. While Refugee status is a limited status in political terms, it can enable refugees to make progress in repairing the "rupture of their private lives" that they experience in becoming displaced. The underlying logic of solving 'the refugee (as) problem' emerges here in the ability of the rules of the refugee regime itself to become complicit in making the refugee worldless and superfluous once again by leaving any such progress made by the refugee open to destruction once more.

The underlying population/migration management approach of the refugee regime is also evident in the way in which the cessation clauses have been applied in practice. As Chimni highlights in his analysis of the shift towards involuntary repatriation since the end of the Cold War (2004: 55–73), the material change in circumstances which should prompt cessation of Refugee status has been interpreted more and more loosely, to the point where the country of origin (or, if applying the Internal Flight Alternative, merely a part of the country of origin) is deemed merely "safe enough". Refugees can be repatriated, against their will, even to "less than optimal conditions" in their country of origin (Chimni, 2004: 63). While Northern states rarely apply the cessation clauses, and certainly not on a group level, Southern states – where the majority of the global refugee population reside – have employed the cessation clause 25 times between 1973 and 2008 (Siddiqui, 2011: 4), often resulting in uncertain legal status and vulnerability to arbitrary arrest and imprisonment, forced repatriation to unsafe circumstances, and economic and social deprivation on the part of refugees whose recognition has been removed (Siddiqui, 2011). The way that the cessation clause seems to have been put into practice simply assumes – but itself does nothing to ensure or require – that the country of origin can actually be a home – a place in the world – again for the returned citizen, as it focuses (in theory but even less so, it would seem, in practice) merely on the presence or absence of the factors that produced the original "well-founded fear of persecution" prompting initial flight. In other words, neither the durable solutions, nor the cessation clause, appear to be about the possibility of *effective citizenship*, but about finding places to put people; it is about population management and solving the problem of the refugee, rather than solving the problems of worldlessness and superfluity that refugees themselves face.

Does this suggest, then, that conceptualising the right to have rights as citizenship in the nation-state is the way to go in addressing these problems? The final section of this chapter argues that while this would be an improvement over Refugee status, it is not, in and of itself, unproblematic. Focusing simply on legal status, and the rights attached to that status, even a (theoretically) more expansive one such as citizenship, is to fall into the legalistic thinking about human rights that Arendt felt was so problematic. Her critique of rights, it should be remembered, turns on the observation that absent a community willing and able to guarantee rights – which is a matter of political *practice* – we are rightless, regardless of whether, on paper, we possess a legal status which entitles us to such rights. While citizenship is an important status for Arendt, it has become in many ways merely a degraded legal formality – merely the last bulwark against complete worldlessness, rather than a facilitator of worldliness.

World Alienation and Modern Citizenship: The Degradation of Political Life

Arendt considered the stateless to be the most symptomatic group of contemporary politics (Arendt, OT: 277). Why is this? It is tempting to interpret this statement in purely structural terms. She does, after all, state that since "the Peace Treaties of 1919 and 1920 the refugees and the stateless have attached themselves like a curse to all the newly established states on earth which were created in the image of the nation-state" (Arendt, OT: 290). Since the internal structural logic of the nation-state system will continue to produce refugees, refugees are thus a reflection of the structural problems plaguing our system. I contend, however, that there is another reason why refugees are the most symptomatic group of contemporary politics, which underpins this structural reality: the world alienation which characterises modernity.

World Alienation

Arendt's entire political theory is an attempt to understand how totalitarianism, and the unprecedented crimes committed by its agents and by the many ordinary people swept along in its march, could have happened at all. Rather than searching for its 'origins', as the title of *The Origins of Totalitarianism* might suggest, she sought to isolate certain elements of modernity that crystallised into totalitarianism. Her subsequent work was oriented towards trying to understand how these elements developed, in the hope of recovering aspects of our experience and existence that could help us to prevent its recurrence. *The Human Condition* is, in addition to an examination of the general human capacities of the *vita activa*, a historical and philosophical analysis of modern 'world alienation', by which Arendt means the "twofold flight from the earth into the universe and from the world into the self" (Arendt, HC: 6). This flight is one of the processes which made totalitarianism historically possible – not which directly caused it, but which made it possible by destroying the common world and public reality, resulting in the continual creation of lonely and isolated masses, unrelated either to each other or to the common world, and uniquely vulnerable to the logic and meaning offered by mass movements. The world alienation that characterises existence under modernity renders "lonely mass man" particularly vulnerable to the allure of mass movements and the 'belonging' that they promise. The loss of meaning resulting from not having a home in the public world constitutes what Arendt calls the basic experience of our century. If the world that humans make and preserve provides the most striking evidence of their self-interpretation (McCarthy, 2012: 66) then humans today appear to interpret themselves primarily as *animal laborans* – members of the animal species, Man – for whom life and productivity are the highest goods, who relate to each other and to the world as consumers, and who behave, rather than act in concert. This 'triumph' of *animal laborans* and his values of life, productivity and abundance, is the outcome of a process of world alienation facilitated by social, philosophical and scientific developments of modernity. The innermost story of the modern age concerns the destruction of the common world and public reality, a story at the threshold of which stand three great events: the so-called 'discovery' of the New World, the Reformation, and the invention of the telescope. These events mark a fundamental transformation in Western man's relation to his surroundings, his "being-in-the-world" (Villa, 1996: 190). Each event represents a different form of retreat from the worldly dimension of our lived experience, and each is significant because, in "the ways of knowing and form of life it instantiates, reality is neither verified nor engendered through the presence of others" (Curtis, 1999: 77).

The 'discovery' of the Americas, and the subsequent age of exploration, had the paradoxical effect of shrinking the earth and making it seem much smaller, ultimately enabling man to "take full possession of his mortal dwelling place and gather the infinite horizons" in the representable and objective form of 'the globe'. In so doing, man has become as much an inhabitant of the earth as he is an inhabitant of his country or community (Arendt, HC: 250), and gained a perspective on the world more akin to that of the cartographer looking down upon the earth, rather than a situated individual as a spectator in the human world (McCarthy, 2012: 83–84). The Reformation began the process of expropriation through which millions ultimately lost their property – their privately owned place in the world to which they could retreat for the shelter and quiet Arendt thought necessary for a good life – and thus became subject to an unlimited, socialised accumulation of wealth (Villa, 1996: 190). Property is "an essentially worldly phenomenon, as a source of stability and temporal continuity, and, as such, differs significantly from the creation and amassing of wealth which, in modernity, has often depended on confiscating property and destroying durable artefacts" (McCarthy, 2012: 85). The expropriation of the peasantry which accompanied the Reformation laid the foundations for a capitalist economy in Europe by creating a class of 'labouring poor', retaining only their labour power once their place in the world was taken from them. This initial expropriation of the peasantry was the first stage in what turned out to be a process whereby society became the subject of the new life process, membership in a social class came to replace the protection previously offered by membership in a family, and society as a whole came to be identified with a "tangible, albeit collectively 'owned' piece of property, the territory of the nation-state" (Arendt, HC: 256). The invention of the telescope and Galileo's observation of the heavens confirmed the Copernican theory that the earth orbits the sun, and delivered the secrets of the universe to "human cognition 'with the certainty of sense-perception'" (Arendt, HC: 260). The abolition of "the old dichotomy between the earth and the sky" and the unification of the universe effected by Galileo's discoveries meant that from then on nothing occurring in earthly nature was viewed as a merely earthly happening (Arendt, HC: 262–263). As Curtis explains, with each of these processes, the self was required to habitually rip itself, or be ripped, from its embeddedness in the world of things and others in its local and immediate world (Curtis, 1999: 78). Earth alienation became the hallmark of modern science, but this flight from the earth is intimately connected with the withdrawal from the world into the self.

The confirmation of the Copernican theory of the universe demonstrated that man had been deceived by his senses, and this initiated an assault on the adequacy of our body-bound senses to reveal truth. The response to the nightmare that reality is only a dream, expressed most clearly in Descartes' doctrine of radical doubt, is to save reality by shifting inwards, by making representations, rather than appearance, the benchmark of the real. In making this move, Descartes explicitly articulates what Arendt calls

> the most obvious conclusion to be drawn from the new philosophy of science: though one cannot know truth as something given and disclosed, man can at least know what he makes himself, namely, the clear and distinct ideas of mathematical science.
>
> (Villa, 1996: 193)

This Cartesian subjectification of the real is, for Arendt, a sign of common sense in retreat in that men have only the structure of their minds in common, rather than the world. By giving primacy to the experiences of an isolated subject, thought as the essence of the human mind has been endowed with the power to determine reality. The cost of this new approach to reality, in making it a purely private affair, is the loss of its inter-subjective meaningfulness (Passerin d'Entrèves, 1994: 24).

After being and appearance parted company there arose, Arendt claims, a "veritable necessity to hunt for the truth behind deceptive appearances ... in order to know one had to do" (Arendt, HC: 290). If, Villa explains, man can know or be certain only of that which he, as representing subject, produces and arranges, then it follows that *fabrication* provides the new paradigm for securing truth (Villa, 1996: 196). The rise of *homo faber* is clear not only in the seventeenth-century 'mechanistic' political philosophies of, among others, Thomas Hobbes, which sought to *make* a commonwealth, but also in the hegemony of a broad set of attitudes including the instrumentalisation of the world, confidence in tools and in the productivity of the maker of artificial objects, and the conviction that every issue can be solved and every human motivation reduced to the principle of utility (Arendt, HC: 305). The implication of this for our attitude towards the world is that it comes to be thought of in terms of means and ends: the common world ceases to be characterised by *meaning* and comes instead to be characterised in terms of *utility*. However, since this is not the inevitable outcome of the process of fabrication itself, but rather the generalisation of the fabrication experience in which usefulness and utility are established as the ultimate standards for life and the world of men (Villa, 1996: 199), the triumph of work atop the hierarchy of the *vita activa* was to be short-lived. The knowledge obtained by the evolution of modern science organised by the fabrication process was, Arendt claims, no longer concerned (or at least not primarily) with the *why* or the *what* of the phenomena under study, but with the *how*; with the *process* of generation and development of that knowledge (Passerin d'Entrèves, 1994: 43). By shifting emphasis to the process over the end product, concern with stability, permanence and durability – which characterise the work of *homo faber* – is gradually eroded, and this erosion is further enabled by the rise of the historical sciences, which understand history as well as nature to be subject to process. The discovery of processes by the natural sciences "coincided with the discovery of introspection in philosophy" and so, Arendt claims, "it was only natural that the biological process within ourselves as members of the human species should eventually become the very model of the new concept" of 'process'. Within "the framework of experiences given to introspection we know of no other process but the life process within our bodies, and the only activity into which we can translate it and to which it corresponds is labour" (Arendt, HC: 116). The secularisation and loss of faith simultaneously developing (and in many ways also connected to the rise of Cartesian doubt) stripped individual life of its immortality (or at least of the certainty of immortality), rendering individual life, once again, mortal. Arendt claims that, under these circumstances, what was left was a

> 'natural force', the force of the life process itself, to which all men and all human activities were equally submitted and whose only aim, if it had an aim at all, was survival of the animal species man. None of the higher capacities of man was any longer necessary to connect individual life with the life of the species; individual life became part of the life process, and to labour, to assure the continuity of one's own life and the life of his family, was all that was needed.
>
> (Arendt, HC: 321)

With the triumph of *animal laborans* over *homo faber* and over man as an acting and speaking being, man became alienated as much from the world as human artifice as he did from the world as the inter-subjective in-between (Passerin d'Entrèves, 1994: 44). The values characteristic of the world as human artifice – permanence, stability, durability – as well as those characteristic of the inter-subjective world of action and speech, were sacrificed in favour of the values of life, productivity and abundance. It is important to understand that these values of life, productivity and abundance are not themselves based upon a strong conviction about human dignity or the sanctity of human life. They are, rather, the root of an ethos of consumption: "the idea that the essence of life is the appropriation of material objects, and that human productivity is the preeminent criterion of human well-being" (Isaac, 1996: 65).

In charting this process of world alienation, Arendt does not mean to claim that no one any longer engages in any of the activities of the *vita activa*. Rather, in losing our understanding of these activities as *worldly* activities they have become corrupted, or perverted, and their ability to affirm existence, reality, and meaning have diminished to the point where we no longer act, but behave; the end product of work is no longer an object for use, with the durability and stability that use implies, but for consumption; and the pain, from which we derive the pleasure, of the labouring process is not something that affirms the reality of existence and provides us with an elemental joy in being alive and in connection with nature, but is something to be avoided or emancipated from entirely. This process of world alienation has, Arendt claims, had a profound effect on political life in modern times.

The Shortcomings of Modern Citizenship

As someone who lived the precarious existence of a stateless person for 18 years, Arendt recognised the importance of citizenship. However, as the brief discussion of legal personhood above indicates, she did not consider citizenship to be simply a formal legal status, but a lived experience and, importantly, one that not only connected the individual to the state but also to their fellow citizens in a meaningful community *in (and of) practice* and not merely on paper. However, modern states are ill-suited for the kind of politics, the kind of belonging, that Arendt felt characterised citizenship.

The political and cultural outcome of world alienation, with its victory of the process character of labour and the concerns of *animal laborans*, is "the dubious equation of the common good with the production, distribution and consumption of non-worldly objects" (McCarthy, 2012: 86). In such a system, the promotion of the life process of society takes precedence over every other public concern, and the purpose of government (to whose field of activity all politics is assigned) becomes "to protect the free productivity of the society and the security of the individual in his private life" (Arendt, PP: 142). This is facilitated by, and occurs within, a realm unknown either to antiquity or the medieval period: the social. Neither properly private nor properly public, the social realm developed from the eighteenth century onwards and is defined by the fact that it is directed towards the necessities of life – a 'private' concern – but is, nevertheless, 'public' (Walsh, 2014: 129).[5] Arendt writes, in *The Human Condition*, that

> Perhaps the clearest indication that society constitutes the public organiza- tion of the life process itself may be found in the fact that in a relatively short time the new social realm transformed all modern communities into societies of labourers and job holders; in other words, they became at once centred around the one activity necessary to sustain life. (To have a society of labourers, it is of course not necessary that every member actually be a labourer or worker ... but only that all members consider whatever they do primarily as a way to sustain their own lives and those of their families.) Society is the form in which the fact of mutual dependence for the sake of life and nothing else assumes public significance....
>
> (Arendt, HC: 46)

Mass society is, thus, a novel form of communal life characterised by the fact that individuals are united only by their common membership of the human species; that is, by the common biological needs of life, and not by the common world of action and speech (Passerin d'Entrèves, 1994: 47). Since the biological needs of life are secured by production and consumption, government is organised for securing and maximising the benefits of these processes for all, by dedicating itself to the 'rational', bureaucratic management characteristic of the social (or behavioural) sciences. Action in the social realm is not really action at all, but behaviour, which can be predicted, moulded, and channelled. What society expects from its members is conformity to certain standards of behaviour, and that they share the same private interests (i.e. economic interests). As behaviour replaces action, and bureaucratic management replaces government by public participation, individuals become increasingly dependent on administrative organisations to govern, and, by focusing on their private interests, become increasingly alienated from each other and from the reality of world. The upshot of this is that individuals become identifiable only by their function in society, rather than by their innate individuality. The members of mass society are superfluous "in the sense that their active participation becomes increasingly dispensable in economic and political life", and the concentration of political power within bureaucratic structures, and processes of capital accumulation, continually produce and reaffirm this dispensability (Isaac, 1996: 62).

Politics under such a system is also massified, to the extent that it cannot really be called politics at all – it is more akin to administration. Ronald Beiner's summary of Arendt's critique of modern mass democracy is instructive here. Politics, in our present consumer society, has been reduced to an instrumental apparatus at the service of individual consumption. The political system is understood as a process whose function is to channel and fix priorities among the demands made by individual consumers. The 'clients' of this system are either satisfied that it has successfully 'delivered the goods', or, as is more likely, they are dissatisfied that it has failed to do so, and this dissatisfaction is duly registered at the ballot box. Political discourse, in such a system, similarly serves an instrumental function: "speech is used for *bargaining*, for getting the best deal for oneself and one's immediate family" (Beiner, 1984: 366). Such a system is one in which members relate to each other as rivals, with whom one competes for the most advantageous share possible of the goods to be distributed. The problem with such an understanding of politics is that individuals fail to see others as "partners in a common discourse concerning the best way of life or the good common to all" (Beiner, 1984: 366–367). The kind of political activity open to most individuals in modernity is restricted to voting, an infrequent act through which the voter "can only consent or refuse to ratify a choice which [through the operation of internal selection mechanisms of political parties] is made without him". This choice is embellished by the "obvious phoniness" of political campaigns, "through which the relationship between representative and elector is transformed into that of a seller and a buyer" (Arendt, OR: 276). Public discourse is reduced to a public relations game, and citizenship, in turn, is reduced to infrequent forms of vicarious participation (Isaac, 1994: 157). Such a system seems ill capable of ensuring that one's opinions are significant and one's actions effective.

Citizenship, for Arendt, is a practice in which one is driven by concern for the *world* and not one's private interests:

> Throughout his life man moves constantly in two different orders of existence: he moves within what is his own and he also moves in a sphere that is common to him and his fellow men. The 'public good', the concerns of the citizen, is indeed the common good because it is located in the world which we have in common without owning it. Quite frequently, it will be antagonistic to whatever we may deem good to ourselves in our private existence.
>
> (Arendt in Mooney and Stuber, 1977: 104)

Engaging in the practice of citizenship – not in the sense of rituals or routine/ routinised practices but participating directly in common action and in public deliberation – creates that public space where freedom can appear, in which we disclose *who* rather than *what* we are, which in turn assures us not only of the reality of the world but of the value, or meaning, of our own existence to and within that world. A couple of examples from Arendt's own work are instructive here. The first concerns the French resistance to Nazi occupation during the Second World War. As Isaac explains, the collapse of French society during the war created a vacuum in French politics into which tens of thousands of resisters were drawn who had never before participated in the 'official' business of the country (Isaac, 1993: 536). As Arendt writes in the preface to *Between Past and Future*:

> Without premonition and probably against their conscious inclinations, they had come to constitute willy-nilly a public realm where – without the paraphernalia of officialdom ... – all relevant business in the affairs of the country was transacted in deed and word.... [They] had become challengers, they had taken the initiative upon themselves and therefore ... had begun to create that public space between themselves where freedom could appear.
>
> (Arendt, BPF: 3–4)

In their active resistance to oppression, these subjects became citizens, albeit citizens defined in opposition to the existing state (Isaac, 1993: 536). Civil disobedience is another example which allows us to understand how Arendt conceptualises citizenship and its worldly focus. Arendt contrasts the conscientious objection of someone like Henry David Thoreau, whose refusal to pay poll taxes resulted in him spending a night in jail, with the civil disobedients of the civil rights movement. While Thoreau's actions are often called 'civil disobedience', Arendt felt this was an example of conscientious objection, a course of action governed by individual conscience and conscience's moral obligation. While he opposed the Mexican-American War and the institution of slavery, and cited both as a reason not to pay his taxes, Thoreau's concern was to avoid self-reproach, to avoid being implicated in something he considered wrong (Passerin d'Entrèves, 1994: 150). His actions were not motivated by, or directed towards, fighting for the redress of injustice. In fact, he expressly stated that this was not his role as an individual:

> it is not man's duty to devote himself to the eradication of any, even the most enormous, wrong; he may still properly have other concerns to engage him; but it is his duty, at least, to wash his hands of it.
>
> (Thoreau quoted in Arendt, CR: 60)

While Thoreau may be justified in arguing that this may not be the duty of a man, such action would certainly be the duty of the citizen. This was understood, Arendt claims, by those – both the enfranchised and the disenfranchised – who joined together in the civil rights movement. These citizens were not trying to save their conscience; rather, they were struggling to improve their polity to establish standards of universal justice (Passerin d'Entrèves, 1994: 151). Bound together by common opinion rather than common (i.e. similar private) interests, and motivated by concern for the world where a wrong is being committed or an unjust action perpetrated, these individuals become citizens through their collective action in pursuit of greater justice. Finally, in what may come as a surprise to readers of Arendt convinced that she felt that economic or social concerns are unpolitical 'by definition' (Cohen, 1996; Pitkin, 1981; Wolin, 1983), the labour movement is also lauded by Arendt as an example of political action constituting citizenship. The labour movement, which rose up time and again between the revolutions of 1848 and the Hungarian revolution of 1956, was extraordinary because it forged a political approach to social and economic injustices that "tied together questions of economic justice, social change, and democratic government" (Gündoğdu, 2015: 83). Its power arose from the fact that the workers who had been given formal entrance to the political sphere – in that they had been given the right to vote – refused to accept the position of a special interest group seeking the resolution of its problems within the existing configuration of the system (as trade unions had done and still do) (Gündoğdu, 2015: 86), and organised themselves, instead, as struggling for equality and freedom through "a transformation of society together with a transformation of the political institutions in which this society was represented" (Arendt, HC: 216). While these actions are (but need not necessarily be) directed towards the state, they are examples of citizenship in an Arendtian sense because of the relationships formed between those who act and their orientation towards the common world we share, rather than because these individuals possess birth certificates or passports attesting to a legal relationship between them and the state. In a society of alienated individuals, such a legal status is not in itself capable of creating the conditions for worldliness.

For action and speech to occur, to be significant, and to be effective, it is "not enough to have a collection of private individuals voting separately and anonymously according to their private opinions" (Passerin' d'Entrèves, 1994: 146). Rather, these individuals must be able to see and talk to one another in public, to meet in a public space so that their unique perspectives on the world and issues of common concern can be shared, and courses of action can be debated. There is no inherent reason why this public space must be 'the national' or 'state' space, or that the citizenship effected through such action must only be citizenship in the nation-state since, as we have seen, citizenship is not just a legal status. Arendt's call to re-imagine the very nature of the communities to which the right to have rights would correspond needs to be understood in light of the broader reflections we have examined on what it means to belong to a community. It is, Isaac argues, above all "participation in self-government that Arendt wishes to rescue from a world overcome by a preoccupation with mass consumption and the ritualised spectacles of mass politics" (Isaac, 1994: 157). It is through the *pluralisation* of political space; through breaking up, rather than replacing, mass society, that the displaced can regain a foothold in the common world, and overcome the worldlessness and superfluity that they experience in their ejection from the state-people-territory trinity.

Arendt is often criticised for offering a view of politics which reifies the activity itself at the expense of explaining what its substance is. Moreover, she is criticised for banishing economic and social issues from the political sphere, and thereby banishes from political action all those who live lives so constrained by necessity – the poor, the disenfranchised, the marginalised of society – that they have neither the luxury nor the opportunity to engage in a life of speech and action. But, I would argue, these criticisms are based on too narrow a reading of *The Human Condition* and a selective reading of *On Revolution*, ignoring Arendt's work on the world. Arendt's politics is a matter of people sharing a common world and common spaces of appearance in which public concerns can emerge and be articulated from different perspectives. It is not the 'issues' or contents of debate that define politics for Arendt. It is a distinctive mode of being with others, manifest in speech and action, and marked by a concern for the public world itself (Owens, 2012: 306). Caring for the world may even take the form of activities associated with the social realm, and with economic concerns – as Arendt's praise for the labour movement, highlighted above, demonstrates. Arendt's concern for the public character of the world and its ability to affirm the reality of our existence and the significance and value of our opinions and actions, means that action to counter the economic and social marginalisation of the poor, the homeless, women, refugees, the disabled, and others, would be precisely the kinds of activity that she would consider to be political action. For such action is, in targeting the causes of marginalisation, directed towards the inclusion of these individuals and their unique perspectives in our common care for the world, and in so doing, recognising them as equals in recreating the human world, and all the public spaces within it, anew.

Conclusion

This chapter has, through a close reading of Arendt's work, argued that the problems that refugees face in becoming displaced are best understood in terms of worldlessness and superfluity. To become displaced, for Arendt, is not simply a matter of physically being where one does not 'belong'. Her examination of statelessness reveals that to be displaced is to be superfluous, to lose one's place in the world, on the (existential) level of lived experience, and is not simply a matter of losing a formal legal status. It follows, then, that these are the problems which need to be the focus of our attention. But in order to address these problems of worldlessness and superfluity we need to understand ourselves once again as worldly beings, and politics as a worldly activity. By shifting our understanding of the problem to be addressed to the problems of worldlessness and superfluity that refugees face, and our understanding of the right to have rights beyond citizenship in the nation-state and understanding it, instead, as a ground upon which to build a home in the world with others, we can move forward in more imaginative ways and being to think of how we might address the problems faced by refugees beyond the confines of the state. As Passerin d'Entrèves explains:

> The reactivation of the public sphere, of the sphere within which the activity of citizenship can flourish, depends upon both the recovery of a common, shared world, and the creation of numerous spaces of appearance in which individuals can disclose their identities and establish relations of reciprocity and solidarity.
>
> (Passerin d'Entrèves, 1994: 140)

It is to this task that the final chapter of this book now turns.

Notes

1 Arendt considered the core of refugeehood to be identical with statelessness (Arendt, OT: 279 and 281), and so I will use the terms interchangeably in what follows.
2 It is worth noting that Arendt wrote *The Human Condition* at the advent of the nuclear age when, for the first time in history, mankind possessed both the knowledge and the capability to destroy all life on earth – a circumstance that Arendt specifically references in the introduction to the book.
3 The *vita contemplativa* – human life in so far as we think, will and judge – is also a vital part of our worldly existence. While the *vita contemplativa* will not be the focus of this chapter, we will return to it in the next.
4 See, for example, the growing literature on Protracted Refugee Situations: Hyndman and Giles, 2011; Lindley, 2011; Loescher and Milner, 2005; Loescher *et al.*, 2008.
5 This resonates with our analysis in Chapter Two of the gradual emergence of "life problems" for political power in the form of biopower/biopolitics, and with the emergence of social welfare in the nineteenth century.

References

Agier, M., *Managing the Undesirables: Refugee Camps and Humanitarian Government* (Cambridge: Polity Press, 2011)
Arendt, H., "On Humanity in Dark Times: Thoughts about Lessing" in *Men in Dark Times* (New York: Harcourt, 1968): 3–31

Arendt, H., "Civil Disobedience" in *Crises of the Republic* (Middlesex: Penguin Books, 1972): 43–82

Arendt, H., *The Origins of Totalitarianism* (New York: Harcourt, 1973)

Arendt, H., "Public Rights and Private Interests" in Mooney, M., and Stuber, F. (Eds), *Small Comforts for Hard Times: Humanists on Public Policy* (New York: Columbia University Press, 1977): 103–108

Arendt, H., *The Life of the Mind* (New York: Harcourt, 1978)

Arendt, H., *On Revolution* (London: Penguin, 1990)

Arendt, H., *The Human Condition* (Chicago: University of Chicago Press, 1998)

Arendt, H., "Prologue" in *Responsibility and Judgment* (New York: Schocken Books, 2003): 3–14

Arendt, H., "Socrates" in *Promise of Politics* (New York: Schocken Books, 2005): 5–39

Arendt, H., "We Refugees" in *The Jewish Writings* (New York: Schocken Books, 2005): 264–274

Arendt, H., "Preface: The Gap between Past and Future" in *Between Past and Future: Eight Exercises in Political Thought* (New York: Penguin Books, 2006): 3–15

Arendt, H., "Truth and Politics" in *Between Past and Future: Eight Exercises in Political Thought* (New York: Penguin Books, 2006): 223–259

Beiner, R., "Action, Natality and Citizenship: Hannah Arendt's Concept of Freedom" in Pelczynski, Z. A., and Gray, J. (Eds), *Conceptions of Liberty in Political Philosophy* (New York: St Martin's Press, 1984): 349–375

Benhabib, S., *The Rights of Others: Aliens, Residents and Citizens* (Cambridge: Cambridge University Press, 2004)

Chétail, V., "Are Refugee Rights Human Rights? An Unorthodox Questioning of the Relations between Refugee Law and Human Rights Law" in Rubio-Marín, R. (Ed.), *Human Rights and Immigration* (Oxford: Oxford University Press, 2014): 19–72

Chimni, B. S., "From Resettlement to Involuntary Repatriation: Towards a Critical History of Durable Solutions to Refugee Problems" in *Refugee Survey Quarterly* 23(3) (2004): 55–73

Cohen, J. L., "Rights, Citizenship, and the Modern Form of the Social: Dilemmas of Arendtian Republicanism" in *Constellations* 3(2) (1996): 164–189

Curtis, K., *Our Sense of the Real: Aesthetic Experience and Arendtian Politics* (Ithaca, NY: Cornell University Press, 1999)

Dubernet, C., *The International Containment of Displaced Persons: Humanitarian Spaces Without Exit* (Aldershot: Ashgate, 2001)

Fuss, P., "Hannah Arendt's Concepts of Political Community" in Hill, M. A. (Ed.), *Hannah Arendt: The Recovery of the Public World* (New York: St Martin's Press, 1979): 157–176

Gündoğdu, A., "Perplexities of the Rights of Man: Arendt on the Aporias of Human Rights" in *European Journal of Political Theory* 11(1) (2011): 4–24

Gündoğdu, A., *Rightlessness in an Age of Rights: Hannah Arendt and the Contemporary Struggles of Migrants* (Oxford: Oxford University Press, 2015)

Hayden, P., "From Exclusion to Containment: Arendt, Sovereign Power, and Statelessness" in *Societies Without Borders* 3(2) (2008): 248–269

Hayden, P., *Political Evil in a Global Age: Hannah Arendt and International Theory* (London: Routledge, 2009)

Herzog, A., "Responsibility" in Hayden, P. (Ed.), *Hannah Arendt: Key Concepts* (Durham: Acumen, 2014): 185–195

Hill, M. A., "The Fictions of Mankind and the Stories of Men", in Hill, M. A. (Ed.), *Hannah Arendt: The Recovery of the Public World* (New York: St Martin's Press, 1979): 275–300

Hyndman, J., and Giles, W., "Waiting for What? The Feminization of Asylum in Protracted Situations" in *Gender, Place and Culture* 18(3) (2011): 361–379

Ingram, J. D., "What is a 'Right to Have Rights'? Three Images of the Politics of Human Rights" in *The American Political Science Review* 102(4) (2008): 401–416

Isaac, J., "Situating Hannah Arendt on Action and Politics" in *Political Theory* 21(3) (1993): 534–540

Isaac, J., "Oases in the Desert: Hannah Arendt on Democratic Politics" in *The American Political Science Review* 88(1) (1994): 156–168

Isaac, J., "A New Guarantee on Earth: Hannah Arendt on Human Dignity and the Politics of Human Rights" in *The American Political Science Review* 90(1) (1996): 61–73

Kesby, A., *The Right to Have Rights: Citizenship, Humanity and International Law* (Oxford: Oxford University Press, 2012)

Lindley, A. "Between a Protracted and a Crisis Situation: Policy Responses to Somali Refugees in Kenya" in *Refugee Survey Quarterly* 30(4) (2011): 14–49

Loescher, G., and Milner, J., *Protracted Refugee Situations: Domestic and International Security Implications*, Adelphi Paper No. 375 (London: Routledge, 2005)

Loescher, G. *et al.* (Eds), *Protracted Refugee Situations: Political, Human Rights and Security Implications* (Tokyo: United Nations University Press, 2008)

McCarthy, M. H., *The Political Humanism of Hannah Arendt* (Plymouth: Lexington Books, 2012)

Michelman, F., "Parsing 'A Right to Have Rights' " in *Constellations* 3(2) (1996): 200–208

Näsström, S., "The Right to Have Rights: Democratic, Not Political" in *Political Theory* 42(5) (2014): 543–568

Oudejans, N., "The Right to Have Rights as the Right to Asylum" in *Netherlands Journal of Legal Philosophy* 43(1) (2014): 7–26

Owens, P., "Reclaiming 'Bare Life'? Against Agamben on Refugees" in *International Relations* 23(4) (2010): 567–582

Owens, P., "Not Life but the World is at Stake: Hannah Arendt on Citizenship in the Age of the Social" in *Citizenship Studies* 16(2) (2012): 297–307

Parekh, S., "A Meaningful Place in the World: Hannah Arendt on the Nature of Human Rights" in *Journal of Human Rights* 3(1) (2004): 41–52

Parekh, S., *Hannah Arendt and the Challenge of Modernity: A Phenomenology of Human Rights* (London: Routledge, 2008)

Passerin d'Entrèves, M., *The Political Philosophy of Hannah Arendt* (London: Routledge, 1994)

Pitkin, H. F., "Justice: On Relating Private and Public" in *Political Theory* 9(3) (1981): 327–352

Rancière, J., "Who is the Subject of the Rights of Man?" in *The South Atlantic Quarterly* 103(2/3) (2004): 297–310

Schaap, A., "Enacting the Right to Have Rights: Jacques Rancière's Critique of Hannah Arendt" in *European Journal of Political Theory* 10(1) (2011): 22–45

Siddiqui, Y., "Reviewing the Application of the Cessation Clause of the 1951 Convention Relating to the Status of Refugees in Africa" in *Refugee Studies Centre Working Paper Series* 76 (2011): 1–52

UNHCR, "Statute of the Office of the United Nations High Commissioner for Refugees", annexed to *General Assembly Resolution: A/Res/428(V)*, access via: www.unhcr.org/3b66c39e1.html (last accessed 21 April 2017)

UNHCR, "Cessation of Refugee Status under Article 1C(5) and (6) of the 1951 Convention Relating to the Status of Refugees (the "Ceased Circumstances" Clauses)" *Guidelines on*

International Protection, HCR/GIP/03/03 (February 2003) access via: www.unhcr. org/3e637a202.pdf (last accessed 21 April 2017)

United Nations, "Status of Refugees and Stateless Persons – Memorandum by the Secretary General", ad hoc *Committee on Statelessness and Related Problems*, E/AC.32/5 (1950)

United Nations, *Convention Relating to the Status of Refugees* (United Nations Treaty Series Vol. 189, No. 2545) (1951): 138–220

Villa, D., *Arendt and Heidegger: The Fate of the Political* (Princeton, NJ: Princeton University Press, 1996)

Walsh, P., "Hannah Arendt on the Social" in Hayden, P. (Ed.), *Hannah Arendt: Key Concepts* (Durham: Acumen, 2014): 124–137

Wolin, S., "Democracy and the Political" in *Salmagundi* 60 (1983): 3–19

Xenos, N., "Refugees: The Modern Political Condition" in *Alternatives: Global, Local, Political* 18(4) (1993): 419–430

5 Making Oneself at Home in the World
Solutions to Refugees' Problems

The dual-track discussion in the previous chapter of the plight of refugees, and of 'world' and 'world alienation' posited that government protection – (re)gaining legal status or citizenship – should not be conflated as a matter of course with the establishment of a home in the world. By understanding the worldlessness and superfluity that refugees suffer as symptomatic of the world alienation characterising life in modernity for all, not just refugees, the 'right to have rights' can be understood as more than a right to citizenship within the nation-state. It is perhaps more accurately understood as a ground upon which to create a home in the world with others, where 'home', importantly, need not necessarily or only mean nation-state. The task that befalls us in this chapter is to reflect upon how we might conceptualise the building of such 'homes'.

The 'national order of things' characterising the 'refugee (as) problem' understands 'home' as an essentialised point on a map, a national territory to which the refugee 'naturally' belongs by birth, citizenship or ethnicity. As Malkki highlights, the assumption underlying such understandings is that the homeland, or country of origin, is "not only the normal but the ideal habitat for any person, the place where one fits in, and has an unproblematic culture and identity" (Malkki, 1995: 508). To speak of refugees in this context as 'uprooted' or 'homeless' is to imply that to leave a national community is automatically to lose one's identity, traditions and culture. While it is not my intention to suggest that this is never the case, there are perhaps two important points to be borne in mind. First, that such displacement and uprooting seem to occur at precisely the time when one is either no longer welcome in one's 'own' society, or when it has become "strange and frightening" due to war or other forms of violence, meaning that it is far from clear that returning to that society can so easily be understood as 'going home' (Malkki, 1995: 509; Den Boer, 2015). The second point is that it is only possible to rebuild or experience an identity, culture, traditions – a 'life-world' – in one's country of origin and nowhere else (Brun, 2001; Malkki, 1992); in other words, that homes are only ever given, never made. For the refugee regime, as we saw in Chapter 3, any choice of a new home by the refugee made on the basis of anything other than physical safety is illegitimate and leaves her open to being defined as an 'illegal immigrant', an 'economic migrant' in disguise, and thus not a 'genuine' refugee. The asylum country is only supposed to be a *temporary* haven until the refugee can 'return home'. The securitisation and externalisation of asylum that has come to characterise the attitude and specific policies towards refugees in many Western states, and the proliferation of camps throughout Africa and Asia, become, Malkki argues, naturalised and rendered reasonable by such functionalist visions of identity and home (Malkki, 1995: 509), and thus can in fact reinforce the worldlessness and superfluity experienced by the displaced. To (implicitly) deny that refugees can or should build new homes for themselves elsewhere than their country of origin is not only to deny agency, but is to reduce a 'home' to a function of legal status expressed as some physical (read, 'national') space. The problem for the international community and the refugee regime, therefore, is to *find places to put people* until such time as their legal status has been restored by their country of origin – i.e. until such time as their country of origin can be recognised by the international community as 'home' again.[1]

Understanding the plight of the refugee not in terms of this state-centric understanding of 'homelessness' – as loss of the state–citizen relationship and being outside of one's 'home' country – but as 'worldlessness', this chapter seeks to employ Arendt's understanding of the 'world', and how individuals come to be 'at home' in it, as an alternative frame of reference to the population management approach of the refugee regime and sovereign state. Building on Arendt's insight that to become displaced is to lose one's place in the world, in the sense of our lived experience and our sense of belonging to particular communities, this chapter investigates the potential of refugee protest, and the UK City of Sanctuary movement, as ways in which to address this problem. I reflect upon refugee protests as instances of performative rights-claiming, a practice which not only reveals the refugee as a political actor but also begins the work of building new 'worlds' to which to belong with others, through the mutual recognition of rights between those engaged in the protests. However, due to the dynamic nature of power relations and efforts by the state to reclaim the political ground from the refugee evident in these protests, these actions stand in need of greater support if refugees are to mount an effective challenge to their exclusion. It is necessary, therefore, to focus not only on the political action of these non-political subjects, but also on the role to be played by those already 'included' in the community in supporting such action. City of Sanctuary is explored as one such avenue of support. An examination of its activities, the role that refugees and 'asylum seekers'[2] play within it, and its focus on re-fashioning the city as a place of belonging for all those present within it, reveals the potential the movement possesses to alter what Markell (2010) refers to as the 'horizons of practical engagement' of citizens, so as to enable them, and perhaps prompt them, to act in solidarity with those claiming rights and inclusion. Doing so, it will be argued, is to take an important step, on the part of those already 'included' as well as those 'excluded', towards transfiguring, or modifying, the games of truth and power in which refugees and others find themselves governed, and in refashioning the very nature of the communities to which the right to have rights would correspond. In exploring refugee protest movements and the City of

Sanctuary movement I am neither constructing case studies, nor offering comprehensive examinations of these movements in the hope of isolating common characteristics, an 'essence' of refugee protest, or the 'defining' features that must typify any 'true' sanctuary movement. To attempt to do so would detract from the specificity that will inevitably characterise each movement. These movements are, rather, offered as illustrative examples of broader theoretical points, the individual characteristics and challenges of which are intended to prompt thinking rather than provide answers. Research into all three movements was primarily desk-based, drawing on the extensive public outreach material made available by the movements themselves, although my reflections on City of Sanctuary are also drawn from observing the activities of various groups involved in the movement and from observing meetings with the national organisation.

From the 'Outside': Refugee Protest

As the asylum system in the European Union has become ever more restrictive, protests by refugees, failed asylum seekers, and EU citizens acting in solidarity have grown in frequency (McGuaran and Hudig, 2014). The forms that such protests take, their size, duration, and focus are as varied as the individuals and groups initiating them, and the exact conditions in each state to which they are directed. Protest camps and marches have occurred in opposition to proposed legal changes relating to status, welfare provision, and access to due process rights, and in opposition to the deportation of specific individuals. Demonstrations against detention and deportation have been frequent occurrences, often triggered as acts of solidarity with inmates engaging in hunger strikes; and coordinated campaigns allied with NGOs working with and on behalf of refugees and asylum seekers have been directed at ending destitution, lobbying against proposed legislation, safeguarding access to support, and many other issues. The diversity of these protest movements renders a comprehensive account impossible, and so in what follows I reflect upon two protest movements in the heart of Europe – in Austria and in Germany.

On 24 November 2012, approximately 100 refugees, asylum seekers, and their supporters marched the 35 km from the refugee reception centre in Traiskirchen to the centre of Vienna, and erected a Refugee Protest Camp in front of the Votive Church in Sigmund Freud Park. The camp remained in the park until it was broken up by police and the inhabitants evicted on 28 December 2012, at which point the protestors were welcomed into the church itself to maintain their camp. At the beginning of March 2013, remaining protestors were invited by Cardinal Shönborn to move the camp into the Serviten Monastery, in Vienna's ninth district, where it remained until 30 October 2013 (Grzinic, 2013: 1–2). During the eleven months of sustained camping and protesting, the refugees and their supporters held a series of press conferences, engaged in hunger strikes when ignored by the Austrian authorities, and marched to, and demonstrated outside, the Ministry of the Interior, the Parliament building, and

UNHCR headquarters. The camps in the park, the church and the monastery were characterised by communal living, and featured regular workshops on human rights and collective action, talks by invited speakers, a protest song writing competition, and public demonstrations at which refugees related their experiences of persecution and detention. Deteriorating conditions of detention had provided the initial catalyst for the protests, but the refugees' demands went beyond improved detention conditions. They had two Urgent Demands and a series of broader Concretised Demands, arrived at after a series of discussions among the refugees during the first weeks of the protest. The Urgent Demands were that the refugees be granted the right to remain in Austria or, at the very least, to have their fingerprints deleted from EURODAC should Austria decide to deport them; and that they be granted permission to work, wishing to sustain themselves rather than rely on the state (Refugee Protest Camp Vienna, 2012a). The six Concretised Demands were as follows: basic support for asylum seekers in Austria, an end to enforced transfer; access to employment, educational institutions and social security; a halt to all deportations associated with the EU's Dublin regulations; the establishment of an independent review and appeal authority for asylum applications; and the recognition of the validity of socio-economic motives behind refugee flight (Refugee Protest Camp Vienna, 2012b).

The marches and demonstrations that became a regular feature of the Protest Camp featured a series of chants, including 'No borders! No nations! Stop Deportations!', 'We are here, we will stay, we won't give our rights away!', and one in particular served as a mantra of sorts for the movement: 'We demand our rights!' The Refugee Protest Camp sparked marches and demonstrations in solidarity all over Europe (Refugee Protest Camp Vienna, 2013b). However, while the Refugee Protest Camp was supported by Austrian citizens, NGOs and activists from elsewhere in the EU, it was organised and carried out by the refugees themselves, and this was a message they were keen to impart to their supporters:

> We ourselves, the refugees, make the demonstration, and we are the ones who want it. It is our fight. We thank everybody for their help, but we don't allow anybody to use us. This is a self-organised struggle of and by refugees, one that needs your support, your presence on the street....
>
> (Grzinic, 2013: 1)

While the refugees were able to rely on Austrian citizens acting in solidarity at their marches, and in the camp, they ultimately were unable to achieve the policy changes they sought. The Refugee Protest Camp no longer exists as a camp, and some of the original protestors have been deported, but self-organised refugee protest continues in Austria under the name of Refugee Protest Camp Vienna.

Refugee protests in Germany have many similarities with those in Austria, namely in the use of protest camps, similar slogans, and the nature of the demands, and they began in earnest at roughly the same time.[3] But there are a few features of the movement in Germany that warrant special attention. In

September 2012, March 2013, and April/May 2015, the refugee protest camp movement based in Berlin, called Refugee Tent Action, was accompanied by Refugee Liberation Bus Tours. The broader protest movement and the Bus Tours demand the abolition of the 'Residenzpflicht, Lager, and Deportation' system in Germany. The *Residenzpflicht* is a mandatory residence system whereby asylum seekers in Germany may not leave the district in which they are registered with the immigration authority office without permission, for any reason. They must apply, and pay, for permits to travel outside of this area. While the law governing this system was amended from 1 January 2015, to apply only to the first three months of an asylum claim, asylum seekers in Germany still have little or no real freedom of movement. Asylum seekers are housed in reception centres for the first three months of their claim, and are then moved to collective accommodation centres, which the refugees refer to as 'Lagers' (camps), and protests and demonstrations outside of these centres have become an ever more frequent occurrence (Linke, 2013). The Bus Tours have mobilised hundreds of refugees and their supporters and travelled to dozens of towns and cities across Germany. When the first Bus Tour arrived back in Berlin it was met with a solidarity protest of approximately 6,000 people (Linke, 2013). At each stop on the tour, the protestors set up a camp and hold a demonstration outside the reception or accommodation centre, and hold informal gatherings to connect asylum seekers and refugees resident in the area with local social and political groups, and to offer information on the campaign.

Beyond the placards and chants accompanying each stop of 'Kein Mensch ist Illegal!' ('No One is Illegal!'), and calling for an end to deportations and detention, the Bus Tour, as a *mobile* demonstration, is both a call for, and manifestation of, the right to freedom of movement in a system in which this right has become a commodity that increasingly destitute asylum seekers must pay for. Indeed, the asylum seeker participants on the Tour are violating the *Residenzpflicht* by travelling outside of their registration area, and so risk arrest and imprisonment just for participating in the protest. The organisers and members of the Bus Tour see it as an expressly political movement, seeking to build a network of asylum seekers, refugees, and other activists within Germany, but also as a movement oriented beyond Germany to the EU as a whole:

> We organised this Bus Tour because the situation of refugees in Europe has gotten worse.... The Bus Tour wants to give self-organised refugee groups the possibility to exchange about the protest and about the situation of refugees in their area and develop a political strategy together.
>
> (Refugee Tent Action, 2015)

The protestors on the Bus Tour and in the various camps of Refugee Tent Action link their protest against local conditions as exemplars of EU policy to the global, and colonial, policies of Western states in general, challenging the presumption that socio-economic reasons cannot be grounds for asylum. The protestors demand recognition of *all* asylum seekers as political refugees, arguing that all reasons, including the socio-economic, compelling one to flee one's country are, ultimately, political. A message often heard at the protests is that the poverty of the countries from which the refugees have fled is due to their exploitation by the countries to which they flee (Linke, 2013). Refugee and 'asylum seeker' activists in Germany arrested for violating the *Residenzpflicht*, or other restrictive laws, have taken to releasing statements on social media sites to draw attention to these broader socio-economic policies within which they frame their protest. More than merely an accusation, these messages invoke a right to remain in Germany, and other EU states, and a responsibility on the part of these states to accept them and treat them with equality and dignity, defying the simplistic distinction between 'there', where 'they' belong, and 'here', where 'we' belong.

Protest as Rights-Claiming: The Refugee as Political Agent

Several scholars have begun to analyse protest movements by irregular migrants and the non-status (e.g. Ataç *et al.*, 2017; Borren, 2008; Erensu, 2016; Johnson, 2012 and 2015; Nyers and Rygiel, 2012), including as instances of performative rights-claiming (Gündoğdu, 2015; McNevin, 2011). To say that rights-claiming is a performative practice, Zivi explains, is to say that the act of claiming a right is itself a practice which *does* something. In making a rights claim, claimants are "doing more than accurately (or perhaps inaccurately) representing a pre-existing moral, legal or political reality" in regard to the particular right or set of rights in question (Zivi, 2012: 8). This is because speaking is a social practice through which we both represent and shape, reflect and constitute the world in which we live. To say, then, that refugees demanding the right to work is an act of performative rights-claiming is to move beyond the question of whether, as a matter of legal or political fact, they do or do not possess this right, to the question of what they are *doing* in the act of claiming it (Zivi, 2012: 8). Through the act of claiming rights, the protesting refugees gather together to create a space of appearance, sustained by the power created through their action in concert, in pursuit of a common goal. In other words, they act *politically*, and become political actors rather than humanitarian objects, and they begin to create a 'world' between themselves.

The protesting refugees in Austria and Germany made their demands explicitly by invoking human rights. They demanded recognition of specific rights, and framed their demands within the language of the Universal Declaration of Human Rights. The various mantras of the movements, such as 'We demand our rights!' position the rights being demanded as those the protestors already possess: 'We demand *our* rights!' Rather than being a case of linguistic confusion on the part of non-native English speakers, this is what Butler refers to as a 'performative contradiction'. When a disenfranchised group make a universal demand, she explains, they lay claim to something from which they have been constitutively excluded. At that moment, the limiting reach of the 'universal' is divulged and challenged (Lloyd, 2008: 36–37). By demanding Convention rights when lacking the status that would entitle them to those rights, but doing so by invoking the UDHR (rights which their human status is supposed to guarantee), the protestors draw attention to the injustice of being denied something that is supposed to be theirs. To draw attention to the injustice of their exclusion is to reveal that the 'universal' upon which these rights depend – human status – is not in fact, in its present configuration, a universal at all. The performative contradiction of demanding *their* rights draws attention to the extent to which the universal – human – rests on the particular and exclusionary – legal status – precisely in order to challenge this exclusion.

The political nature of these acts of rights-claiming emerges clearly in the physical and spatial aspects of the rights claim (Ataç, 2016). The mobile demonstration of the Bus Tour in Germany can be seen as a concrete manifestation of the right to freedom of movement that the *Residenzpflicht* system denies to asylum seekers. In openly violating the laws restricting movement, the protestors are not simply violating the law, but exposing the law's complicity in the denial of rights to those who arrived in Germany seeking the protection of those very rights. The refugees themselves recognise the complicity of the law in the denial of their human rights:

> The conditions in which refugees live are excluding ... because states with economic and nationalist interest are capable to write laws against refugees and migrants which violate human rights. The same human rights that they have written and signed: the prohibition of freedom of movement, the banning of the right to free choice of residence and the banning of social participation, for example, participation in elections, etc., which have become law in the form of residential obligation/*Residenzpflicht*, camps/*Lager*, and deportation. This is the open contradiction to human rights. This means that a refugee and/or migrant who is not from here has not the same human rights as a citizen of this country.
>
> (Refugee Tent Action, 2014)

As Butler and Spivak assert, "to exercise a freedom and to assert an equality precisely in relation to an authority that would preclude both is to show how freedom and equality can and must move beyond their positive articulation" (2011: 67). In Arendtian terms, the protestors enact, or manifest, a principle – freedom and equality – in innovative and unexpected ways, and thus transform the principles themselves (Cane, 2014: 69). Freedom and equality are not simply principles framing the interaction and rights of already recognised members of a community, but are claimed by those yet to be recognised as also theirs 'by right'.

In a similar manner, the asylum seekers protesting in public parks in Austria appropriated a public space (both physical and symbolic) in gathering together and camping, demonstrating and marching. In gathering together in the park, the refugees and their supporters created a public political space out of a public recreational space, through both their presence and their activities. The space of appearance, Arendt reminds us, becomes manifest, and is sustained, whenever individuals gather together in the manner of speech and action. Collective action "reconfigures the materiality" of public space (Butler, 2011: 1) – a park ceases to be a park and becomes a protest camp in which those who lack the formal right to act politically nevertheless do so. Importantly, rather than seeking permission from the authorities to camp in the park, or to protest outside official buildings or detention centres, the refugees *appropriated* the space. In marching to Parliament, demanding to meet with Ministers, moving around the country of their own accord, and in demanding rights, the refugees were engaging in actions usually associated with citizens, and certainly actions we would usually classify as 'political'. They were acting *as if* they were members of the polity of which they were making demands for rights (cf. Isin and Nielsen, 2008). To make a rights claim is, thus, to engage in an activity *with* others, in which previously marginalised individuals take part in the practice of speaking and acting in public and to create new forms of political subjectivity. As Butler explains, those who are excluded from existing polities may be 'unreal' to those who seek to monopolise the forms of reality, and yet, as these brief examples have shown, even after the public sphere has been "defined through their exclusion", and even after they themselves have been defined as non-political and voiceless, they act, and they act together (Butler, 2011: 4); they appear in public and reveal their unique perspectives on the world. In Arendtian terms, in coming together and claiming rights, refugees, asylum seekers, and their supporters create a public realm sustained by power within which they act and speak with each other, a public realm in which they *appear* to each other. Or, to put it in Foucauldian terms, they engage in 'counter-conduct', and thus exercise freedom. Implicit in Foucault's understanding of power, as the capacity to act upon the actions of others, is the possibility of resistance. Power, Foucault states, can only function between subjects so long as they are free, so long as they are capable of acting differently (Foucault, HS: 95). The lack of prior authorisation, the lack of formal inclusion in the wider polity, does not definitively prevent them from acting and speaking together since action, for Arendt, is *ontologically rooted* in the fact of natality. Natality, the fact that human beings are themselves beginnings, and thus capable of manifesting that beginning in action and speech with others (Arendt, HC: 177), is what enables individuals to act; to insert themselves through word and deed into the human world, thereby forging relationships with others (becoming recognised as belonging to the common world), in which they reveal themselves as distinct 'whos', with unique perspectives on the world in which they act, rather than merely 'whats'. Foucault appears to echo this position in support of a lack of pre-requisite permission on the part of anyone to speak and act politically. In his statement on the solidarity movement in support of refugees from Vietnam he asserts that the right of those involved to speak is constituted precisely because those involved appoint themselves (Foucault, EWP: 474–475). This is not, however, to claim that such action is easy, or lacking in risk and danger for those involved. Indeed, the protestors took great risk in making themselves visible, talking openly about their lack of status and their intentions to remain in Austria and Germany, and in provoking the state. Many others similarly situated do remain silent, afraid to speak up, and so the constraints against the political action of these 'non-political' subjects are very real. And yet, we need not go so far as Agamben, and others, in their analyses of the space of exception occupied by these marginalised subjects, and assert that such subjects are, quite literally, *incapable* of such action. In the face of a structure and regime that constructs them as voiceless victims, or anomalies to be managed, they do, nevertheless, take the initiative and become, even if just for that brief time of protest, political subjects.

But therein, we might posit, lies the problem. Only for the time the protest lasts are they political subjects. Once their protest is over, if no significant changes are guaranteed, would they not be relegated to the very same condition of rightlessness from which they rose up? The short answer may well be "yes". It is by no means certain that any of these efforts, or any future protests, will be 'successful'. As Butler rightly highlights in her analysis of the performativity of irregular migrants in the US, it is not that everything is accomplished by language, by the act of claiming rights: "it's not as if 'I can say I'm free and then my performative utterance makes me free'" (Butler and Spivak, 2011: 68). The act of claiming rights, and manifesting oneself as a political actor in doing so, is not sufficient for the enjoyment of that right, or for the recognition of the polity of your speech as political or your presence as legitimate. Arendt herself states as much in her critique of human rights treaties. The performative rights-claiming perspective does not claim that these acts are *sufficient*. But it does allow us to see the transformative *potential* of this kind of action, rather than focusing solely on the success or failure to achieve state recognition of the specific rights being claimed. In other words, it allows us to shift our focus away from the status-giver and onto the rights-agent and the *meaning* of her action. The assertion of a right, on a Foucauldian understanding, "functions both to remake and contest relations with others but at the same time establishes a particular relation to, and conception of, the rights holder herself" (Golder, 2015: 57) The rights claim, in other words, presents a challenge to those who encounter it. As Arendt writes in her analysis of Kafka's *The Castle*, although K.'s quest for rights and an ordinary life within the village ultimately failed,

> the very fight he has put up to obtain the few basic things which society owes to men has opened the eyes of the villagers, or at least some of them. His story, his behaviour, has taught them both that human rights are worth fighting for and that the rule of the castle is not divine law, and, consequently, can be attacked.
>
> (Arendt, JW: 295)

But, just as the authorities at the castle frustrate K.'s attempts to officially belong to the village "using a thousand and one excuses", so too can the state respond negatively to the challenges posed by the rights claims and concerted action and speech of refugees. States, and other regime actors such as UNHCR, have responded in a variety of ways to refugee protest, ranging from refusals to engage with protestors on the terms of their protest and employing the coercive arms of the state to break up protests, to a range of discursive tactics to shift the frame or terms of the debate and attempt to re-silence those engaging in protest. In the Austrian case, for example, government officials refused to engage in direct talks with the protesting refugees and framed the problem as one of slow status determination, rather than addressing the concrete problems of exclusion from work, education, social services, and the lack of free movement around Austria, created by the asylum system itself. The Austrian President, in a letter to one of the protestors, rhetorically removed the asylum system itself from focus, emphasising that the authorities are doing everything they can "within the boundaries of the prevailing law" to ameliorate the situation (Refugee Protest Camp Vienna, 2013a). This refusal to address the substantive issues of the refugee protests and attempt to shift the frame of reference to the bureaucratic procedures of refugee status determination can be interpreted as a strategic move by the state to reclaim the grounds of legitimate action: persons without legal status in Austria may not question Austrian law itself, and the state will not even recognise challenges posed by such individuals as challenges to the law. The state refused to engage with the protestors as political subjects, emphasising instead concern for their health and a desire to ameliorate their situation – the hunger strike, rather than the politico-legal situation they find themselves in as a result of Austrian asylum procedures. Moreover, insulating the asylum system itself from challenge, the state maintained a separation from the political sphere of what, for the refugees, is a political issue, and maintained it purely as a problem of slow and inefficient bureaucratic procedure. The eviction of the protestors from the park, removing them from the public eye and public space, is an additional tool – an 'erasing' tactic – that the state can employ to maintain the distribution of power relations.

Rather than being a cause for despair, what such reactions reveal is the *dynamic nature* of the relationship between those who seize rights – the protesting refugees – and those who 'grant' them, or, to use Foucault's terms, between the governors and the governed, over the nature of the (power) relationship itself. The government of men, Foucault explains, is a practice that is not merely imposed on the governed, at least not totally and definitively, but by "action between", by a series of conflicts, agreements, discussions, and reciprocal concessions (Foucault, BB: 12). By acting on this 'transactional field', those engaged in 'counter-conducts' – the protestors and government ministers – act on their respective positioning as governors or governed, and seek to modify the 'game' "through which the truth of the governed subject is produced" (Cadman, 2010: 549). Such counter-conducts bring into relief the regime of truth through which subjects are known and acted upon, and, by problematising the way in which they are governed, they also problematise their subjective identities as players in these games of truth (Cadman, 2010: 550). Power relations, as we saw in Chapter 3, can never be transcended or escaped, but this does not mean that they are totalising in a negative sense. Precisely because they are *relations*, they can be modified, and this is what the actions of the protesting refugees seek to accomplish. To make the demand on freedom is already to *begin* its exercise. To

ask for its legitimation is to announce the gap between its exercise and its realisation and to put both into public discourse in such a way that the gap is seen
and can be mobilised (Butler and Spivak, 2011: 68). If rights, as Arendt argues,
are recognised claims of agents within political communities, and to be rightless
is to be deprived of such a community and so be deprived of the relations of
recognition and reciprocity which guarantee the effective exercise of such rights,
then rights-claiming can be seen as the performative activation of a sense of
shared collective responsibility, of recognition, and a re-constituted web of relationships, or world. However, the key to the guarantee of rights, for Arendt, is
mutual recognition. The act of claiming is a necessary first step, but it cannot on
its own achieve the recognition of others. For this, they are reliant on the
response of the community to which their claim is directed. And it is to such
communities that our attention now turns.

From the 'Inside': City of Sanctuary and Remaking Cities

The asylum system in the UK has undergone a series of profound changes in the
past two decades. The Immigration and Asylum Act 1999 introduced a dispersal
system for asylum applicants in need of housing support for the duration of their
claim. If, after the initial screening interview, an asylum seeker is not detained,
she may apply to the Home Office for housing support. Housing is offered on a
'no choice' basis in local authorities in one of a number of dispersal zones, to
'spread the burden' of the housing and support of asylum seekers away from
London and the south-east (Stewart, 2012; Robinson *et al.*, 2003). In April 2000
the government entered into contracts with local authorities to house dispersed
asylum seekers in 'hard-to-let' social housing and in private sub-contracted
rentals. This led to the emergence of an uneven geography of asylum provision,
and a political economy of dispersion across the UK (Darling, 2015). Since 2011
the provision of housing has been contracted out in its entirety to private companies, including Serco and G4S. The dispersal policy has received criticism
from many quarters. Many see it as part of a wider range of punitive policies
seeking to deter asylum seekers from the UK (Bloch and Schuster, 2005), and
attention has been drawn to the negative effects of the policy on asylum seekers,
such as social exclusion and harassment. Dispersal has met with opposition from
host cities, fed, in large part, by an inflammatory media portrayal of asylum
seekers as illegal immigrants using asylum as a means to circumvent migration
controls, as unworthy burdens on social services, and as threats to 'community
cohesion' (Darling, 2015). It is in this context that, in 2005 in Sheffield, the City
of Sanctuary movement began.

City of Sanctuary is an idea, a formal movement, and an informal coalition of
practice. It began as a local movement oriented towards (re)creating Sheffield as
a city of welcome, safety, and inclusion for those seeking asylum, and has, over
the past twelve years, grown into a national coalition of over eighty towns and
cities across the UK and Ireland, each with their own local City of Sanctuary
initiative. As an *idea*, City of Sanctuary seeks to develop and foster a 'culture of

welcome' in towns and cities across the country, with the hope of influencing national asylum policy "through the bottom-up process of cultural change" (Barnett and Bhogal, 2010: 86). As a *formal movement*, the recognition of a place as an official City of Sanctuary involves gaining resolutions of support from local groups and organisations from a variety of sectors (not only the 'refugee sector'), involving local refugee communities in the movement, achieving the support of the City Council or other local authority, and producing a strategy for the greater inclusion of refugees and asylum seekers within the city (Darling and Squire, 2013: 192–193). There is a national organisation, established at the request of the local groups, to facilitate greater collaboration and communication across the country. As an *informal coalition of practice*, City of Sanctuary operates as an umbrella under which existing organisations, groups, and initiatives can come together to share best practice and ideas, to support each other in efforts to include refugees and asylum seekers in their activities, to provide volunteering opportunities to asylum seekers and refugees, and to intervene in local media and politics to change local attitudes to asylum as a moral and political issue.

The spatial and relational nature of the politics of the movement has been of particular interest to political geographers. Darling has characterised City of Sanctuary as being an outward-looking, place-based rather than place-bound movement (Darling, 2010). The focus of each City of Sanctuary initiative is the city or town in which it works, seeking to build relationships between different residents of the city in order to change the 'culture' of the city towards asylum politics. But, while each movement is focused on its own city, it is also oriented outwards, towards the national framing of asylum policy, and globally, in seeking to foreground through its activities "questions of responsibility for the 'stranger without' as well as the 'stranger within'" (Darling, 2010: 131–132). The work of City of Sanctuary cannot completely escape the statist logic of asylum and immigration, but the focus on re-creating the city anew as a place of meaningful belonging for all who inhabit it, for however short a time and regardless of status, makes City of Sanctuary a potentially fruitful example of how we might *begin* to re-imagine the communities of belonging to which the right to have rights could correspond. The initiative in each city is different, but there are three inter-related themes which unite the different groups across the network: testimony, countering isolation, and building relationships.

Testimony, Isolation, and Relationships

Opening up spaces for a different narrative of asylum in the UK is central to City of Sanctuary's aims, and so providing opportunities for refugees to tell their stories is a key concern for the movement in each town and city. Dedicated events at which those seeking asylum can tell their stories of displacement and their experiences of coming to the UK – outside of the hierarchical 'economy of truth' of the formal asylum process – and for those local residents engaging with the movement to share their stories, provide opportunities for people to get to know refugees as individuals and not simply as victims, and play an equally important reflexive role in building a culture of welcome and hospitality.[4] In February 2009, for example, Bradford held a "Stories of Sanctuary" event at which refugees from Iran, Congo, Nigeria, and Pakistan told their stories of persecution, exile, and their efforts to make a new life in the UK. The event was attended by around 120 people from Bradford, including other asylum seekers, who expressed to the organisers how helpful it had been to them to hear the stories of others. Leeds City of Sanctuary provides training in media and public speaking for refugees and asylum seekers who would like to tell their stories and engage with the public, and encourages local businesses and organisations to contact them about including refugee speakers at sanctuary events. Coventry City of Sanctuary organises interactive workshops as part of the City Council's annual Peace Month, which have included short film screenings and roundtable discussions with migrants about their experiences of coming to Coventry, and exhibitions on the impact of the arms trade on African history and the conflicts from which many refugees have fled. The interactive nature of these events enables those attending to discuss what they have heard, how it affects them, and what they can do moving forward. Theatre productions have proven a creative and effective way to engage audiences in a more reflexive way. In 2011, a group of failed asylum seekers in Glasgow put on a play, entitled *The Roundabout*, about the frustrating and angering experience of waiting for status, and the obstacles continually put in their way while trying to navigate the legal and social maze of appealing Home Office determinations. Rather than passively watching the play, the audience were made participants in the scenes, being challenged at a series of intervals with questions such as 'what do you think?' and 'what are your experiences with destitution?' These questions sparked debate among the audience members, which continued with small-group discussions as the play ended. Many of the audience members related during these discussions how uncomfortable they had felt at first, but how they had been drawn in as the play progressed, and made them reflect upon the asylum seeking process and the challenges it poses to those seeking asylum (Bagelman, 2013).

By finding creative ways to include refugees in the life of the city and the everyday activities of a wide variety of organisations, City of Sanctuary actively seeks to counter the isolation that characterises the lives of many refugees and asylum seekers in the UK. Beyond this inclusion in everyday activities, the movement also seeks to counter isolation at the physical/spatial and official levels, through the 'visual production of welcome', and through Meet & Greet, and visiting initiatives at local sites at which national asylum policy manifests itself. When City of Sanctuary began in Sheffield, the organisers developed a series of visual tools to help 'mark' the city as a welcoming place, to reassure those arriving in the city, and sign-posting places where they would find support, advice and welcome. They produced welcome signs for organisations that had pledged their support to display in their windows, and a series of coasters designed to question dominant myths about asylum, which were distributed to local pubs, and council offices (Darling, 2010: 129). Visual markers of welcome and support can take on real significance for refugees in an environment in which a threatening and fear-inducing public discourse has been accompanied by equally hostile visual markers. In 2013, for example, the Home Office trialled two new immigration enforcement advertising campaigns. The first involved a fleet of vans mounted with billboards deployed through six London boroughs 'encouraging' those in the UK illegally to voluntarily self-deport or face arrest. The second involved posters featuring the statement "Is life here hard? Going home is simple" in UKBA (now UKVI) reporting centres in Glasgow and London, centres which asylum seekers must visit on a regular basis. Nyers, in his work on the sanctuary movement in Canada, highlights the negative impact that the visual production of 'unwelcome' can have on those without secure status trying to access services. Posters by Citizenship and Immigration Canada, in agencies, hospitals and other organisations, have acted as visual cues to memories of border experiences, discouraging individuals from accessing services, including those to which they are legally entitled (Nyers, 2008: 168).

Beyond the visual production of welcome, City of Sanctuary groups across the UK have instituted Meet & Greet schemes and visiting programmes to counter isolation. Loughborough is the site of the East Midlands Reporting Centre, to which asylum seekers housed in Derby, Leicester and Nottingham must report on a weekly, bi-weekly, or monthly basis. The City of Sanctuary group there has a dedicated group of volunteers who travel to the reporting centre every week and meet with those reporting and take them for coffee or lunch. The reporting process can be particularly stressful for asylum seekers as many worry that they could be arrested and detained at any time given the frequent changes in policies affecting the asylum process and the difficulties posed by language. Many new arrivals have not yet had the opportunity to orient themselves in their new town and so the group offers much needed advice, friendly faces, and sympathetic ears. Leeds has an Asylum Seeker Support Service, which runs a Befriending Scheme in which trained refugee and local resident volunteers are matched with asylum seekers, failed asylum seekers, and refugees who seek support from LASSS. Volunteers visit asylum seekers in their homes every week and show them where various services in Leeds are located, accompany them to appointments with lawyers and doctors, translate letters and documents, or just talk with them, go out and have fun, and just be a friend – whatever the individual feels that (s)he needs.

Such befriending schemes are not the only way in which City of Sanctuary seeks to build relationships between different residents of the city. Great emphasis is placed on providing volunteering opportunities within the organisations involved with the movement, and the formal network itself. The Terminus Initiative, in Sheffield, was started in 2002 by four churches working in a deprived area of the city called Low Edges, and is a well-established example, and now part of the City of Sanctuary network. The Initiative includes a café and a healthy living centre, run by volunteers, and has actively sought to include refugees who come to live on the estate into these activities by establishing a Conversation Club where women, of any background and status, can come and practise their English in a friendly and safe environment, and by encouraging refugees to volunteer in the café. As one of the ministers involved in the project explains, in addition to providing work experience, the project emerged out of, and advances engagement between, 'established residents' and new arrivals (Squire, 2011: 297). Another supporting organisation in Sheffield offering volunteering opportunities is a local radio station, Sheffield Live! 93.2 FM. The station offers free training in radio journalism, making a particular effort to engage with young people who have no formal education. The station manager opened up this training to refugees in Sheffield, and when they have completed their training they have the opportunity to present their own radio show, and some of the initial volunteers help to train new arrivals and local young people (Barnett and Bhogal, 2010: 18). City of Sanctuary itself also seeks to incorporate asylum seekers and refugees into its organisation, both nationally and locally: five seats on the national Board of Trustees are reserved for refugees and asylum seekers, and the recently revamped website for the network was created by an asylum seeker volunteer. Moreover, each town or city working towards 'official' City of Sanctuary status needs to incorporate refugees and asylum seekers into their local working groups. Not all supporting organisations are able to offer volunteering opportunities, but whatever other activities they are able to open up to refugees and asylum seekers, the important point for City of Sanctuary is that they enable those involved to establish relationships with each other and with people that they may otherwise never have met, despite living in the same city. The most effective way to achieve this is for each organisation to decide for themselves how they can best support, welcome and include those seeking asylum, rather than the City of Sanctuary group dictating this to them. Examples of this have typically included local football teams, athletics clubs, theatre groups, churches, mosques, synagogues and other religious communities, and youth clubs.

Cities of Sanctuary as 'Worlds'

In 'We Refugees' and *The Origins of Totalitarianism*, Arendt highlighted the two primary losses suffered by refugees in being forced to flee their state: the loss of government protection, and the loss of their homes. In losing their homes, the refugees lost the "familiarity of daily life", the "social texture within which they established for themselves a distinct place in the world" (Arendt, OT: 293). They lost their occupations, and with them the confidence that they were of some use in this world; and they lost their language, "the naturalness of reactions, the simplicity of gestures, the unaffected expression of feelings" (Arendt, JW: 264). The asylum process has been characterised as one of temporal limbo, isolation and uncertainty. The Home Office endeavours to make decisions on asylum claims within six months of a claim being filed, but it has become increasingly common for applicants to wait up to nine years for a final decision and any form of legal status (Bagelman, 2013: 56). The activities of various City of Sanctuary groups surveyed above each contribute, in their own way, to the ability of refugees to begin to repair the "rupture of their private lives", and weave a new social texture within which they can carve out a distinct place for themselves in the world again.

'Asylum seekers', and 'failed asylum seekers', are legally precluded from paid employment while their claim is processed or deportation arranged, leaving them entirely dependent on the meagre cash support from the National Asylum Support Service. This support is, at the time of writing, £36.95 per week for a single adult, in cash, for an individual with a claim on-going, and a similar sum for 'failed asylum seekers', but as a payment card accepted at a restricted number of outlets. By establishing links with local businesses, charities and community groups to coordinate and facilitate volunteering opportunities for asylum seekers, City of Sanctuary offers a means of reconnecting, even if only for a few hours or days a week, with a sense of regularity of life that Arendt states labour affords the individual (Gündoğdu, 2015: 135), and therefore a means of coping with the logic of waiting built into the asylum system, even if such opportunities cannot escape, or mount a sustained challenge to, the dependency on others for income. Volunteering within the community presents opportunities for refugees to establish links, build relationships, and feel a part of their new community. In a study on asylum seeker perspectives of belonging in Greater Manchester, Darling and Healey highlighted the importance of volunteering on the part of the asylum seekers they interviewed. Irfan, from India, for example, volunteers with a range of different groups in the city – asylum seekers, the homeless, the LGBT community – to address issues of exclusion, marginalisation and hate crimes. As a part of Refugee Week in 2011 he organised and chaired a 'No to Cashlessness' conference at the University of Salford, attended by 250 people from the city and a variety of organisations (Darling and Healey, 2012: 24). Through his volunteer and advocacy work, and organising events such as the conference, Irfan developed a sense of his own worth to the community. Sofia, a 'failed asylum seeker' interviewed in the same study, also spoke of the sense of belonging she developed despite her status as a failed asylum seeker, through the support she offers in her voluntary work to other women seeking asylum.

Volunteering opportunities can help to counter the isolation and inertia that refugees often feel while waiting for legal status. The attempts that City of Sanctuary groups make to mark the city as a place of welcome and inclusion can also play an important role here. In a particularly poignant remark in 'We Refugees', Arendt draws attention to the role that a hostile environment can play in adding to the considerable weight that comes with lacking legal status when she explains that:

> Once we could buy our food and ride on the subway without being told we were undesirable. We have become a little hysterical since newspapermen started detecting us and telling us publicly to stop being disagreeable when shopping for milk and bread ... We try the best we can to fit into a world where you have to be sort of politically minded when you buy your food.
>
> (Arendt, JW: 269)

In a social and political climate hostile to immigrants and suspicious of refugees, and in which specific documents alert others to the status of an individual as an asylum seeker, knowing that there are places in the city where you can go and feel welcome, safe and included can have important psychological effects. For those newly arrived in the city, the signs and posters that organisations support-ive of City of Sanctuary display, and the information provided by Meet & Greet groups at the reporting centres, provide the sign-posts to a welcome they may not find otherwise. This can be especially helpful given that City of Sanctuary seeks to work with groups and organisations not already focused on refugees – groups where new arrivals might expect to feel welcomed anyway. The conver-sation clubs that have sprung up across many of the cities in the network provide opportunities to meet new people and make friends, but also enable those for whom English is not their first language to learn and develop their language skills, gradually breaking down a significant barrier to inclusion and accessing services.

Beyond these more practical areas of focus of City of Sanctuary, the 'crea-tive' aspects of its activities can be important and helpful to refugees in carving out a place for themselves in a new environment. Dedicated art exhibitions, poetry evenings, and museum exhibits enable refugees to display their work and, in Arendtian terms, make a distinct contribution to the human artifice we share with others. Museum exhibits held by Sheffield City of Sanctuary actively sought to show the links and relationships of refugees past and present with the city, thereby including them in the life of the city through the pieces they created for the exhibit (Squire and Darling, 2013: 67). Theatre productions in particular have potential not only as an outlet for creativity, but as a way for refugees to work through their experiences, share them with others, and be encountered as actors, interpreters, musicians and comedians, in addition to being refugees, and, in McNevin's words, "become political" (McNevin, 2010). The community theatre project she examines was developed and written over the course of a series of workshops designed to build the confidence of the refugees to share their often deeply tragic stories with each other and with strangers. The produc-tion's narratives of what it means to be a refugee were presented as counter-narratives to the 'queue-jumper', 'illegal immigrant' and 'security threat' of those hostile to refugees, but also to the narrative of the 'damaged' or 'broken' victim to be saved by well-meaning idealists and humanitarians, many of whom were in the audience (McNevin, 2010: 154–155). While focused on a project in Australia, McNevin's insights into the potential of theatre to be a public stage in the (Arendtian) political sense of the term, through the transformation from humanitarian subjects to spokespersons for themselves effected by the act of per-forming, are useful also for understanding the theatre projects supported by City of Sanctuary.

All of City of Sanctuary's activities are, ultimately, aimed at challenging the discourse on asylum in the UK, not only in Westminster but also on the streets, and in the pubs and workplaces of the city, by establishing relationships between refugees and ordinary residents of the city. And so, encounters with refugees, in many forms, and the testimony of those who have been displaced, those who have come to know the displaced, and those whose opinions have been changed through these encounters, is central to the movement. Storytelling is an activity of particular *political* significance for Arendt, and can thus help draw out the connections between the activities of City of Sanctuary and acts of rights-claiming on the part of refugees, and provide a different framework, or narrative, through which to approach responding to the problems faced by the displaced. It is to the link between storytelling, understanding, action, and the world, that I now turn.

The Interdependence of Action: Outside/Inside

Storytelling, or narrative, is, for Arendt, a uniquely human experience, or activity, that straddles the *vita contemplativa* and the *vita activa*. While Arendt dealt with these two realms of human existence in separate works, *The Life of the Mind* and *The Human Condition*, she never considered them to be strictly separate from each other in reality. They are dependent upon each other and both, ultimately, make the earth into a world for human beings and allow us to orient, or make ourselves at home, in it. We saw in the previous chapter that, being born into the world as strangers, we need to engage in various activities to make ourselves at home in it, namely labour, work, action, and speech. Further, we have seen that it is possible to be made a stranger to the world once more – to become worldless – through refusing to partake in these activities, or by being denied the possibility to partake in them. Speaking and acting with others are crucial for a sense of reality and, hence, worldliness, dependent as these activities are on the presence of and dialogue with others. But, to reconcile ourselves to the world in which we must carve a distinct place, and to be able to act and speak with others in pursuit of this, we need to engage in understanding.

Understanding, Arendt states, is "the other side of action" and is that form of cognition by which "acting men eventually can come to terms with what irrevocably happened and be reconciled to what unavoidably exists" (Arendt, EU: 321–322). Action is by nature boundless and unpredictable. The actor cannot control the consequences of her actions, and, moreover, will inevitably be the sufferer of the actions of others. Understanding is the process, or mode of existence, by which we make sense of and derive meaning from what might otherwise appear as "an unbearable sequence of sheer happenings" and take our bearings in the world (Arendt, MDT: 104). Storytelling is the form such understanding takes. It is the fundamental form of thinking about experiences, the "form of dialogue in which I think with myself about what happened, and in thinking through how the event unfolded I am presented with its story" (Hill, 1979: 287–288). In the form of a story, I can derive meaning from what has happened by understanding how it came about, and storytelling thus offers us the means of reconciliation with reality. But storytelling also makes a *common understanding of reality* possible for us in our plurality (Hill, 1979: 289). Reality, Arendt states, is "different from, and more than, the totality of facts and events, which anyhow is unascertainable" (Arendt, PP: 257), and plurality is not simply the totality of unique individuals, but the unique perspectives on the world we share in common. Reality, then, is both the totality of facts and events that, regardless of anyone's interpretation of them, irrevocably occurred, and the way in which the world appears to each living being (Biser, 2014). But our sense of reality, our trust in the world as it appears to us, depends upon the presence of others with whom to relate our individual perspectives on the world. Story-telling, then, is also the way in which we communicate with each other about experience. In addressing the question of how we understand what has happened, from the point of view of the present, storytelling gives us the chance to keep up with what happens in the world: the end of the story returns us to the possibility of action (Hill, 1979: 289).

Our capacity for narrative understanding not only reconciles us to reality, and enables a common understanding of reality, but also grounds the quintessentially political art of representative thinking – political judgement – which can provide the impetus for further action, and open up space for new actions and actors. Judgement, for Arendt, is an inter-subjective and public enterprise, intrinsically related to the essential plurality of human beings, and to our living in a common world, which is opened up by speech. The validity of judgement depends upon our ability to think 'representatively'; that is, from the standpoint of everyone else, and this ability, in turn, can only be acquired and tested in a public forum where individuals can exchange opinions on particular matters and see whether they accord with those of others (Passerin d'Entrèves, 1994: 123–124). To put this another way, judging creates worldly relations that turn on the ability to see the same thing from multiple points of view, which is identical to what it means to see politically (Zerilli, 2005: 166). This 'enlarged mentality' developed through judgement involves 'imaginative visiting' through which we come to see the same world in very different aspects – we imaginatively seat ourselves in different seats around the table that is the common world in order to reflect on what the same world looks like from the perspective of another. The telling and hearing of stories – of others' perspectives on any given issue or event – is vital to this process, as the Greeks of the *polis* understood only too well:

> In this incessant talk, the Greeks discovered that the world we have in common is usually regarded from an infinite number of different stand-points, to which correspond the most diverse points of view. In a sheer inex-haustible flow of arguments, the Greeks learned to understand – not to understand one another as individual persons, but to look upon the same world from one another's standpoint, to see the same in very different and frequently opposing aspects.
>
> (Arendt, BPF: 51)

If to *see* politically means to see the same thing from multiple points of view, and come to an opinion on the basis of reflecting upon these different perspec-tives, then to *speak* politically is to share these opinions, to attempt to persuade others of the validity of your perspective on the issue or event at hand. Politics, thus, consists of the exchange of opinions, of "it appears to me", in the sense of opening up the world that appears to us. Opening up, Zerilli explains, creates a context within which a change in perspective may happen and things we may have known all along get counted differently (Zerilli, 2005: 166). The ability to persuade depends upon "the capacity to elicit criteria that speak to the particular case at hand and in relation to particular interlocutors" (Zerilli, 2005: 171). Returning to the protesting refugees with which this chapter began, we can see the ways in which they sought to persuade others in just such a manner, rendering their speech and action political not simply because they 'took a seat at the table', so to speak, but because their speech consisted, fundamentally, of 'saying what is'; of telling stories, relating their diverse 'it appears to me', but doing so in a way that *solicits the responsiveness of others.*

The framing of the protests in Germany within continental and global socio-economic processes takes on added significance here. The Refugee Convention, and European asylum policy in general, attempts to maintain a strict separation between 'political' and 'economic' reasons for leaving one's country of origin, recognising only political reasons as valid for recognition as a Refugee. This distinction, for the protesting refugees, is untenable for two reasons: first, political and socio-economic conditions cannot be so arbitrarily divided – as the 'migration-asylum nexus' shows; and second, that such separation serves as a way for affluent (especially former colonial) states to absolve themselves of responsibility for the consequences of their policies. One particularly impassioned example of this view is in the statement issued by a protestor, Arash, upon his arrest in Munich in January 2014:

> The reasons for flight or migration are: dictatorships, poverty, oppression and war. Those causes, forcing people to flee, have their roots in the mutual relations between countries of origin and destination ... [and] formed in this globalised economic system and the resulting distribution struggles over resources and power. The resulting imbalance is the main reason for displacement and migration. The existence of this system is made possible by a network of neo-colonial exploitation and oppression. That circuit is formed by both the 'democratic' and/or 'liberal' states, and maintained by dictatorial states. In countries such as ... Iran and Pakistan, the system is protected with a visible state violence. In countries such as Germany and France, the same system is protected with 100 billion Euros of arms exports.
>
> (Refugee Tent Action, 2014)

In drawing attention to the links between European social, economic, and military policies, and the situations from which refugees flee, the protestors seek to validate their claims for rights beyond the criteria of the Refugee Convention, by foregrounding the fundamentally interconnected nature of global economics and politics. Strict separations between 'there' and 'here' become troubled by such accusations, and the target audience of these claims are not only those already acting in solidarity, but wider members of society, the media, and the governing elites. These accusations question the very framework within which, and the basis upon which, status determination and access to rights are made and granted.

The creative appropriation of language is another way of seeking to persuade others and garner support for the claiming of rights. The official names for the reception and accommodation centres housing refugees in Germany are *Aufnah-meeinrichtung* (initial reception centre) and *Gemeinschaftsunterkünfte* (collective accommodation centre), but the refugees and other activists call them *Lagers*, to draw parallels with the *Konzentrationsläger* (concentration camps) of the Nazi regime. Demonstrations outside these centres are designed to raise awareness among the local population that they have such a centre in the vicinity, as well as to protest against the detention system itself. Drawing the attention of local people to the existence of this 'Lager-system', and using language reminiscent of the darkest period of German history, can be interpreted as an attempt to shine a light on the disparity between professed German support for human rights and its domestic policies curtailing or denying these very rights to those lacking formal legal status. These actions are challenges to the community, to be sure, but they are challenges which seek to elicit a response. However, since the meaning of an action is never simply what its initiator says it is but is, rather, the sum of the responses it provokes (Thiele, 2009), the response provoked by these actions – or indeed whether their action will provoke a response at all – depends upon those to whom the action is *directed*. It depends upon *their* ability to inter-pret what they hear as something to respond to, and their recognition of their own ability to respond. And so, we are returned to what Arendt refers to as the 'original interdependence of action'.

The Interdependence of Action and the Horizons of Practical Engagement

In the existence in Greek and Latin of two different yet inter-related words with which to designate the verb 'to act' lies evidence, Arendt writes, for the original interdependence of action – the dependence of the beginner upon others for help in bearing an enterprise to the finish, and the dependence of these others on the initiator for an occasion to act themselves (Arendt, HC: 189). Our contemporary vocabulary of action obscures its interdependent nature and construes it on the model of sovereignty or mastery, which can only compound the frustration felt when our actions, as they so often do, fail to achieve or obtain the goal sought. The interdependence of action implies that the recognition of any particular action as a beginning or event to which to respond is the prerogative of the responder, rather than the initiator, and, further, that whether or not an action constitutes a beginning depends upon our attunement to it as an occasion for response (Markell, 2010: 75). For this reason, Markell claims, it might be more helpful for our understanding of action as beginning to speak of action as "some-thing that is, at various times and places, coming into being or passing away, as the intensity of responsiveness in a space of potential circulation waxes and wanes, but which never simply or definitively *is*" (Markell, 2010: 76). This implies that the significance of events is a matter of judgement, which is under-taken within "horizons of practical engagement". When we act, we confront pat-terns of engagement and response which are, in part, the effects of social and political practices and institutions, which structure and mediate people's experi-ences of the world (Markell, 2010: 80) – we can think, perhaps, of the world ali-enation discussion in Chapter 4, and also the discussion of the role of discipline, norms and power which structure our actions, in Chapter 3. What this approach to action has the potential to do is to shift our focus to the question of how to "sustain, intensify and democratise the beginnings with which we are con-fronted". Importantly, this is a question of worldly relationships – between persons, and between persons and the happenings they encounter (or fail to encounter). Our responsiveness to events can be enhanced or weakened by a range of practices and institutions, both formal and informal, and so these prac-tices and institutions present opportunities upon which to work to broaden our horizons of practical engagement, in order to recover and enhance our attune-ment to events as occasions to which we *can* and should respond (Markell, 2010: 80–81). City of Sanctuary – its activities, goals and the relationships it enables and fosters – has the potential to do just this, albeit in smaller, localised spaces than those of the nation-state as a whole. But therein, perhaps, lies its power.

The spatial, relational, and localised nature of City of Sanctuary contains the potential for the movement to refashion our horizons of practical engagement and make us more attuned to recognising and responding to the voices of refugees. The volunteering opportunities, and the inclusion of refugees in the everyday activities of a vast range of groups and organisations, creates literal space within which refu-gees can appear, speak and act with others. The importance placed on testimony and engagement with those relating their experiences also creates figurative space in enabling conversation, not just among the 'converted' but with the indifferent, the sceptical, and the hostile. By actively seeking to establish relationships between organisations not already working with refugees, and to foster relationships between the individuals involved with them, City of Sanctuary has the potential to facilitate a move away from the idea of a distinct 'refugee sector' to refocus atten-tion on the structural sources of exclusion in our societies. This can broaden the interested, concerned, and active audience for addressing the problems faced by the displaced beyond those who we may think already have the 'job' of dealing with these issues, by focusing on how what we do in our own groups and organisa-tions may contribute to the exclusion and isolation faced by refugees. The local-ised, grass-roots nature of the movement mobilises support from the ground up in ways that established national organisations, such as the Refugee Council, are not best suited to do. Those involved with City of Sanctuary are able to reach audi-ences and address issues which, being local in character, are often not within the purview of nationwide charitable organisations.

The spaces created by the activities of the movement are, importantly, not only spaces for refugees to re-establish lives in their new surroundings, but also spaces for more established residents of these cities and towns to forge relationships with people they may otherwise never have met, despite living in the same city, and therefore change the relationship they have with the city itself. By understanding the city not as a container for social interactions between 'rightful residents' but as a dynamic space created and continually recreated by the diverse relationships established within and beyond it, not only does the space of the city become reconfigured, but the relationships of those resident within it change (Darling, 2009b). One of the more recent developments in the City of Sanctuary network is Streams of Sanctuary, covering education, healthcare, the arts, sports, and faith, in which initiatives focused on these areas connect across towns and cities to add another layer of cooperation and coordination between the localised City of Sanctuary groups in their attempt to influence the national framing of asylum. This is another way in which City of Sanctuary is a place-based, rather than place-bound movement.

The potential of these new and diverse relationships is evident in the importance placed on testimony and the soliciting of, listening to, and reflecting upon the stories of the displaced. This provides opportunities for the displaced to regain access to the inter-subjective world of stories, opinions and judgement, which we have seen presupposes the presence of others, and to make their mark within it. But it can also influence the capacity for judgement, representative thinking and imaginative visiting on the part of those who listen, leading to a broadening of the 'mental' space of appearance, and, potentially, a more open attitude towards newcomers to the 'physical' space of appearance. If one of the major obstacles for marginalised subjects who wish to speak publicly and lay claim to a stake in the public realm is to have that speech recognised as speech (Malkki, 1996; Nyers, 2006; Rancière, 2001) – to be listened to – then the relationships forged by these activities and the various organisations involved with City of Sanctuary can provide a receptive and growing audience willing to at least listen. There is, of course, the danger of merely preaching to the converted, but the pace at which the movement has grown, the number of organisations outside of the 'refugee sector' pledging their support, and the growing visibility of campaigns around refugee rights suggest that perhaps the movement does have the potential to change more sceptical and hostile minds. But, even if this is not the case, as McNevin highlights, the 'already converted' often have a view of refugees as victims in need of charity, rather than as individual actors in their own right (2010: 154–155). It is important to recognise that it is not a simple task for grass-roots movements such as these to navigate the difficult, and potentially problematic, dynamics of "host and guest" and the implications of "gratitude" that these can produce (Darling and Squire, 2013; Darling, 2013). However, by providing opportunities for individuals to engage with each other on the basis of shared interests, skills, and opinions, relationships can be built not on the dynamic of host and guest, or victim and protector, but on a more equal footing, where what is of primary importance is the goal or the activity itself, and the joint action in pursuit of it, rather than the immigration statuses of those involved in it (Squire and Bagelman, 2012).

There does appear to be some, albeit anecdotal, evidence for the activities of City of Sanctuary having broadened the horizons of practical engagement of those involved, and attuned them to events as occasions for response, including the actions of refugees both 'at home' and abroad. When City of Sanctuary began in 2005 the organisers considered themselves expressly to be eschewing political action in favour of action directed at cultural change (Barnett and Bhogal, 2010). While they sought the support of organisations that were involved in political campaigning they did not become directly involved in such campaigns themselves. This does appear to be changing. As the movement has grown, it has begun to involve itself more openly in political campaigns for the inclusion and rights of refugees, and many of the individuals involved are also involved in these campaigns – such as Still Human, Still Here (a campaign to end enforced destitution), and the recent, and ongoing, campaign to end asylum seeker detention in the UK. City of Sanctuary has now held two 'Sanctuary in Parliament' events, which saw dozens of members of the movement spend the day at Westminster speaking with MPs about their experiences, the goals of the movement, and the problems with national asylum policy. A Sanctuary Summit was held in November 2014 in Birmingham, which brought together over 100 civil society organisations and 400 delegates to discuss the formation of a broad alliance to end destitution and detention of asylum seekers. The purpose of the summit was also to translate what the organisations perceive to be the growing support of the public for a change in approach to asylum policy into practical action.

As we have seen in the work of Foucault and Arendt, with the rise of the modern nation-state and the development of government as a nation-wide administration of housekeeping, individuals have become increasingly superfluous to the life of their communities in the sense that their *active* participation becomes increasingly dispensable in economic and political life. As the communities of belonging grew ever larger, from the family, to class, to society, and finally to the nation-state, the ability of individuals to belong to the world with others – to create worlds with others – diminished. What the development of City of Sanctuary perhaps indicates is the possibility of making the communities of belonging smaller, making the city a meaningful world for those who come to live in it, and pluralising political space within the state. This is not to escape the statist logic of the refugee regime. The state, after all, has final say over who may stay and who must leave. But to focus solely on who has the power to dictate the grant of legal status is to fall into a number of traps: the trap of thinking that this grant of legal status is all that matters; the trap of thinking that the state is the only meaningful community in which, and to which, individuals belong (Isin and Nielsen, 2014: 2); the trap of thinking that the relationship of the individual to the state is the only meaningful socio-political relationship; and the trap of thinking that such decisions resolve all the problems that refugees face. What I have sought to show in this chapter and the previous chapter is that refugees have not *only* lost legal status, and so the granting of legal status, given the political conditions under which we live, including the nature of formal citizenship, is insufficient in and of itself to address all of the losses that refugees have incurred in becoming displaced. City of Sanctuary is not a once-and-for-all 'solution' to 'the refugee problem', but perhaps the logic of 'solutions' – or the permanence implied in it – is precisely what stands in need of critique. This is an issue with which the book concludes, in the next chapter.

Conclusion

Neither self-organised refugee protest, nor sanctuary and solidarity movements, are unique to Europe. Refugee protests have occurred in places as diverse as Indonesia, Bangladesh, Japan, Egypt, Canada, Australia, and Namibia. In Indonesia, in 2015, 120 refugees went on hunger strike to protest the lack of action on their resettlement. All have received recognition of their Refugee status from UNHCR, and yet they remain stuck in Indonesia, as UNHCR has been unable to find a state willing to accept them, and Indonesia refuses to allow them to stay (Topsfield, 2015). Rohingya refugees from Myanmar, many of whom live unregistered in Bangladesh, face discrimination and repression both in their country of origin and of 'asylum'. Both UNHCR and the Bangladeshi authorities have been the focus of repeated protests by Rohingya refugees over the discriminatory treatment that they face, and against forced repatriation back to Myanmar (Uddin, 2015; Loescher, 2001: 286). Asylum seekers in Tokyo have staged sit-in protests outside UNHCR buildings to protest the refusal of the Japanese authorities to grant them Refugee status (Shindo, 2009). Similar sit-in protests have also occurred in Cairo, although the target was UNHCR and its 'monopoly' of decisions over solutions to refugees' problems that were the focus of the 3,000 Sudanese refugees who occupied Mustapha Mahmoud Square in September 2005 (Moulin and Nyers, 2007). Refugees in the Osire camp, in Namibia, have engaged in a range of political acts designed to draw attention to, and protest against, violations of their human rights (Ilcan, 2014). A group of refugees from the Democratic Republic of Congo, for example, formed their own human rights organisation, the *Association for the Defence of Refugee Rights* (ADR), and its members have protested against their treatment at the hands of Namibian state officials and the UNHCR (Ilcan, 2014: 100). Refugee protest, and solidarity protests, against the country's 'stop the boats' and mandatory detention policies have become a semi-permanent fixture of Australian politics. In July 2011 a protest occurred outside the Melbourne Immigration Transit accommodation centre, captured by photographer John Englart. In one picture, a teenage girl and young boy draw in chalk on the sidewalk. Behind them, watching over them, two adults hold a large banner, reading: "Treating refugees as the problem *is the problem*" (Englart, 2011). Both the US and Canada have active sanctuary movements, both of which are rooted in church-based initiatives to give physical sanctuary to asylum seekers in danger of deportation, beginning in the 1980s (for good summaries of both movements, see the edited volume by Lippert and Rehaag, 2013). These initiatives expanded, in the 2000s, into broader-based rights and justice movements in cities across both countries, focused on improving relations, access to services, integration, and living conditions for refugees and undocumented immigrants (for an overview of both movements, see Goodall, 2011).

Just as with the refugee protests in Germany and Austria, and with the UK City of Sanctuary movement, each of these movements is unique and prompted by local conditions. And yet, while place-based, each movement appears also not to be place-bound, connecting their actions and struggles not only to immediate local circumstances and policies, but towards national, regional and global dynamics of refugee protection. But in their actions these diverse actors seem also to recognise, and to seek to counter, the tendency of both UNHCR and the state to treat the refugee as the problem, and to expect that refugees will simply sit quietly and wait – even if that means indefinitely – and simply trust that their particular problems are also at the centre of state and global concern.

The solution to the 'refugee (as) problem' is to find places to put people who have been ejected from the state-citizen-territory trinity, until such time as their state of origin can be recognised by the international community as 'home' again. To understand 'home' in this way is to reduce it to a function of legal status expressed as some physical point on a map. An Arendtian understanding of 'the refugee problem' as the problems of worldlessness and superfluity *for* the refugee lends itself to an understanding of home as 'world'. This requires an approach to addressing the problem from an understanding of the *character* of this thing called 'world', and how what we do, or fail to do, can undermine its existence and thus, also, our human existence within it. In other words, it requires an approach oriented by the *lived experience* of being in the world, which, for Arendt, is the experience of being-in-the-world-*with-others*, and the different modes that such being takes, and is not reducible to legal status or simply having a physical place to which to 'belong'.

Notes

1 The concept of 'home' has become a growing area of interest in anthropological approaches to refugees and forced migration, often focused on individual countries or groups of refugees. A recent issue of *Refuge* – 31(1) (2015) – is devoted to conceptualising 'home' in the context of protracted displacement.
2 In this chapter I use the term 'asylum seeker' or Refugee when it is the status of the individual in the eyes of the Home Office, or other authorities, that is central to the point being made. Otherwise I refer to these individuals as refugees.
3 The Voice Refugee Forum is an online platform which collects information about protests, demonstrations and campaigns of refugees and 'asylum seekers' across Germany, and links to various groups and organisations, giving an indication of how large and diverse the refugee rights movement is in Germany: http://thevoiceforum.org/.
4 The City of Sanctuary website is an extensive resource for the activities of the network as a whole, the activities and initiatives undertaken by each local group, and the campaigns in which the network is engaged with others.

References

Arendt, H., *Men in Dark Times* (New York: Harcourt, 1968)
Arendt, H., *The Origins of Totalitarianism* (New York: Harcourt, 1973)
Arendt, H., *The Human Condition* (Chicago: University of Chicago Press, 1998)

Arendt, H., "Understanding and Politics (The Difficulties of Understanding)" in *Essays in Understanding 1930–1954: Formation, Exile and Totalitarianism* (New York: Schocken Books, 2004): 307–329

Arendt, H., "Introduction into Politics" in *The Promise of Politics* (New York: Schocken Books, 2005): 93–200

Arendt, H., "The Concept of History: Ancient and Modern" in *Between Past and Future: Eight Exercises in Political Thought* (New York: Penguin Books, 2006): 41–90

Arendt, H., "The Jew as Pariah: A Hidden Tradition" in *The Jewish Writings* (New York: Schocken Books, 2007): 275–297

Arendt, H., "We Refugees" in *The Jewish Writings* (New York: Schocken Books, 2007): 264–274

Ataç, I,. "Refugee Protest Camp Vienna: Making Citizens through Locations of the Protest Movement" in *Citizenship Studies* 20(5) (2016): 629–646

Ataç, I., Rygiel, K., and Stierl, M. (Eds), *The Contentious Politics of Refugee and Migrant Protest and Solidarity Movements: Remaking Citizenship from the Margins* (London: Routledge, 2017)

Bagelman, J., "Sanctuary: A Politics of Ease?" in *Alternatives: Global, Local, Political* 38(1) (2013): 49–62

Barnett, C., and Bhogal, I., *Becoming a City of Sanctuary* (Ripon: Plug and Tap, 2010)

Biser, A. N., "Calibrating Our 'Inner Compass': Arendt on Thinking and the Dangers of Disorientation" in *Political Theory* 42(5) (2014): 519–542

Bloch, A., and Schuster, L., "At the Extremes of Exclusion: Deportation, Detention and Dispersal" in *Ethnic and Racial Studies* 28(3) (2005): 491–512

Borren, M., "Towards an Arendtian Politics of In/Visibility: On Stateless Refugees and Undocumented Aliens" in *Ethical Perspectives: Journal of the European Ethics Network* 15(2) (2008): 213–237

Brun, C., "Reterritorialising the Relationship between People and Place in Refugee Studies" in *Geografiska Annaler Series B, Human* Geography 83(1) (2001): 15–25

Butler, J., "Bodies in Alliance and the Politics of the Street" *The State of Things Lecture Series* (Venice: 7 September 2011)

Butler, J., and Spivak, G. C., *Who Sings the Nation-State? Language, Politics, Belonging* (Oxford: Seagull Books, 2011)

Cadman, L., "How (Not) To Be Governed: Foucault, Critique, and the Political" in *Environment and Planning D: Society and Space* 28 (2010): 539–556

Cane, L., "Hannah Arendt on the Principles of Political Action" in *European Journal of Political Theory* 14(1) (2014): 55–75

City of Sanctuary, http://cityofsanctuary.org/ (last accessed 6 July 2017)

Darling, J., "Becoming Bare Life: Asylum, Hospitality, and the Politics of Encampment" in *Environment and Planning D: Society and Space* 27(4) (2009a): 649–665

Darling, J., "Thinking Beyond Place: The Responsibilities of a Relational Spatial Politics" in *Geography Compass* 3(5) (2009b): 1938–1954

Darling, J., "A City of Sanctuary: The Relational Re-imagining of Sheffield's Asylum Politics" in *Transactions of the Institute of British Geographers* 35 (2010): 125–140

Darling, J., "Moral Urbanism, Asylum, and the Politics of Critique" in *Environment and Planning A* 45(8) (2013): 1785–1801

Darling, J., *Producing Urban Asylum*, www.producingurbanasylum.com/four-cities/dispersal-in-the-uk/ (2015) (last accessed 6 July 2017)

Darling, J., and Healey, R., "Seeing the City Anew: Asylum Seeker Perspectives of 'Belonging' in Greater Manchester" in *North West Geography* 12(1) (2012): 20–28

Darling, J., and Squire, V., "Everyday Enactments of Sanctuary: The UK City of Sanctuary Movement" in Lippert, L., and Rehaag, S. (Eds), *Sanctuary Practices in International Perspectives: Migration, Citizenship and Social Movements* (London: Routledge, 2013): 20–28

Den Boer, R., "Liminal Space in Protracted Exile: The Meaning of Place in Congolese Refugees' Narratives of *Home* and *Belonging* in Kampala" in *Journal of Refugee Studies* 28(4) (2015): 486–504

Englart, J., "Treating refugees as the problem is the problem – Refugee Rights Protest at Broadmeadows, Melbourne" (9 July 2011), photograph available at: www.flickr.com/photos/takver/5918017660 (last accessed 6 July 2017)

Erensu, A. I., "Notes from a Refugee Protest: Ambivalences of Resisting and Desiring Citizenship" in *Citizenship Studies* 20(5) (2016): 664–677

Foucault, M., "Confronting Governments: Human Rights" in Faubion, J. (Ed.), *Essential Works of Foucault, Volume 3: Power* (London: Penguin, 1994): 474–475

Foucault, M., *The History of Sexuality, Volume 1: The Will to Knowledge* (London: Penguin, 1998)

Foucault, M., *The Birth of Biopolitics: Lectures at the Collège de France, 1978–1979* (Basingstoke: Palgrave Macmillan, 2010)

Golder, B., *Foucault and the Politics of Rights* (Stanford, CA: Stanford University Press, 2015)

Goodall, C., "Sanctuary and Solidarity: Urban Community Responses to Refugees and Asylum Seekers on Three Continents" *New Issues in Refugee Research* 221 (2011): 1–45

Grzinic, M., "A Refugee Protest Camp in Vienna and the European Union's Processes of Racialization, Seclusion, and Discrimination" in *e-Flux Journal* 43 (2013): 1–9

Gündoğdu, A., *Rightlessness in an Age of Rights: Hannah Arendt and the Contemporary Struggles of Migrants* (Oxford: Oxford University Press, 2015)

Hill, M. A., "The Fictions of Mankind and the Stories of Men", in Hill, M. A. (Ed.), *Hannah Arendt: The Recovery of the Public World* (New York: St Martin's Press, 1979): 275–300

Ilcan, S., "Activist Citizens and the Politics of Mobility in Osire Refugee Camp" in Isin, E. F., and Nyers, P. (Eds), *Routledge Handbook of Global Citizenship Studies* (London: Routledge, 2014): 186–195

Isin, E., and Nielsen, G. (Eds), *Acts of Citizenship* (London: Zed Books, 2008)

Isin, E., and Nyers, P., "Globalizing Citizenship Studies" in Isin, E. F., and Nyers, P. (Eds), *Routledge Handbook of Global Citizenship Studies* (London: Routledge, 2014): 1–11

Johnson, H., "Moments of Solidarity, Migrant Activism and (Non)citizens at Global Borders: Political Agency at Tanzanian Refugee Camps, Australian Detention Centres and European Borders" in Nyers, P., and Rygiel, K. (Eds), *Citizenship, Migrant Activism and the Politics of Movement* (London: Routledge, 2012): 109–128

Johnson, H., "These Fine Lines: Locating Non-citizenship in Political Protest in Europe" in *Citizenship Studies* 19(8) (2015): 951–965

Linke, L., "This is Our Battleground: How a New Refugee Movement is Challenging Germany's Racist Asylum Laws" (2013), available at: https://ceasefiremagazine.co.uk/this-battleground-germanys-refugee-movement-challenges-racist-asylum-laws/ (last accessed 6 July 2017)

Lippert, R., and Rehaag, S. (Eds), *Sanctuary Practices in International Perspectives: Migration, Citizenship and Social Movements* (London: Routledge, 2013)

Lloyd, M., "Performing Radical Democracy" in Little, A., and Lloyd, M. (Eds), *The Politics of Radical Democracy* (Oxford: Oxford University Press, 2008): 33–51

Loescher, G., *The UNHCR and World Politics: A Perilous Path* (Oxford: Oxford University Press, 2001)

Malkki, L., "The National Geographic: The Rooting of Peoples and the Territorialization of National Identity Among Scholars and Refugees" in *Cultural Anthropology* 7(1) (1992): 24–44

Malkki, L., "Refugees and Exile: From 'Refugee Studies' to the National Order of Things" in *Annual Review of Anthropology* 24 (1995): 495–523

Malkki, L., "Speechless Emissaries: Refugees, Humanitarianism and Dehistoricization" in *Cultural Anthropology* 11(3) (1996): 377–404

Markell, P., "The Rule of the People: Arendt, *Archê*, and Democracy" in Benhabib, S. (Ed.), *Politics in Dark Times: Encounters with Hannah Arendt* (Cambridge: Cambridge University Press, 2010): 58–82

McGuaran, K., and Hudig, K., "Refugee Protests in Europe: Fighting for the Right to Stay" in *Statewatch Journal: Reflections on the State and Civil Liberties in Europe* 23(3–4) (2014), available at: http://database.statewatch.org/article.asp?aid=33230 (last accessed 4 July 2017)

McNevin, A., "Becoming Political: Asylum Seeker Activism through Community Theatre" in *Local-Global: Identity, Security, Community* 8 (2010): 142–159

McNevin, A., *Contesting Citizenship: Irregular Migrants and New Frontiers of the Political* (New York: Columbia University Press, 2011)

Moulin, C., and Nyers, P., "We Live in a Country of UNHCR – Refugee Protests and Global Political Society" in *International Political Sociology* 1(4) (2007): 356–372

Nyers, P., "Taking Rights, Mediating Wrongs: Disagreements over the Political Agency of Non-status Refugees" in Huysmans, J., Dobson, A., and Prokhovnik, R. (Eds), *The Politics of Protection: Sites of Insecurity and Political Agency* (London: Routledge, 2006): 48–67

Nyers, P., "No One is Illegal: Between City and Nation" in Isin, E., and Nielsen, G. (Eds), *Acts of Citizenship* (London: Zed Books, 2008): 160–181

Nyers, P., and Rygiel, K. (Eds), *Citizenship, Migrant Activism and the Politics of Movement* (London: Routledge, 2012)

Passerin d'Entrèves, M., *The Political Philosophy of Hannah Arendt* (London: Routledge, 1994)

Rancière, J., "Ten Theses on Politics" in *Theory & Event* 5(3) (2001)

Refugee Protest Camp Vienna, "Urgent demands" (2012a), available at: https://refugeecampvienna.noblogs.org/demands/urgent-demands/ (last accessed 6 July 2017)

Refugee Protest Camp Vienna, "Demands by the protesting refugees" (2012b), available at: https://refugeecampvienna.noblogs.org/post/2012/11/26/refugee-demands-24th-nov-2012/ (last accessed 6 July 2017)

Refugee Protest Camp Vienna, "Letter from the Federal President of Austria to the protesting refugees" (2013a), available at: https://refugeecampvienna.noblogs.org/post/2013/02/14/nach-langem-schweigen-schreiben-des-bundesprasidenten-an-fluchtling-in-der-wiener-votivkirche/ (last accessed 6 July 2017)

Refugee Protest Camp Vienna, "Report: Feb. 16, International Day of Action" (2013b), available at: https://refugeecampvienna.noblogs.org/post/2013/02/17/16-2-das-war-der-international-day-of-action-report-feb-16-international-day-of-action/ (last accessed 6 July 2017)

Refugee Tent Action, "In Solidarity with our comrade and friend Arash D." (2014), available at: http://refugeestruggle.org/en (last accessed 6 July 2017)

Refugee Tent Action, "First Bus Tour stop in Hamburg" (2015), available at: http://oplatz.net/2015/04/20/first-bustour-stop-in-hamburg/#more-6711 (last accessed 6 July 2017)

Robinson, V., Andersson, R., and Musterd, S. *Spreading the Burden? European Policies to Disperse Asylum Seekers* (Bristol: Policy Press, 2003)

Shindo, R., "Struggle for Citizenship: Interaction between Political Society and Civil Society at a Kurd Refugee Protest in Tokyo" in *Citizenship Studies* 13(3) (2009): 219–237

Squire, V., *The Exclusionary Politics of Asylum* (Basingstoke: Palgrave Macmillan, 2009)

Squire, V., "From Community Cohesion to Mobile Solidarities: The City of Sanctuary Network and the Strangers into Citizens Campaign" in *Political Studies* 59(2) (2011): 290–307

Squire, V., and Bagelman, J., "Taking Not Waiting: Space, Temporality and Politics in the City of Sanctuary Movement" in Nyers, P., and Rygiel, K. (Eds), *Citizenship, Migrant Activism and the Politics of Movement* (London: Routledge, 2012): 146–164

Squire, V., and Darling, J., "The 'Minor' Politics of Rightful Presence: Justice and Relationality in City of Sanctuary" in *International Political Sociology* 7 (2013): 59–74

Stewart, E., "UK Dispersal Policy and Onward Migration: Mapping the Current State of Knowledge" in *Journal of Refugee Studies* 25(1) (2012): 1–25

Thiele, L. P., "The Ontology of Action: Arendt and the Role of Narrative" *Theory and Event* 12(4) (2009) available at: http://muse.jhu.edu/journals/theory_and_event/v012/12.4.thiele.html

Topsfield, J., "Refugees in Indonesia Go on Hunger Strike to Protest Delays in Resettlement" (15 October 2015), access via: www.smh.com.au/world/refugees-in-indonesia-go-on-hunger-strike-to-protest-delays-in-resettlement-20151015-gka7bs.html (last accessed 6 July 2017)

Uddin, N., "State of Stateless People: The Plight of Rohingya Refugees in Bangladesh" in Howard-Hassmann, R. E., and Walton-Roberts, M. (Eds) *The Human Right to Citizenship: A Slippery Concept* (Philadelphia: University of Pennsylvania Press, 2015): 62–77

Zerilli, L. M. G., "We Feel Our Freedom: Imagination and Judgment in the Thought of Hannah Arendt" in *Political Theory* 33(2) (2005): 158–188

Zivi, K., *Making Rights Claims: A Practice of Democratic Citizenship* (Oxford: Oxford University Press, 2012)

Conclusion

On Durability and Permanence

> Who says what is always tells a story, and in this story the particular facts lose
> their contingency and acquire some humanly comprehensible meaning.
>
> (Arendt, BPF: 257)

This book set out to unpack a deceptively simple term: 'the refugee problem'.
Used by a wide range of different actors and often without any accompanying
explanation of what exactly they mean by 'the refugee problem', this term
obscures more than it illuminates. Setting aside both the assumption that 'the
refugee problem' means the same thing to everyone who uses it, and that those
actors, namely states, who employ the term while simultaneously instituting policies that result in restricting the access of refugees to the rights and protections
to which they are legally and morally entitled are being disingenuous when they
claim to be acting to solve 'the refugee problem', necessitates addressing a series
of inter-related questions: Which 'problem' was the refugee regime established
to solve? If established to solve more than one 'problem', to what extent is it
able to solve each one? Who gets to have a say in how these problems are
solved? What assumptions and interests underpin each 'problem' and the solutions conceived? In asking these questions, my goal with this book was that we
become more attentive to how the way in which we construct problems will
influence the kinds of solutions that we seek, and that these decisions have profound consequences for those people supposedly at the centre of all our concerns: refugees themselves. However, this attentiveness brings with it its own
complexities, raising additional questions about how we conceptualise and enact
our political lives.

The story of the development of the international refugee regime is, at its
heart, a story about a battle between two different problems: the problems that
refugees pose to states and the international order, and the problems that refugees themselves face. If we take only a cursory look at the various international
agreements and conventions drafted between 1921, when the League of Nations
first turned its attention to 'the problem' of population displacement, and 1951
when the United Nations drafted the Refugee Convention which forms the
bedrock of the refugee regime to this day, then it is easy to conclude that the

refugee regime was created "out of profound concern" (United Nations, 1951: Preamble) with the plight of the displaced, and to remedy the problems they faced by lacking the protection of their country of origin. If we look a little more closely, and at a wider range of sources from this period, however, a more nuanced picture emerges. While concerns for the plight of the displaced were undoubtedly at work, and efforts to address these problems were at the centre of concern for a great many of the individuals and groups working 'on the ground' with refugees, these concerns were arguably not of primary importance to the states that created the formal refugee regime. The problem that they seemed keen to solve was the problem that the existence, presence, and potential onward movement of refugees posed to them: to their social cohesion, and to their economic stability. The creation of a new, but limited, legal status, access to protection of a limited set of economic and social – but not political – rights, abdication of formal financial responsibility for the costs of the regime, the creation of a limited and hampered organisation to oversee the Convention, and the insurance policy of national security qualifiers attached to even the most basic of protections for refugees (including protection from *refoulement*) formed a regime of marginalistic inclusion of refugees emblematic of the desire to avoid, where at all possible, responsibility for providing the refugee with a new home and the conditions for a new start in life.

This 'refugee (as) problem' lends itself to an approach to solutions that could be called population or migration management. Places must be found to put refugees and, in the context of increased, and increasingly complex, migratory movements, mechanisms must be established to enable states and regime actors to sort through the body of people 'on the move', to assign them to the correct category of migrant, to expedite the process of identifying, and moving the individual to, the appropriate place. The establishment and effective functioning of such mechanisms requires knowledge and expertise, both about migration as a phenomenon and about migrants 'themselves'. The active engagement of and with refugees, however, is neither sought nor welcome in this process. The 'expertise' of border agents, of Country of Origin Information Services, of language analysts, and of academics, is sufficient to enable the state, or UNHCR, to 'discover' the 'true' identity of each individual who presents herself to authorities in search of protection, and to provide either for her exclusion from, or her marginalistic inclusion in, the state. Assigning individuals to various migratory subject-positions, facilitated by processes and practices of knowledge production, (re)produces the silences and denial of agency so characteristic of humanitarian aid practices.

To be sure, there are aspects of the refugee regime that lend themselves to addressing the problems that refugees face. Many of the rights enumerated in the Refugee Convention are undoubtedly important ones for helping refugees to re-establish some degree of normality in their lives, and that so many people make a claim for Refugee status indicates that this, albeit limited, legal status is considered to be valuable. But the logic of temporariness built into the refugee regime prevents it from effectively addressing the problems that refugees face in becoming displaced. Refugee status is, by definition, a limited one, both temporally and substantively. Refugee status is not, as states were at pains to emphasise in creating the regime, akin to, or a guaranteed step on the road to, citizenship. Refugee status does not entitle the refugee to civil and political rights in her country of refuge. And the cessation clauses of the Refugee Convention make even the 'durable solutions' of resettlement, assimilation, and repatriation much less 'durable' than they may at first appear.

It does not seem unreasonable, therefore, to posit that perhaps states are not simply being disingenuous when they claim to be trying to solve 'the refugee problem'. In many ways, contemporary state practices of securitisation and externalisation of asylum, and of limiting access to resettlement or local assimilation, are in accord with what they understand 'the refugee problem' to be, and with the broad contours of the regime they established to address it: 'the refugee (as) problem'. What is clear, however, is that this is not the only way to understand or approach 'the refugee problem', and is certainly not one that puts the problems that refugees themselves face at the centre of concern. Having to flee one's home, as an immediate 'solution' to the dangers or problems one faces, not only causes problems for the idealised, sedentary international order, but also for refugees themselves, but this is a problem of a different, existential, kind. Precisely because the whole world has come to be organised on the model of the sovereign nation-state, being ejected from one of these tightly organised communities turns out to be akin to being ejected from humanity altogether. This is not only because in being ejected one becomes isolated from one's 'own' community of equals, to whom one's opinions are significant and with whom one can act, but because this isolation is compounded by lacking the right to be admitted to a new community of equals. To be displaced in such a system is to be rendered worldless and superfluous: what the refugee thinks or does is of absolutely no consequence to anyone. Deprived of the opportunity, and of the right, to contribute, through labour, work, and action, to the co-constitution of the common world that gives individual lives a meaning and existence more permanent than life itself, refugees find themselves in a position not dissimilar to the obscurity of slaves: that they are in danger of passing through this world leaving no trace that they ever existed; that they appear to others only as 'whats' – refugees, figures of burden and pity – not 'whos' – unique and irreplaceable individuals whose perspectives and actions are vital to the continuation of 'the world' itself as a home on earth fit for human habitation and flourishing.

To address 'the refugee (as) problem' it is sufficient to find a physical place to put refugees until such time as they can return 'home' again – until they can return to their state of origin. To address refugees' problems of worldlessness and superfluity requires an attentiveness to the fact that in becoming displaced refugees have not simply lost a physical place to which to 'belong', where such belonging is determined and facilitated by legal status, but have lost the lived experience of being-in-the-world-with-others. Addressing these problems necessitates a focus on the ways in which such being-with-others can manifest and be encouraged and facilitated. And it is here that efforts made by refugees themselves to address the problems they face, and efforts undertaken by others in solidarity with them, come to play such a central role in (understanding) contemporary political life.

The practices of rights-claiming on the part of protesting refugees, and the City of Sanctuary movement, with its goal to remake the city into a place of belonging for all who come to live within it, can be understood as attempts, on the part of those who have been ejected from the shared common world of a community willing and able to guarantee the right to have rights, to gain a foothold in the world. Arendt's recognition of the need to remake the communities to which the right to have rights would correspond, given the inability of the modern nation-state to be such a community, for anyone, is not accompanied by any sustained insight into, or blueprint for, what these communities should look like. The difficult relationship that Arendt charts between the state as an institution, citizenship, and politics as action in concert and the manifestation of freedom, and that permeates her political writings, indicates that this was not an oversight, and this has direct bearings on the question of how 'durable' the City of Sanctuary and practices of rights-claiming might be for combating the worldlessness and superfluity suffered by the displaced.

Responding to the hypothetical question of whether it would not be better to outline a set of concrete institutional solutions that can enforce a right to have rights instead of "finding some vain solace in the fleeting moments of political action", Gündoğdu highlights that Arendt would reject the false choice implied in the question between action and institution, radical novelty and relative permanence (Gündoğdu, 2015: 201). For Arendt, institutions are vital for providing relatively stable guarantees for rights and the possibility of action in concert, but they can only provide these guarantees if they retain their character as *political* institutions. We should not, therefore, understand institutions (including those of the law and political communities) strictly, or primarily, as the products of making, governed by the means–end logic of *homo faber*, whereby the end of the process of making comes when a "thing with enough durability to remain in the world as an independent entity has been added to the human artifice" (Arendt, HC: 143). While we may need to create stable boundaries/walls/laws/rules that could give these institutions shape, the purpose, or end, of these institutions is not independent existence but political action, freedom, and equality. In other words, the work of founding political communities or institutions for the protection and realisation of rights and action in concert is not complete once we formally establish such institutions. Whereas the products of work possess the durability to remain within the human world independent of their use by humans, political institutions, if they are to retain their character as *political* must be continually maintained by the speech and action of individuals in their plurality. In 'What is Freedom' Arendt writes that:

> Political institutions, no matter how well or badly designed, depend for continued existence upon acting men; their conservation is achieved by the same means that brought them into being. Independent existence marks the

work of art as a product of making; utter dependence upon further acts to keep it in existence marks the state as a product of action.

(Arendt, BPF: 152)

In her examination of the American Revolution, Arendt continuously returns to the failure of the Founding Fathers to carve out spaces within the new republic where freedom could appear, where the people could gather and deliberate together about matters of public concern. In short, the "Constitution had given all power to the citizens, without giving them the opportunity of *being* republicans and of *acting* as citizens" (Arendt, OR: 253). This was the result, Arendt claims, of the triumph of the drive for stability as permanence over the durability, or preservation, of the revolutionary spirit. For the practice of freedom characteristic of the revolution to become durable, and the revolutionary spirit of public happiness and the freedom to act to be preserved, a space for the manifestation of this spirit through action needed to be created. The "little republics", or "wards" of which Thomas Jefferson spoke towards the end of his life could have been the organs to save the republic from the lethargy which he predicted would develop among a people relegated from the public realm. These "little republics" would be

the main strength of the great one; for inasmuch as the republican government of the Union was based on the assumption that the seat of power was in the people, the very condition for its proper functioning lay in a scheme to divide government among the many, distributing to every one exactly the function he was competent to. Without this, the very *principle* of republican government could never be *actualised*, and the government of the United States would be republican *in name only*.

(Arendt, OR: 253–254; emphasis added)

What this points to, for our purposes here, is that a political community (such as a city or a state) and institutions (such as citizenship, and laws guaranteeing human rights) can become empty shells, hollow promises, without continued action which manifests the principle – of equality and freedom – which brought them into being. We are not faced, then, with a choice between establishing lasting institutions or celebrating (or deriving solace from) moments of political action; a choice between having the state, or having some other institution which could more 'perfectly' guarantee rights; a choice between having citizenship within the state as a guarantee, or creating a new form of membership. *All* institutions and communities – no matter how 'perfectly' or in how much detail they may be 'designed' – contain the risk that they may decay and cease to be 'worlds' within which individuals can act and speak together, and assure themselves of the reality and meaning of their existence, if the possibility and spaces do not exist for such action and speech which could maintain them.

As *practices* of action manifesting freedom and creating nascent 'worlds', City of Sanctuary and rights-claiming cannot provide guaranteed, fixed, permanent worlds to which to belong for those involved now, or to those who may come to live in these communities in the future. Durability, in human affairs, is, for Arendt, always a relative durability, and should individuals decide that they no longer wish to contribute to the building of these worlds through joining the endeavour, then these worlds may disappear again. City of Sanctuary and rights-claiming, as ways to address the refugee problem of worldlessness and super-fluity, are, therefore, risky. They cannot offer permanence. But the maintenance and care of continued action which they require does, I posit, render them more faithful to the kind of politics and 'belonging' that lie at the heart of Arendt's call for a right to have rights – a right to live in a framework where one is judged by one's actions and opinions, a right to a place in the world which makes opinions significant and actions effective.

This relative durability of human affairs is not to be mistaken for the 'durability' of the 'solutions' of repatriation, resettlement or assimilation. The relative durability of political institutions of which Arendt speaks requires continued action of the sort that is not required by the three 'durable solutions' to 'the refugee (as) problem', which depend simply upon state decision-making. A different kind of politics, community and belonging is implied in Arendt's understanding of the durability of institutions: a kind of politics that involves grappling with the challenges of responsibility implied in an approach to 'solutions' which problematises the spatiality and modes of belonging in contemporary political life. What becomes clear through the actions undertaken by refugees and asylum seekers who take to the streets and parks of the states in which they have sought refuge and demand to be heard and to have a say in the politics of their futures, and through the actions of those involved in the City of Sanctuary movement is that responsibility, spatiality and belonging are conceived of in a fundamentally different way to the spatiality and belonging permeating the politics of 'the refugee (as) problem'.

The actions of refugees, and of sanctuary/solidarity movements, reconfigure the spatiality of contemporary politics; or, perhaps more accurately, they bring out into the open how the spatiality of contemporary politics fails to conform to the idealised, sedentarised world of 'the refugee (as) problem': the world of the maps that adorn our walls and the world in which citizenship, polity, and rights seamlessly coincide in the institution of the state. Refugee protests and City of Sanctuary are localised movements triggered by the specific circumstances operative in a particular place, whether state, region, city, village, or detention centre and, as McNevin highlights, where the local emerges as "a site of contestation", it becomes clear that the state is neither the sole nor the primary space in which political belonging takes shape (McNevin, 2011: 139). But while these localised movements may be place-*based*, they are not place-*bound*. The protesting refugees in Germany engaged in a *mobile* demonstration, taking their action 'on the road' and in doing so exposed the complicity of the law in denying their freedom of movement. The protesting refugees in Austria and Germany explicitly linked the individual state policies against which they rose up, to broader European policies, and even to the global system of structural economic inequality:

The struggle against the capitalist isolation system is an important fight for our future. We do not want to live in refugee camps, in which we are isolated. We do not want to be victims of racist measures … We want to connect our struggle with all anti-capitalist and anti-fascist forces, with all our comrades in the streets of the world. We do not want to pay the bill for the wars and crises of the capitalist-imperialist system.

(Refugee Tent Action, 2012)

Streams of Sanctuary connect the actions of diverse City of Sanctuary groups around issues including education, healthcare, and the arts, expanding the horizons of such action beyond the city itself to the national space. The emphasis and importance placed on the testimony and experiences of the displaced also open the city to the wider world through foregrounding the histories, experiences, links, and routes which connect the city, through its newest residents, to the places and conditions from which these refugees have fled. And the relationship of those engaged in such action and the places and spaces within which their actions take shape changes through their mobilisation. The park and the city become meaningful places of belonging, in which relationships are forged not on the basis of shared nationality, but on the responsibility and solidarity engendered by presence and common goals.

In the world of 'the refugee (as) problem', belonging is simple: humanity is divided into distinct (national) groups of citizens, each of which is 'housed' within a strictly delimited territory (states), the borders of which are the limits of responsibility and obligation of that state's government. The status of citizen comes with a set of rights, protections, and responsibilities, but these extend only so far as the body of one's fellow citizens, and this belonging is effected primarily through each individual citizen's relationship with the state. But refugee protest and sanctuary/solidarity movements belie this simplistic picture of citizenship and belonging in the contemporary world. The refugees protesting in Austria and Germany did not make simplistic claims for belonging or status, but complex claims, full of contradictions. They actively made claims for Refugee status, thereby recognising its importance in contemporary world politics and 'buying into' the state-based framing of 'the refugee problem', but made such a claim in ways which simultaneously *challenged* the parameters of that same status and framing. They did so by demanding recognition as Refugees on the basis that socio-economic reasons behind displacement are, by definition, political; a claim difficult to reconcile with the definition in Article 1 of the Refugee Convention. But their actions also laid claim to citizenship: in demanding to meet with state representatives, in appropriating public spaces, in challenging, and subjecting to critique, the laws of Germany and Austria, the refugees act as if they are members of the Austrian and German polities. In Isin's terminology, they enacted themselves as citizens (Isin and Nielsen, 2008). In connecting their struggle for rights, recognition and inclusion with their "comrades in the streets of the world" engaged in a struggle against the global economico-political system which they hold, in part, responsible for the conditions from which they fled, the protestors not only enact themselves as German and Austrian citizens, but as global citizens. These actions reveal, as Isin and Nyers explain, that individuals never belong only to one polity, but to "several, nested, if not overlapping and conflicting, series of polities, ranging from the city, the region, the state, and the international" (Isin and Nyers, 2014: 2). In responding to the actions of refugees, citizens acting in solidarity similarly recognise that we are all placed in a web of rights and duties which often are, but need not necessarily be, mediated through the relationships that individuals hold with the state. Action in common, for Arendt, is a collective activity in the double sense that more than one actor is required for action to be common, but also in the sense that action *constitutes* a collective through its very exercise, a collective through which we take responsibility for our world and our mutually interdependent existence within it. Cities of Sanctuary, through the actions taken to create and sustain them, become new polities in which new citizens are created, not on the basis of possessing the correct birth certificate or passport as evidence of an enduring relationship with the state, but on the basis of mutual recognition and collective action between individuals *regardless* of legal status.

All of this points to a responsibility that similarly exceeds the bounds operative in the world of 'the refugee (as) problem'. Not only are states and the UNHCR bearers of responsibility in addressing refugees' problems; so are refugees themselves, as well as ordinary citizens. The protesting refugees in Austria and Germany recognise their own responsibility not to remain silent any longer, but to take to the streets and make a stand, to take an active role in the politics of their futures: "to bring this inhuman system to an end ... we have to organise and to take to the streets. We have to put pressure on those in power, but at the same time get active ourselves. We are all responsible!" (Refugee Protest Camp Vienna, 2013). Those involved in the City of Sanctuary movement understand themselves as taking up a responsibility to change the narrative of asylum in the UK through refashioning the cities and towns within which they live into spaces which welcome and include refugees, rather than treat them with hostility and exclude them. Reflecting on how the activities of their own sports clubs, youth groups, schools, and religious communities, may exclude non-citizen residents of the city, precisely so that avenues for inclusion can be opened up, can be understood as recognition of a responsibility towards refugees and towards creating the kind of communities in which we live, that resides with the individual, the church group, the football club, and the university, and not only with the state.

If Arendt is right and refugees are indeed the most symptomatic group of contemporary politics (Arendt, OT: 277), and if my interpretation of this assessment as rooted in the world alienation that characterises modernity is valid, then the value and importance of refugee protest and of movements like City of Sanctuary lie not in their immediate potential to prevent mass displacement or to find a place to put every refugee for the duration of their displacement. They lie, rather, in their potential to push back against this alienation, to recognise ourselves once again as worldly beings, to reactivate the public sphere, to recover a common, shared world, and "create numerous spaces of appearance in which individuals can disclose their identities and establish relations of reciprocity and solidarity" (Passerin d'Entrèves, 1994: 140). Their potential lies, in other words, in their ability to help us to *begin* the task of refashioning the very nature of the communities to which the right to have rights can correspond.

References

Arendt, H., *On Revolution* (London: Penguin, 1963)

Arendt, H., *The Origins of Totalitarianism* (New York: Harcourt, 1973)

Arendt, H., *The Human Condition* (Chicago: University of Chicago Press, 1998)

Arendt, H., "Truth and Politics" in *Between Past and Future: Eight Exercises in Political Thought* (London: Penguin, 2006): 223–259

Arendt, H., "What is Freedom?" in *Between Past and Future: Eight Exercises in Political Thought* (London: Penguin, 2006): 142–169

Gündoğdu, A. *Rightlessness in an Age of Rights: Hannah Arendt and the Contemporary Struggles of Migrants* (Oxford: Oxford University Press, 2015)

Isin, E., and Nielsen, G. (Eds), *Acts of Citizenship* (London: Zed Books, 2008)

Isin, E., and Nyers, P., "Globalizing Citizenship Studies" in Isin, E. F., and Nyers, P. (Eds), *Routledge Handbook of Global Citizenship Studies* (London: Routledge, 2014): 1–11

McNevin, A., *Contesting Citizenship: Irregular Migrants and New Frontiers of the Political* (New York: Columbia University Press, 2011)

Passerin d'Entrèves, M., *The Political Philosophy of Hannah Arendt* (London: Routledge, 1994)

Refugee Protest Camp Vienna, "New wave of deportations from Austria: get active for concrete solidarity to stop deportations" (14 December 2013), available at: https://refugeecampvienna.noblogs.org/post/2013/12/14/new-wave-of-deportations-from-austria-get-active-for-concrete-solidarity-to-stop-deportations/

Refugee Tent Action, "Why we marched to Berlin and why we continue our resistance" (29 December 2012), available at: http://thecaravan.org/node/3619

United Nations, *Convention Relating to the Status of Refugees* (United Nations Treaty Series Vol. 189, No. 2545) (1951): 138–220

Index

Taylor & Francis eBooks

Helping you to choose the right eBooks for your Library

Add Routledge titles to your library's digital collection today. Taylor and Francis ebooks contains over 50,000 titles in the Humanities, Social Sciences, Behavioural Sciences, Built Environment and Law.

Choose from a range of subject packages or create your own!

Benefits for you

» Free MARC records
» COUNTER-compliant usage statistics
» Flexible purchase and pricing options
» All titles DRM-free.

Benefits for your user

» Off-site, anytime access via Athens or referring URL
» Print or copy pages or chapters
» Full content search
» Bookmark, highlight and annotate text
» Access to thousands of pages of quality research at the click of a button.

REQUEST YOUR **FREE** INSTITUTIONAL TRIAL TODAY

Free Trials Available
We offer free trials to qualifying academic, corporate and government customers.

eCollections – Choose from over 30 subject eCollections, including:

Archaeology	Language Learning
Architecture	Law
Asian Studies	Literature
Business & Management	Media & Communication
Classical Studies	Middle East Studies
Construction	Music
Creative & Media Arts	Philosophy
Criminology & Criminal Justice	Planning
Economics	Politics
Education	Psychology & Mental Health
Energy	Religion
Engineering	Security
English Language & Linguistics	Social Work
Environment & Sustainability	Sociology
Geography	Sport
Health Studies	Theatre & Performance
History	Tourism, Hospitality & Events

For more information, pricing enquiries or to order a free trial, please contact your local sales team: www.tandfebooks.com/page/sales

Routledge
Taylor & Francis Group

The home of Routledge books

www.tandfebooks.com